UTOPIAN ESSAYS
AND
PRACTICAL PROPOSALS

PAUL GOODMAN

Utopian Essays

AND

PRACTICAL PROPOSALS

VINTAGE BOOKS

A Division of Random House

NEW YORK

Acknowledgments

The following essays first appeared as magazine articles:

"Utopian Thinking," in *Commentary*, July, 1961.

" 'Applied Science' and Superstition," under the title "The Human Uses of Science," in *Commentary*, December, 1960.

"Pornography and the Sexual Revolution," under the title "Pornography, Art and Censorship," in *Commentary*, March, 1961.

"Designing Pacifist Films," in *Liberation*, May, 1961.

"Post-Christian Man," in *WMFT Prospective*, November, 1961.

"On the Intellectual Inhibition of Explosive Grief and Anger," in *Complex*, spring, 1950.

"My Psychology as a 'Utopian Sociologist,' " in *Anvil*, winter, 1960.

"On a Writer's Block," in *Complex*, winter, 1952.

"Notes on a Remark of Seami," in *The Kenyon Review*, autumn, 1958.

"Dr. Reich's Banned Books," in *Kulchur*, 1960.

"Banning Cars from Manhattan" (with Percival Goodman), in *Dissent*, summer, 1961.

"What Is a Picture," in *Art News*, April, 1959.

"Advance-Guard Writing in America: 1900-1950," in *The Kenyon Review*, summer, 1951.

"Good Interim Writing—1954," under the title "Good Enough Long Enough," in *The Kenyon Review*, winter, 1955.

"Underground Writing, 1960," under the title "Notes on the Underworld," in *The Nation*, March 11, 1961.

TO ELLIOTT SHAPIRO

Preface

Frequently in the following essays I return to the characteristic moral dilemma of the Americans today: "It is only by the usual technological and organizational procedures that anything can be accomplished. But with these procedures, and the motives and personalities that belong to them, fresh initiative is discouraged and fundamental change is prevented." There is a style in which problems are stated, there are established techniques, there are channels of influence; often all these are pretty irrelevant. If there's an increase of delinquency or addiction, our only recourse is more repressive legislation, although experience and theory prove that this does not work and creates worse problems. If there are urban problems of congestion, poor transportation, and slums, our recourse is to new and bigger technological wonders, although experience and theory prove that these soon create worse problems. When economic expansion begins to produce a glut of goods more and more dubious in value and threatening unemployment, our recourse is to increase the rate of expansion and to step up the advertising, though the goods become even more useless and the jobs that provide these goods even more meaningless. A psychologist would say that our people suffer from a compulsion neurosis; they are warding off panic by repeating themselves; inevitably, they are very busy and very conformist. There is no effort radically to remedy the causes and improve the center, and there is little effort to think up new directions that would offer opportunities for more normal growth, and to educate to more prudent motives and methods. Indeed, given our usual agencies and offices, and the kind of technicians and even the kind of social scientists that we have, it is hard to see who *could* make the effort. Therefore the logical conclusion of the American moral dilemma is the conclusion that dilemmas generally have: "Really, we cannot do anything. We are trapped by modern times."

Naturally, as a live animal and the heir of a great culture, I cannot accept this unsatisfactory syllogism, although, like everybody else, I have had occasion to experience its validity. I do not grant the premises. By analyzing the usual procedures and motivations, it can be shown, I think, that they are *not* always necessary and that they are rarely the best. And indeed, one can make bold to suggest better things that *can* be done by better means. So this is a book of Utopian Essays and Practical Proposals. Partly I have a spiteful motive in writing such a book in the present climate of our society. It is to establish that if you do not do better, it is not because there are no alternatives, but because you do not choose to. Modern science and modern cities need not work out as they do with us. Our problems are *not* technological and sociological; they are moral and political. The question is, is it worth while to bring this home to people? Does it not merely arouse guilt and anxiety? For, if we conclude that our problems are moral and political, a more glaring problem at once presents itself: Why do people not choose better? What are they afraid of? They are afraid of losing their jobs; each one is afraid to be embarrassed by thinking and acting differently from his fellows; nobody really knows enough to risk a radical change, and so forth. But such surface explanations accept, and buttress, the very system of procedures and motivations that is at issue. Why isn't everybody eager to make his job worth while? Why is there not a premium on originality? How, in social and also technical matters, have people become so distrustful of the evidence of their senses and feelings? Frankly, I find these questions puzzling. I do not know the answers, but I think I know where to look.

2

As my books and essays have appeared, I have been severely criticized as an ignorant man who spreads himself thin on a wide variety of subjects, on sociology and psychology, urbanism and technology, education, literature, esthetics, and ethics. It is true that I don't know much, but it is false that I write about many subjects. I have only one, the human beings I know in their man-made scene. I do not observe that people are in fact subdivided in ways to be conveniently treated by the "wide variety" of separate disciplines. If you talk separately about their group behavior or their individual behavior, their environment or their characters, their practicality or their sensibility, you lose what you are talking about. We are often forced, for analytic purposes, to study a problem under various departments —since everybody can't discuss everything at once, but woe if one then plans for people in these various departments! One will never create a community, and will destroy such community as exists.

The separate disciplines are the best wisdom we have; I wish I knew them better. But there is a real difficulty with them that we might put as follows: In my opinion, it is impossible to be a good lawyer, teacher, statesman, physician, minister of religion, architect, historian, social worker, or psychologist, without being a good deal of all of them at once; yet obviously—especially today when there is such a wealth of indispensable specialist knowledge—it is impossible to be expert in more than one or two "fields." Again, I do not have an answer; but I prefer to preserve the wholeness of my subject, the people I know, at the cost of being everywhere ignorant or amateurish. I make the choice of what used to be called a Man of Letters, one who relies on the peculiar activity of authorship—a blending of memory, observation, criticism, reasoning, imagination, and reconstruction—in order to treat the objects in the world concretely and centrally. And may I say this?—if to many people my thinking seems always to have a kind of surprising optimism, a foolish optimism, my hunch is that it is because I keep trying to see people whole and beginning—still growing—and then they seem less limited than they do to sociologists or psychologists, politicians or journalists. But it doesn't much matter whether one has an "optimistic" or a "pessimistic" outlook, for the question still remains, Now what?

I seem to be able to write only practically, inventing expedients. (When I write as a poet, my poems are my expedients.) My way of writing a book of social theory has been to invent community plans. My psychology is a manual of therapeutic exercises. A literary study is a manual of practical criticism. A discussion of human nature is a program of pedagogical and political reforms. This present book is no exception. It is social criticism, but almost invariably (except in moments of indignation) I find that I know what I don't like only by contrast with some concrete proposal that makes more sense.

I have arranged these essays under the usual "wide variety" of headings—social-psychology, architecture, youth problems, literature, etc. As I have explained, I do not take these divisions very seriously. But there is, instead, in all these essays a certain unity of method, and I should like to spell it out.

(1) Whatever the subject, I try to keep it *imbedded in its social-psychological causes*, relying heavily on the familiar authors in psychoanalysis, functionalist anthropology, and social history. (I here regret the lack of a medical training, for I am sure that physiological causes are relevant, but I do not know them.)

(2) I try to find in the subject *a structural idea that I can show actually operating*. When I have this, I have

something to say. For instance, when I see that there is an intrinsic relation among a certain stage of life, a certain kind of work, and a certain kind of community, I have an essay on Youth Work Camps. Or I understand Advance-Guard art when I see that it is an "inner" response to an indigestible "introjected" social norm. Sometimes I use the same device negatively, pointing to an evident incoherence or failure of structure in order to define the nature of a situation—for example, the contradiction in the University between its tradition and its practice; or the incoherence in recent painting between the framing and the thing that is being framed.

(3) But finally, I tend to see the subject as *ongoing into the immediate future, requiring to be coped with.* That is, characteristically I choose subjects that are political, personal, or literary problems of practice, and this is why my essays come so often to suggesting expedients, "just to live on a little," as Goethe said. And the problems are my problems. As a writer I am hampered by the present law on pornography, and as a man and a father by the sexual climate of that law; so it is a problem for *me.* It is as a New Yorker that I propose to ban the cars from the streets and create a city of neighborhoods. As an intellectual man thwarted, I write on the inhibition of grief and anger and look for a therapy to unblock them. And it is because I am hungry for the beauty of a practical and scientific environment that I am dismayed by our "applied science" and would like to explain it away.

Apart from history or fiction, a human subject matter is not "explained" unless we cope with its immediate future; what it is is what it is about to be, and this means what we can try to make it. This has an existentialist ring, but I trust that my thinking is less merely willed than French existentialism, less cut off from body, culture, and spirit. The reader will see that by and large I prefer the language of pragmatism and, best, an organism/environment psychology of novelty, excitement, and growth. The existing is prior to hopes and plans; and the "Right Method" is to find in the existing the occasion that has future, freedom to act.

3

The present crisis in which an American writes is a peculiar one. He confronts in his audience the attitude that things are well enough, there is nothing to be grievous or angry about, and anyway our situation is inevitable. This attitude is the audience's technological and organizational helplessness mollified by the famously high standard of living. It puts a writer in the position of, as we Jews say, banging a teakettle, when his readers couldn't care less. At the same time, these same people are evidently in the grip of anxiety in the face of changes and threatening changes that they don't begin to prepare for. Instead, they eat up books that glumly expose our plight; and they turn to the daily headlines for new shocking surprises. So a writer, instead of being able to devote himself to the truth and use of his subject matter, finds himself delivering sermons to rebuild morale and to prove that common reason is, in spite of all, practical. But worst of all, if he can successfully achieve these two marvels, of noisily affirming obvious goods and of proving that where there's life there's hope, the writer is wondered at and praised as a refreshing idealist of the olden times. A hundred years ago, Ruskin said bitterly, "I show men their plain duty and they reply that my style is charming." My own experience is that when I suggest a practical proposal plain as the nose on your face, people weep with pleasure for the reminder of paradise lost.

What idea do these people have? The idea of Jeffersonian democracy is to educate its people to govern by giving them initiative to run things, by multiplying sources of responsibility, by encouraging dissent. This has the beautiful moral advantage that a man can be excellent in his own way without feeling special, can rule without ambition and follow without inferiority. Through the decades, it should have been the effort of our institutions to adapt this idea to ever changing technical and social conditions. Instead, as if by a dark design, our present institutions conspire to make people inexpert, mystified, and slavish.

One is astounded at the general slavishness. The journalists at the President's press conference never ask a probing question; they have agreed, it seems, not to "rock the boat." Correspondingly, the *New York Times* does not print the news, because it is a "responsible newspaper." Recently, the Commissioner of Education of the State of New York spoke of the need for young people to learn to "handle constructively their problems of adjustment to authority"—a remarkable expression for doing what you're told. Then I have heard young people in a philosophy class express their resentment against Socrates as a moral aristocrat who had principles to decide his behavior, whereas "most people are not up to that." To them there are apparently different grades of humanity. Griping sailors sit on a fence and slavishly snicker at the ensigns who walk by with girls; and in the corporations, the junior executives talk about the Rat Race, yet kowtow to rank. This is slavish. It is a short step to the mentality of the operators and hipsters who take it for granted that the legitimate world belongs to the Others, and who then spitefully try to prove that earnest people are frauds or suckers.

So we drift into fascism. But people do not recognize it as such, because it is the fascism of the majority.

Contents

xi   Preface

1

3   Utopian thinking

22   "Applied science" and superstition

49   Pornography and the sexual revolution

70   Designing pacifist films

80   Post-Christian man

2

93   On the intellectual inhibition of explosive
grief and anger

110   My psychology as a "Utopian sociologist"

119   On a writer's block

130   Notes on a remark of Seami

138   Dr. Reich's banned books

3

145   *Banning cars from Manhattan*
       (with Percival Goodman)

156   *Seating arrangements: An elementary lecture in*
       functional planning

182   *What is a picture?*

4

191   *Advance-guard writing in America: 1900-1950*

217   *Good interim writing—1954*

222   *Underground writing—1960*

236   *Some problems of interpretation: silence,*
       and speech as action

5

255   *Vocational guidance*

263   *Youth work camps*

274   *Crisis and new spirit*

UTOPIAN ESSAYS
AND
PRACTICAL PROPOSALS

Utopian thinking

After a long spell of Marxian "scientific" realism and businessmen's† "hard-headed" realism, our social scientists have begun to praise "utopian thinking." Since the war, the cultural anthropology of the Americans has thus taken the following course: first, a flood of popular social criticism, and now an emphasis on goals and utopias. What is meant by such language? When is it used? What does it conceal?

This new praise of utopian thinking occurs in the context of our surplus technology. There is a vast productive capacity already lying idle, and the threat of sharply increased efficiency with automation. It is necessary to use capital and labor for some purpose or other, if only for plausible fantasies, and utopias promise more efficient planned consumption than the synthetic demand created by advertising. This may not be a bad thing. Luxury corrupts, and though moral corruption is wicked and usually foolish, it is rarely explosive and sometimes amiable. For instance, even the Soviet Union, as it tends to become a "have" nation, seems to become less Calvinist and fanatical. And when in our country David Riesman urges the youth of Kansas to build a mountain so that they can have manly work and enjoy skiing, one does not know whether to cry or laugh or cheer. Such an expedient is less morally outrageous than planned obsolescence. And it is certainly no more dismaying than our present Mass Leisure.

Naturally, utopian ideas for using up a surplus will not exhibit the common sense and parsimonious sweetness of Fourier or William Morris trying to remedy harsh conditions of labor by proving that centralized production is not necessary for happiness. Nor will there be a premium on the abstract justice and wisdom that inspired Plato or Thomas More, for it is characteristic of our period (as I shall argue below) that moral choices are considered irrelevant. Our new utopian thinking seems rather to comprise:

(1) A heavy indulgence in the sensational technologism of Bellamy, Sant'Elia, and science fiction; that is to say, visions of vaster and more marvelous achievements in the technical and managerial style that we are already used to. But this is soon admixed with the anti-utopianism of *Brave New World*—the suspicion that more such advancements will settle us for good. A variant of such utopias is the plea for "future-thinkings," like Margaret Mead's proposal to cut History out of the universities and substitute Chairs of the Future. In principle, future-thinking is the extrapolation of our present ways, a combination of market research and the theory of games; the one thing that the "future" must not change is the rules. (History deals, at least, with different kinds of error.)

(2) But a more useful property of our technology is its plasticity, the opportunity it offers for alternative choices of power, raw materials, location, tooling, and a surplus for transition and retooling. Thus, we could decentralize instead of centralizing, with probably

equivalent efficiency. We seem at present to be trying to choose between more public goods or more leisure goods; we could even choose more leisure without more goods, but this would perhaps involve moral and political alternatives that are excluded. Now, to make interesting choices, inventive imagination is indispensable. When people were asked about twenty years ago, "What do you want in your postwar house?" the responses were hopelessly banal, and Catherine Bauer wisely commented, "People can want only what they know." One must invent something and show it to them. But there is nothing utopian about inventions; they either work and win their way, or they fail.

Perhaps ideas are "utopian," however, when they work and do *not* win their way, like the nickel-cadmium battery, or like Fuller's Dymaxion automobile, a better car that did not fit in with the plans of Detroit, which has proceeded for twenty-five years to dole out less drastic improvements, until spurred by Europe. This brings us, I think, to the virulent meaning of "utopian," the sense in which it is controversial.

(3) Ideas are called "utopian" when they seem to be useful but they propose a different style, a different procedure, a different kind of motivation from the way people at present do business. Such ideas may make obvious common sense and may, technically, be very easy to effectuate; all the more will they be called "impractical" and "an imposition on people by experts and intellectuals," with a vehemence that indicates a powerful psychological resistance. Let me tell a melancholy anecdote.

An executive of the Columbia Broadcasting System recently asked me, as an "intellectual," to outline an article critical of TV, for they planned to put out a highbrow magazine to recoup, by self-criticism, the prestige lost in the quiz scandals. He said they were even afraid of losing their franchise. Since I have a positive turn of mind, I dutifully offered as my contribution a few proposals for good programs. (One that I remember was to allow Franz Kline, Picasso, Cocteau, etc., to create half-hour montages on the screen, and so explore what the medium can do. This would evoke a "storm" of ridicule and protest—as many as twenty letters—but it would be looked at and might do a public service.) To my surprise, my innocent proposals cast the executive into consternation. "You don't get the idea at all," he said; "we want you to criticize unsparingly. We can handle that. We know that TV is lousy, but it's inevitably so. But now you try to show that it could be different!" (P.S. I did not get the job.)

There is no doubt that the term "utopian thinking" is importantly used to conceal the statement: *The structure and folkways of our society are absurd, but they can no longer be changed. Any hint of changing them disturbs our resignation and rouses anxiety. Cruelly, for things are well enough as they are.*

The situation was remarkably summarized by the recent remark of an important businessman's wife. "The way this business is run," she said, "we would have failed long ago if we didn't make so much money."

2

In a technical sense, to call a utopian proposal "impractical" is ludicrous. Consider the actualities of the recent generation, since the Depression. In New York City alone there has been built, at more than a million dollars a mile, the entire parkway system: the East and West Side drives; the Belt, Henry Hudson, Saw Mill River, and Bronx River parkways; the Cross-County and Major Deegan expressways; the Thruway; the Whitestone and Triboro bridges; the Holland Tunnel, two Lincoln tunnels, the Queens-Midtown and Brooklyn-Battery tunnels, etc. These have entirely transformed the residential pattern of the city and the behavior of its inhabitants, revolutionized land values, produced a different kind of suburban culture. In the central city itself, whole neighborhoods have been disrupted, razed, replaced by tall housing in low- and middle-income ghettos. No utopian planner would dare propose or would want to propose such vast, disruptive, and expensive changes as this colossal bad planning effectuated by Robert Moses and his associates. Again in less than twenty years the entire pattern of culture and entertainment in the United States has been transformed, centralized, intensified, stereotyped, and debased by TV and the TV networks, invading more than 70 per cent of the homes and hypnotizing more hours of attention per day than anything since the Tibetan prayer wheels. The most misguided religious reformer would not have fantasized a comparable ritual observance. And in the same period, again, the peculiar complex of graduated income taxes, swollen expense accounts, diners' clubs, and the new hotels, has dovetailed with the absolute novelty of standardized air travel and with the American zeal for making casual acquaintances, to create extraordinary institutions like business trips, conventions, panel discussions, and sessions of brainstorming. Thousand-mile journeys that used to be undertaken only by commercial travelers and itinerant lecturers have suddenly become routine for a great segment of the middle class. Naturally, between this and the TV, any regional differences that once existed have vanished into the sameness of Hilton hotels and Hertz drive-yourself cars. (For serious planners, this history is a model of how great and many-sided changes come about through a combination of fiscal, technological, and psychological factors.) And finally, it is barely fifteen years since the atom bomb has altered what we mean by peace and war.

But the other criticism that is made of utopian ideas,

that they propose an unusual dictatorial imposition upon people, is equally unrealistic. Not only has the physical behavior of most of us been rudely altered by the new techniques and institutions, but people are entrapped in them far more totally than we Americans, at least, were ever accustomed to. This has been the chief burden of the social criticism of the organization, the bureaucracy, the status-seeking, the advertising, the standard of living, the methods of wielding control and managing initiative. Immensely proliferating, the system pre-empts nearly all the space, all the channels, and all the resources. As Darwin would have said, this is a successful new species, like the rabbits in Australia. It dictates the style of drama and the format of debate. By its centralizing and stereotyping, it disrupts community and individuality, which are then, for necessary creature comfort and social security, reconstituted by the cult of a pantheon of canned symbols. All human societies are patterns of culture, but the present American—and increasingly world-wide—pattern has superseded the old with great suddenness; and it has certainly had the effect of being imposed, for it has created affectlessness, delinquency, fad without style, role without task, and inquiry after "goals," as if goals were not implicit in concrete activity.

Nevertheless, inept as it seems, the charge that "utopian thinking" is impractical and an imposition does have a meaning. It is a subtle meaning, but devastatingly important.

The rapid changes and impositions that have actually occurred in recent years have not *directly* impinged on each person's sense of his individual "personality," his liberty of choice, his privacy, his bodily intactness, his sexual and family behavior. On a broader view it is obvious that, indirectly, the individual is entrapped, seduced, pushed, limited—in his education, his jobs, his hygiene, his politics, his marriage, and parenthood;

but his "personality" is kept pretty inviolate, perhaps even more so than in previous generations. (The exceptions, the violations of personality, are the draft and desegregation.) The provisions of the Constitution and the immediate moral outrage of all the other personalities protect individuality and the sanctity of the home. (In other, less politically fortunate areas, e.g., Africa, the imposition of our technical ways causes much more personal and community hurt and is reacted to violently.)

Now, it is just this feeling of individual intactness that we "utopians" who think in terms of common sense and direct action toward obvious goods, continually seem to violate. Our simple-minded proposals make people feel foolish and timid; our plea for community wakes up sleeping dogs and rebellious hopes; we mention ancient wisdom that everybody believes but has agreed to regard as irrelevant; and all this among people who *in fact* have little control of the means of production or power, but are nicely habituated to the complicated procedures of the moment and get satisfaction by identifying with them. Therefore, paradoxically, the simpler and more easily effected the ideas we suggest—the less "utopian" they are—the more they are *really* impractical for these people. If we recommend an old-fashioned straightforward procedure, we seem to be asking that a foreign or "advance-guard" way of life be imposed. Naturally, we who are beguiled by the sirens of reason, animal joy, and lofty aims, fail to notice how far out into left field we sometimes stray; but we are most out of contact in naïvely believing that, given simple means and a desirable end, something can be *done*.

This is the crux of the argument over utopian thinking. It *is* true that the organized American system has invaded people's personalities, even though it protects every man's individuality, privacy, and liberty of choice

For the system has sapped initiative and the confidence to make fundamental changes. It has sapped self-reliance and therefore has dried up the spontaneous imagination of ends and the capacity to invent ingenious expedients. By disintegrating communities and confronting isolated persons with the overwhelming processes of the whole society, it has destroyed human scale and deprived people of manageable associations that can be experimented with.

I do not think that this result is inevitable from the use of scientific technology and mass communications. It is not hard to think up industrial arrangements that fire initiative rather than dampen it. There are known methods of education and organs of culture to counteract sheepishness, and they could be encouraged instead of neglected. But the case is that, whether innocently or cynically, our present procedures and those who manage them have exerted and do exert a poisonous moral influence. To demonstrate this point it is not necessary to explore details like subliminal advertising or wire tapping, except to see that they are logical next steps.

Gentlemen of power who claim, perhaps ingenuously, that "we give people what they want, we cannot impose higher standards on them," ought to ask themselves if they are taking responsibility for the sheer quantities of messages and objects with which they swamp the public, for the pre-emption of space and resources, for the monopolistic exclusion of alternatives, and worst of all, for trivializing the earnest by glamorizing the base, catering to a low standard. In a recent address, Dr. Thomas Coffin of the National Broadcasting Company reassured his (Ethical Culture) audience that radio and TV really had little effect on "basic moral values." (He cited a sociological study.) Surprisingly, the audience exclaimed that that was just the worst of it, that such a vast quantity of communication and entertainment filled up the foreground of attention and *had* no moral effect, and this in itself was a disastrous moral effect, for it made moral choice inarticulate and irrelevant. For instance, when thousands of hours are taken up by mere entertainment, we can be sure that there will be little dramatic art that purges and changes the audience; and there will be a jaded audience slow to respond to anything essential. Again like the rabbits in Australia, these enterprises proliferate because they never meet with a moral enemy head-on; but indirectly they win out by eating up the crops. Whether in goods or the communication of ideas, once a market has been cornered—sometimes with collusion among the "competitors"—it can soon become effectually the case that there is no alternative; the way things are is the way they must be.

To give a grim example: in order to batten on Urban Renewal and other money, promoters will get a perfectly savageable neighborhood classified as a slum for demolition. The residents protest; but because of the classification, owners are discouraged from making improvements, banks will not finance renovations, excellent but timid residents move away. So by the time the protest drags through the hostile administrative procedure, the neighborhood *is* certifiable as a slum and is demolished. The example is grim because there is, at the same time, a critical shortage of housing, and a functioning neighborhood has been disrupted.

Recent history, however, seems to show that this system is not altogether viable. Granted that the current "social criticism" and "utopian thinking" are mainly means of griping and being adventurous without acting, yet we must also take them at face value as voices of dissent. A more important symptom is the increasing polarization of attitudes. Among the young, there are those who are content and able to perform, and those who are totally disgusted and withdraw: the squares and the beats—with the hip playing it cool, whether as juvenile delinquents or aspiring junior executives. And in the adult world that the young graduate into, there is a polarizing between economy and vocation; between "communications" and honest speech innocent of public relations; between *Realpolitik* and politics; between scientific technology and the humanities. Put crudely, the means lack goods and the goods lack means. Groups polarize, with mutual resentment, according to whether they need to be in the swim, busy and identifying with power, or are honorably baffled and protestant. "Utopians," however, are praised because they are neither realistic nor resigned, but have, as Riesman once said, "the nerve of failure" (a jolly state of life). They still think that machines are meant to be useful, that work is a productive activity, that politics aims at the common weal, and in general that something can be done. These are now utopian ideals.

3

Let me use ideas of mine as an example, since I am notoriously a "utopian thinker." That is, on problems great and small, I try to think up direct expedients that do not follow the usual procedures, and they are always called "impractical" and an "imposition on people by an intellectual." The question is—and I shall try to pose it fairly—in what sense are such expedients really practical, and in what sense are they really *not* practical? Consider half a dozen little thumbnail ideas:

The ceremony at my boy's public school commencement is poor. We ought to commission the neighborhood writers and musicians to design it. There is talk about aiding the arts, and this is the way to advance them, for, as Goethe said, "The poetry of public occasions is the highest kind." It gives a real subject to the poet, and ennobles the occasion.

Similarly, we do not adequately use our best talents. We ought to get our best designers to improve some of the thousands of ugly small towns and make them unique places to be proud of, rather than delegate such matters to professionals in bureaucratic agencies, when we attend to them at all. A few beautiful models would be a great incentive to others.

In our educational system, too much is spent for plant and not enough for teachers. Why not try, as a pilot project, doing without the school building altogether for a few hundred kids for most of the day? Conceive of a teacher in charge of a band of ten, using the city itself as the material for the curriculum and the background for the teaching. Since we are teaching *for* life, try to get a little closer to it. My guess is that one could considerably diminish the use of present classrooms and so not have to increase their number.

The problem with the old ladies in a Home is to keep them from degenerating, so we must provide geriatric "occupational therapy." The problem with the orphans in their Home is that, for want of individual attention, they may grow up as cold or "psychopathic personalities." But the old ladies could serve as grandmothers for the orphans, to their mutual advantage. The meaning of community is people using one another as resources.

It is false to say that community is not possible in a great city, for 6,000,000 can be regarded as 2,000 neighborhoods of 3,000. These make up one metropolis and enjoy its central advantages, yet they can have a variety of particular conditions of life and have different complexes of community functions locally controlled. E.g., many neighborhoods might have local control of their small grade-schools, with the city enforcing minimum standards and somewhat equalizing the funds. Political initiative is the means of political education.

In any city, we can appreciably diminish commutation by arranging mutually satisfactory exchanges of residence to be near work. The aim of planning is to diminish in-between services that are neither production nor consumption. More generally, if this wasted time of commutation were considered *economically* as part of the time of labor, there would soon be better planning and more decentralization.

In New York City, the automobile traffic is not worth the nuisance it causes. It would be advantageous simply to ban all private cars. Nearly everyone would have faster transportation. Besides, we could then close off about three-quarters of the streets and use them as a fund of land for neighborhood planning.

Now, apart from the particular merits or demerits of any of these ideas, what is wrong with this *style* of thinking, which aims at far-reaching social and cultural advantages by direct and rather dumb-bunny expedients? I think that we can see very simply why it is "utopian."

It is risky. The writers and musicians designing the commencement ceremony would offend the parents, and the scandal would be politically ruinous to the principal, the school board, and the mayor. Nobody expects the ceremonial to be anything but boring, so let sleeping dogs lie. Artists are conceited anyway and would disdain the commissions. So with the small towns: the "best designers" would make the local hair stand on end. As for the thought of children being educated by roaming the streets and blocking traffic, it is a lulu and the less said the better.

Further, such thinking confuses administrative divisions. Community arrangements are always awkwardly multipurpose. What department is responsible? Who budgets? It is inefficient not to have specialized equipment, special buildings, and specialists.

Further, community creates conflict, for incompatibles are thrown together. And there is definitely an imposition of values. "Community" is an imposed value, for many people want to be alone instead of sharing responsibilities or satisfactions; that is why they came to the big city. The notion of living near work, or of a work-residence community, implies that people like their work; but most people today don't.

Further, most such proposals are probably illegal; there would never be an end to litigation. They override the usual procedures, so there is no experience of the problems that might arise; one cannot assess consequences or refer to standard criteria.

Further, they are impracticable. To effect a change in the usual procedures generally requires the pressure of some firm that will profit by it; such things do not happen just because they would be "advantageous"; one can hardly get the most trivial zoning regulation passed.

Finally, such proposals are impractical if only because they assume that the mass of people have more sense and energy than they in fact have. In emergencies, people show remarkable fortitude and choose sensible values and agree to practical expedients because it is inevitable; but not ordinarily. The quotation from Goethe is typical; it is "true," but not for us.

This is a fair picture of our dilemma. A direct solution of social problems disturbs too many fixed arrangements. Society either does not want such solutions, or society is not up to them—it comes to the same thing. The possibility of a higher quality of experience arouses distrust rather than enthusiasm. People must be educated slowly. On the other hand, the only way *to* educate them, to change the present tone, is to cut through habits, especially the character-defense of saying "nothing can be done" and withdrawing into conformity and privacy. We must prove by experiment that direct solutions are feasible. To "educate" in the accustomed style only worsens the disease. And if we do *not* improve the standard of our present experience, it will utterly degenerate.

Therefore we must confront the dilemma as our problem. Our present "organized" procedures are simply not good enough to cope with our technological changes. They debase the users of science, they discourage inventive solutions, they complicate rather than simplify, they drive away some of the best minds. Yet other procedures rouse anxiety and seem unrealistic and irresponsible—whether or not they actually are. The question is, what kind of social science can solve a dilemma of this kind? Let us approach this question by deviating to a more philosophical consideration.

4

In my opinion Americans have lost the spirit of their pragmatic philosophy, even while following the letter. We pay a good deal of attention to "methods" in the solving of problems, just as "scientific knowledge" is applied to technology; but the right method has ceased to be the particular solving *of* the concrete problem. For James and Dewey, the end and the means, the moral-practical and the instrumental, derive meaning from their intrinsic connection in process, and there is no other meaning. One cannot have "usual procedures" or the problems also become empty of value. Problem or goal suffuses and energizes an enterprise from the beginning and creates means and methods; and the problem or goal is transformed and made definite by carrying the enterprise through.

It is this pragmatic idea that we in America have

been losing as we have moved from the expanding industrialism of the nineteenth century to the affluent technologism of today. (Perhaps our "problems" are not serious enough; and the serious problems are disregarded.) Men used to work the machines, also forming themselves to the machine—this was the lesson of Veblen and of the early thinking of Frank Lloyd Wright. Now it is coming to be that the machines work themselves, and the men are formed passively on the system of production and the products; they are creatures of their standard of living and of their roles. In the logic of science, the operational definition of meaning (that the meaning of a proposition lies in the operations that test it), which began as an exquisite refinement of Dewey's instrumentalism, now tends to put both human problems and the nature of things pretty far out of sight, and therefore "truth" is interpreted as the self-expanding and self-correcting system of scientific operations in isolation from anything else—and scientific knowledge is then "applied." In sociology and politics, on the other hand, the noble pragmatic aim of developing a natural ethics and a moral politics has degenerated into a dreary teleology of fixed and arbitrary "values," "national goals," and even profits and ratings. What is the condition of a society whose "goals" are not implicit in its activity, but have to be sought out by a Presidential Commission and imposed! (Of course, they are not even imposed—which would be a political act; the entire procedure is ceremonial and "politics.") In pedagogy, contrast the pragmatic progressive method of learning by experimental work in a functional community, to educate the "whole child," with the technological-teleological program of teaching predetermined lessons by a teaching machine that reinforces lessons. We have come to the very antithesis of pragmatism. In this new climate, where experts plan in terms of an unchangeable structure, a pragmatic expediency that still wants to take the social structure as plastic and changeable comes to be thought of as "utopian." And meantime, of course, the structure is really changing with violent rapidity—impractically.

What would be a pragmatic method in the social sciences?

The closest approximation in official sociology is that caucus of the American Sociological Association that calls itself the Social Problems Approach. The Approach is to choose a problem area, to work it with research and analysis, and to find a solution. But I attended a congress of this group last winter and, to my chágrin, I heard paper after paper choose interesting areas and "do" sociology, but there was hardly ever a solution. Nor could there be, because the sociologists did not have that kind of pragmatic involvement *in* the problem by which a solution might emerge; they were applying "methods." The problem was treated too "objectively," as if it were not a human problem and therefore one that also implicated the investigator personally. There were too many "hypotheses," as though the problems did not require inventive solutions, to be found only *in* the solving. Naturally there was a lot of testing but little experiment. (If there is a real social problem, with stubborn participants who are not fools, something must be changed in how the problem is taken or it will not give way. For instance, we might uncover "inner conflicts" and change the locus, e.g., in racial troubles; or make a new invention and find new resources, e.g., for economically depressed regions; or we might have to change the political structure in which the problem exists, e.g., nuclear war.)

An interesting use of a really experimental approach has been made at Earlham College in Indiana, especially by William Biddle, in a course called Community Dynamics. Here the method is for the professor and students to go into the problem area, to study and work with the people involved; they irradiate the problem from within, with such science and understanding as they have; and, in reported cases, solutions have emerged from their participation. Clearly this is both classical progressive education and classical pragmatic sociology.

Let us attempt a list of postulates for a pragmatic social science:

(1) The fact that the problem is being studied is a factor in the situation. The experimenter is one of the participants and this already alters the locus of the problem, usefully objectifying it.

(2) The experimenter cannot know definitely what he is after, he has no fixed hypothesis to demonstrate, for he hopes that an unthought-of-solution will emerge in the process of coping with the problem. It is an "open" experiment.

(3) The experimenter, like the other participants, is "engaged"; he has a moral need to come to a solution, and is therefore willing to change his own conceptions, and even his own character. As Biddle has said: "A hopeful attitude toward man's improvability may become a necessary precondition to further research," for otherwise one cannot morally engage oneself.

(4) Since he does not know the outcome, the experimenter must risk confusion and conflict, and try out untested expedients. The safeguard is to stay in close contact with the concrete situation and to be objective and accurate in observation and reporting, and rigorous in analysis.

In the context of a pragmatic social science, utopian thinking at once falls into place. Utopian ideas may be practical hypotheses, that is, expedients for pilot experimentation. Or they may be stimuli for response, so that people get to know what they themselves mean.

The fact that such ideas go against the grain of usual thinking is an advantage, for they thereby help to change the locus of the problem, which could not be solved in the usual terms. For instance, they may raise the target of conceivable advantages to a point where certain disadvantages, which were formerly prohibitive, now seem less important. (The assurance of help for an underprivileged child to go to college may make it worth while for him not to become delinquent. This has been the point of the "utopian" Higher Horizons program in the New York City schools.) Further, if a utopian expedient seems *prima facie* sensible, directly feasible, and technically practical, and is nevertheless unacceptable, there is a presumption that we are dealing with an "inner conflict," prejudice, the need to believe that nothing can be done, and the need to maintain the status quo.

5

As an illustration of the several points of this essay, consider utopian planning for increased face-to-face community, people using one another as resources and sharing more functions of life and society. In a recent discussion I had with Herbert Gans of the University of Pennsylvania and other sociologists, it was agreed by all that our present social fragmentation, individual isolation, and family privacy are undesirable. Yet it was also agreed that to throw people together *as they are*—and how else do we have them?—causes inevitable conflicts. Here is our dilemma.

Gans argued that the attempt at community often leads to nothing at all being done, instead of, at least, some useful accommodation. In Levittown, for example, a project in the community school fell through because the middle-class parents wanted a more intensive program to assure their children's "careers" (preparation for "prestige" colleges), whereas the lower-middle-class parents, who had lower status aims, preferred a more "progressive" program. "In such a case," said Gans, "a utopian will give up the program altogether and say that people are stupid."

My view is very different. It is that such a conflict is not an obstacle to community but a golden opportunity, *if the give-and-take can continue, if contact can be maintained.* The continuing conflict cuts through the character-defense of people and *defeats* their stupidity, for stupidity is a character-defense. And the heat of the conflict results in better mutual understanding and fraternity. In Levittown, the job of the sociologist should have been not merely to infer the class conflict, but to bring it out into the open, to risk intensifying it by moving also into concealed snobbery and resentment (and racial feeling?), and to confront these people with the *ad hominem* problem: are such things indeed more important to you than, as neighbors, educating your children together?

In quarrels of ordinary personal life, the conflict consists usually in the *weights* that are assigned to opposing values, and so the argument must finally be *ad hominem.* This is the use of face-to-face community —it prevents going on with stereotypes and rationalizations. It is risky, but there are excellent sociological and psychological techniques for maintaining and increasing contact in conflicts; e.g., the different methods of group therapy, the sociometric methods of Moreno and Infield, Community Dynamics, the proper use of motivational research. Also, it makes no difference if the original issue of conflict is lost, if a better understanding results from the conflict, for then there is a lively future. Just so, it is better if city planning is done by competitive projects, exhibited, explained, and submitted to a popular referendum, rather than handed down by official agencies. People might choose unwisely, but they would be educated in the process, and in the fairly short run there would be better planning.

In our era, to combat the emptiness of technological life, we have to think of a new form, the conflictful community. Historically, close community has provided warmth and security, but it has been tyrannical, anti-liberal, and static (conformist small towns). We, however, have to do with already thoroughly urbanized individuals with a national culture and a scientific technology. The Israeli kubbutzim offer the closest approximation. Some of them have been fanatically dogmatic according to various ideologies, and often tyrannical; nevertheless, their urban Jewish members, rather well educated on the average, have inevitably run into fundamental conflict. Their atmosphere has therefore been sometimes unhappy but never deadening, and they have produced basic social inventions and new character-types. Is such a model improvable and adaptable to cities and industrial complexes? Can widely differing communities be accommodated in a larger federation? How can they be encouraged in modern societies? These are utopian questions.

"Applied science" and superstition

> The contrast between [the consequences and] the expectations of the men who a generation or two ago strove, against great odds, to secure a place for science in education, is painful.
> —JOHN DEWEY, 1916

In the century-old debate between Science and the Humanities, the humanities are now a weak opponent. They are not sure of what they are and they do not seem to have much of use to offer; whereas science looms in the fullness of success, it has made new advances in theory, and its technological applications have transformed the modern world. Yet sadly, perhaps just because our humanities are so weak, we have been losing the basic humane values of science itself. Having lost our firm credulity about what man "is" and what society is "for," we have become confused about what is relevant, useful, or efficient. Thomas Huxley or Thorstein Veblen were thinking of a "scientific society" where people were critical and modest, accurate and objective; where they shared in an international community of inquiry; where they lived "naturally," without superstitions or taboos; and they hoped to make this come to be for every child. Is anybody saying anything like this? With us, the idea of a "scientific society" seems to have degenerated to applying the latest findings of professional experts to solve problems for an ignorant mass, problems often created by the ignorance of the mass, including the scientists. This is neither very noble nor very practical. To give the tone of it (at its worst), let me quote from the pitch of an International Business Machines demonstrator: "The demands that will be placed on us [to sell our machines] can be met, for one must never forget that we are the masters. We alone have that great instrument called the human mind. It weighs 2 pounds. It takes only this much space. It can store 15 billion bits of information. It can be fed on less than ½ an apple a day. If man were to build this mighty instrument, it would take all of the power supplied to the City of Rome and require a space as large as Palazzo dei Congressi. All of us have such a machine. We are the masters and not the servants. We can keep pace. Yes, and ahead of the pace if we wish!"

When I ask, "What is a scientific society?" I am not raising an academic question. In this essay I want to analyze two kinds of confusion that the scientific camp suffers from. There is a confusion between science and technology—this is glaringly displayed by such a spokesman as Sir Charles Snow in his recent book on "The Two Cultures." And there exists in both the popular and the scientific mind—though of course differently—a confusion between science and what has to be called magic and superstition. These confusions are socially disastrous. They cost us billions in social wealth, they damage backward peoples and retard their progress from poverty, they jeopardize our safety, and they distort the education of the next generation.

1. SCIENCE AND TECHNOLOGY

There has always been an intimate and mutually productive relation between science and technology. Let me give only spectacular modern examples. It was a problem of navigation that first led to the momentous measurement of the speed of light. The study of thermodynamics, by Carnot, Joule, Kelvin, grew from experience with steam engines, was advanced by working on practical problems of steam engines, and led to discoveries in refrigeration. Darwin's proof of evolution through natural selection relied heavily on experience of breeding livestock, while Mendel's studies in genetics have led to endless uses in agriculture. At present the very word "technology" is used not so much to refer to practical arts as to the application of fairly up-to-date scientific concepts to the mass production of goods and services. It would be awkward to call carpentry "technology," and it would be wrong to call medicine "technology"; but wallboard, canned foods, ship radar, and the manufacture—and prescription?— of penicillin are parts of our technology. Marxist philosophers have insisted on an indissoluble relation, if not formal identity, between science and technology; and *in a background sense*, this is, in my opinion, true. Especially experimental science would not much exist among peoples who lack elaborate industrial arts; they would not have the data, they would not have the techniques, and they would not consider it important. (Yet such peoples might be excellent naturalists and mathematicians, like the Greeks. And in social psychology, with its techniques of rhetoric and pedagogy, all peoples, of course, have plenty of experimental evidence of behavior—a point that is often overlooked.)

A dangerous confusion occurs, however, when contemporary science and the current style of technology come to exist in people's minds as one block, to be necessarily taken as a single whole. The effect of this is that political arguments for some kind or complex of technology, which indeed has been made possible by modern science, are illogically strengthened by the moral excellence, the prestige, and the superstition of science itself. Contrariwise, if anybody opposes the mass production, the export to underdeveloped countries, or the widespread domestic use of certain machines, technical complexes, or therapies, he is sure to be "refuted" as an obscurantist, an irrationalist or esthete, a pessimist or a Luddite. (Sir Charles Snow is liberal with this kind of logic.) Because the adventure of modern science must be pursued, it is concluded that there are no choices in the adoption of scientific technology. This is an error in reasoning, but unfortunately there are powerful vested interests in business and politics throughout the world, on both sides of the Iron Curtain, that want to reinforce this error and probably believe it.

The criteria for the practice of science and the practice of technology are distinct. One may affirm that the most absolute freedom and encouragement—including a blank check—should be given to the pursuit of scientific knowledge, and yet that the mass application of this knowledge to industrial arts, communications, pedagogy, medicine, etc., should be highly selective and discriminating, and even, at present, rather grudging in some departments and regions. I want to affirm both propositions and go on to suggest some political, moral, and psychological criteria for choosing technologies. (What an odd sound such a reasonable proposal has today!)

My reasons for praising science are, of course, the classical ones, but let me spell them out for the pleasure of it. The pursuit of natural truth is a transcending good that justifies itself, like compassion, social justice, fine art, or romantic love. No superior standard exists by which to limit such pursuits, even though the sky falls. The life of research and theory is one of the forms of human happiness. The submission of the intellect to nature is a kind of humble prayer. Scientific habits are positive virtues, and, negatively, science is the chief antidote to illusion, prejudice, and superstition. The adventure of discovery is itself romantic and delights the animal spirits; conversely, any restriction of curiosity and inquiry very soon proves to be psychologically depressing and morally disastrous, leading to trickery and lies. Sometimes (certainly at present) we may fear that the discovery of truth is dangerous or inopportune; nevertheless, we must risk it.

I have not mentioned the final proposition in the classical eulogy of science: that science is useful, it finds out all kinds of things for the general welfare. Precisely in our times, thoughtful scientists might, on reflection, deny this. "The invention of flight, for example, is probably, on balance, a curse." (John Ullmann.) From Hiroshima on, many scientists, for instance those associated with the *Bulletin of Atomic Scientists*, have shouldered responsibility for the spectacularly bad consequences of their work. This certainly does not mean that they give up studying nuclear physics; it does mean that they try to select and control the technical applications.

When we turn to technical applications we are in the realm of prudence and choice, we weigh and balance values, take account of consequences, and realize that consequences are often incalculable. But —apart from the recent cases of the bombs and fall-out, some smoke control, and the traditional cautiousness of medical men—there have been almost no criteria in this field beyond cost and marketability (and legality). On the contrary, the policy in advanced countries has been "as much as possible of all the latest," and the policy in backward countries is now "all of it, as quickly as possible." Yet this technology determines our ways of life. Ideally we should pay the most serious attention to selecting each particular innovation for mass adoption, and to continually reviewing the technology we have. At least we should be ruthless in halting the further proliferation of those machines and their complexes that have demonstrably become ruinous, like the cars and roads.

2. SOME CRITERIA FOR SELECTING TECHNOLOGY

Start with the criterion of Utility. And consider the limiting case of Afro-Asian regions of dire poverty and drudgery, populous and industrially backward. What capital and technicians are useful?

The demand of the Western-trained leaders in these regions (it is hard to know what the people would choose) is to industrialize totally on advanced Western models as quickly as possible, and attain something like the American standard of living. The policy to accomplish this may be to concentrate at once on heavy industry, steel mills, machine tools; or, less radically, to devote part of the production to native goods for export, to build up a balance of trade. Either way, the policy means hard work without immediate rewards, curtailment of consumption, a stringent and likely totalitarian dictatorship both for work-discipline and for very long-range planning, a corresponding increase of the bureaucracy, the enforcing of new work habits, the disruption of the age-old community forms, occasional famines, sometimes the need to repress tribal revolts. Further, there are bound to be immense mistakes; nor is it surprising if, at the end of the process, much has been created that is already outmoded, and even more that does not, after all, suit the native conditions, materials, and uses. Such things could be docu-

mented again and again from the history of the in-
dustrialization of Russia, India, Israel, China, the
Congo, etc., etc.

This policy is understandable as a reaction of despair to economic and political colonialism, leading
people to produce bombers and bombs before anything
else. Importantly, however, it is an illusion sprung
from a superstitious notion of what it means to be
modern and scientific. As such, it is abetted by foreign
promoters who are interested in exporting pipe lines,
mining machinery, and paved roads. But also govern-
ments and international agencies, claiming to have only
benevolent aims, willingly go along with it. Yet if there
were no wish to make profits or wield political influence, it would certainly be more useful to restrict
the import of technology, specifically to give each
region as soon as possible a self-supporting livelihood:
the industries and techniques directly necessary for the
maximum mass production of basic subsistence, food,
shelter, medicine, and clothing where it is essential.
And otherwise hands off! (It is dismaying to see
photographs proving American benevolence by showing Africans in a school learning business methods and
typing, and dressed in collars and ties. Is *any* of this
package useful? Is even literacy according to *our* methods so indispensable for these people?)

To make people quickly self-supporting would be a
far cheaper gift and in the long run a safer investment.
People would be better off almost at once and could
then think up the advantages that come marginally
next in order. They could make their own community
adjustments to the new conditions. In the production
of subsistence goods there cannot be great mistakes,
for people know the values involved. Less prior training
is required. Less is wasted on politicians and policemen;
it is more difficult for grafters to take their toll. People
come to a higher standard according to their own

style and choice, and therefore can develop a living culture out of what they have, instead of suffering a profound alienation. And the relation of means and ends is fairly direct, so that people are not mystified.

For such a policy, the primary technicians required are geographers and physicians, to ascertain the health and resources of each region; then engineers and anthropologically trained craftsmen-teachers and agronomists. There is not so much need for geologists, metallurgists, etc., nor for economists and urbanists. And no need at all for geopoliticians, promoters, and commissars.

If we turn, next, to our own, the most advanced country, the need for selection is equally obvious, though less drastic. It is now generally conceded that much of our production for consumption is humanly useless, of poor quality, wasteful and demoralizing. (Meantime, economically, 30 per cent of our people live in hardship, there is a critical shortage of housing, and so forth.) But in discussing the Affluent Society, let us by-pass utility as a familiar topic, and develop other criteria.

Efficiency, among us, tends to be measured solely in terms of a particular machine—e.g., gasoline per mile —or in terms of a particular complex of industrial operations—e.g., using the by-products. But if we look at our production more philosophically, in larger wholes and more remote effects, we see that some of our most cherished technical assumptions lead to inefficiency. We centralize as if the prime mover were still a huge steam engine that had to keep hot. For instance, it can be demonstrated that, except in highly automated factories where labor cost is small compared to fixed capital, or in heavy mining attached to its site, for the most part large industrial plants and concentrations of industry are less efficient than smaller ones that assemble parts machined in small shops; it is cheaper to transport the parts than the workers, a worker wastes more than an hour a day going to work and parking, etc. (No doubt an important reason for the concentration of big plants has nothing to do with technical efficiency, but with managerial control. I would strongly urge the unions to ask for some of that travel time to be paid, as the mine workers asked for portal-to-portal pay. Maybe that would lead to more efficient planning. As it is, however—for a reason that quite escapes me—a workman cannot count his carfare or fuel as a business expense against his income tax!) Certainly in the layout of cities, almost any kind of neighborhood plan and community-centered production would be far more efficient than our suburbs.

Similarly, by the evident principle that as the unit cost of production falls, the unit cost of distribution rises, it is likely that much of the vast technology of food processing and transportation is inefficient. Back in the 'thirties, when times were harder, Ralph Borsodi showed experimentally that, using domestic electrical apparatus, it was cheaper in hours and minutes of effort to grow and can one's own tomatoes than to buy the national brands—not to speak of the quality; other items, e.g., wheat and bread, were cheaper not on an individual but on a small co-operative basis; and still other items were cheaper maximum-mass-produced and nationally distributed. (I don't think anybody has ever tried to prove that our actual system of price-controlling semimonopolies is good for anything at all.) My conclusion is not that we ought to produce every item in the most efficient way—we have a surplus and it is not necessary to be all that efficient—but rather that, since our economists do not habitually survey alternate possibilities and make an accounting, our national housekeeping has become slovenly. Because of our slovenliness, we fall in bondage to the supermarket, we cannot get going a co-operative movement, our goods are poor in quality.

A more human-scaled production has obvious political and cultural advantages; it allows for more flexible planning, it is more conducive to scientific education and invention. We complain of the deadening centralism and conformity, and we put up with them because they are "efficient." But they are inefficient.

We hear rhetoric on the theme of learning to master the machine lest the machine master us. Let us consider a couple of criteria for the selection of technology and the users of technology, that directly address this problem. If possible, the operation of a machine should be Transparent and Comprehensible to its users. This can be aided by the design and casing of the machine, and by the education of the users. An important corollary is that a machine ought to be *repairable by its user*. Our present plight is that, in the use of cars, telephones, electricity and gas systems, radio equipment, refrigeration, etc., etc., the mass of people are in bondage to a system of service men for even trivial repairs. The service men notoriously take advantage, but much worse is the tendency of the manufacturers to build obsolescense and nonrepairability *into* the machinery. (This is a negative criterion indeed! But it is inevitable that a caste possessing mysterious knowledge will shear the sheep.) What is the consequence? Psychologically, we have developed an anxious climate in which we don't know how to buy because we can't judge quality. It would be very different if we began to introduce the convention that a consumer must learn to take apart a machine and know how it works before he is encouraged to buy it—much as some of us still frown on an adolescent who cannot fix his broken bicycle. To make an analogy: considering the quantity of cars and mileage, there are remarkably few automobile accidents, but this is because the Americans have been tested and know how to drive.

Fifty years ago, the twin ideas of Progressive Education (learning by doing) and Functionalism in planning and design were matured to meet just this problem of making people more adequate to their new technological means, and of molding the new means into a shape and style more able to be grasped. Both movements, and also the related pragmatic philosophy, were criticized as antihumanistic, as abandoning classical education and traditional canons of beauty. But their principle was precisely humanistic, to reintegrate the new scientific specialism with the common intellectual and moral life. We can see that this is an American hope, to have the industrial revolution *and* a broad fundamental democracy; it still haunts us in our philosophizing about the high schools. (In Europe, similar ideas were almost always far more social-revolutionary, whether we think of Rousseau or Fourier, Kropotkin or the original Bauhaus.)

The British biologist Patrick Geddes, when he championed these ideas fifty years ago, however, saw that we must also select among the technologies. He was in the moral tradition of Ruskin, Morris, and the Garden City planners; they had experienced the profound dehumanization of the coal towns. But Geddes imagined that history was on his side, for the "neotechnology" of electricity had come to replace the "paleo technology" of coal and steam. Electricity satisfied the criterion of cleanliness (Amenity); and its easy transmission allowed ubiquitous sources of power, therefore we could plan more freely, e.g., for the culture of cities (the phrase is Lewis Mumford's, a disciple of Geddes). Some of what Geddes hoped has come about; but on the whole the "forces of history" have not helped us much, in the absence of positive political and moral selection. And by a melancholy irony—history is good at creating melancholy irony—most of us followers of Geddes wryly praise the hideous old slums over the neotechnological slums, for they had more human scale and pullulation of life!

Finally, let us turn to some uncritical applications of science in biology and psychology. The most obvious illustration is the craze for antibiotic drugs. These have been mass produced and promoted—with a simply fascinating lack of corresponding reduction in price—with a now conceded disregard of the organism as a whole. A powerful therapy, indicated for emergencies (e.g., for a dangerous mastoiditis), is used for a quick cure of minor or really systemic infections. Similarly, central-system sedatives and tranquilizers are administered with disregard to malnutrition, bad living habits, and bad environment. Meantime, the scientific "untechnological" tradition of medicine, from Hippocrates on—diet, exercise, natural living, airs, and places—is neglected; and the crucial factor of resistance to disease, the profoundest secret in medicine (just as prevention is its glory), is not studied. Mass immunity to a host of particular symptoms seems to be the sought-for goal, rather than the optimum possible health of each particular organism. But the aim of medicine is not, as such, to increase the average life span of a population—a person can be kept alive as a vegetable for years—but to foster the quality of life. If we want a single word for the criterion of selection that is here being abused, it is perhaps Relevance to the thing being treated.

The irrelevant application of technology to psychology is too rich to cope with; it would carry us away. Let us just mention the usual typical items. Dr. Skinner of Harvard has invented a machine that is useful for reinforcing appropriate responses, so it is now to be mass produced as a teaching machine, though it is irrelevant to the chief factors in either teaching or learning. (The purpose is to save money on teachers and have even bigger classes.) A new computer is installed in Iowa that can score millions of standard tests in very little time, so my boy's class is interrupted to take these tests, and the curriculum will surely be modified for the convenience of a mechanical scorer. In a town in Maine a well-financed research project, involving seventeen variables and plenty of work for the rented computer, discovers that boys tend to elect shop and girls tend to elect cooking; the author of the report comments, "We used to think that this was so, now we know." What criterion is being violated here?

Perhaps it is Modesty: to have as few machines, methods, products (and research projects) as possible. Space is limited; people are multiplying; but the machines have multiplied most, with overpowering effect. The bridges and roads are more impressive than the rivers they span and the places they connect. Most immodest of all are the techniques of communication that have cluttered up the void and silence with images and words. It is now the rule that books are written to keep presses running, and the more radio channels we tap, the more drivel will be invented to broadcast.

Thus I have touched on half a dozen criteria for the humane selection of technologies: utility, efficiency, comprehensibility, repairability, ease and flexibility of use, amenity, and modesty. These values are esteemed by scientists and engineers; they are common ground between science and the humanities; they do not entail any conflict. Why are they not generally evident in our "scientific" society? I have purposely chosen only large and economically, rather than culturally, important examples: the type of foreign aid, the planning and distribution of cities, the organization of production, the American standard of living and public health, the methods of education.

3

Return now to the thread of our argument, the confusion of science and technology and the rhetoric of lumping them together. Let a group that is pushing a particular technology be opposed, and this rhetoric is immediately called on. Thus the big drug companies, being investigated for their outrageous pricing and monopolistic stifling of small competitors, have righteously exclaimed that without their methods of mass production, promotion, and pricing, scientific research comes to an end—there will be no more Listers and Pasteurs. Equally far-fetched is the uncriticized assumption of all the large suppliers of scientific technology that they alone are the right sponsors and entrepreneurs of scientific thought and research: this gives them the license to raid the universities for talent, to fill the public schools with their brochures, to influence the appropriation of school funds, to get tax exemptions for "scientific" foundations that are really parts of the firm, and even to dictate the lines of further research and sometimes actively to discourage "unprofitable" lines of research. In foreign aid and the export of capital, firms that have equipment to sell, and materials and fuels to buy, are wonderfully persuasive about helping backward societies to become modern scientific societies. The Pentagon also is an enthusiastic advocate and underwriter of pure research—though not especially on the genetic effects of radioactive fall-out.

For a couple of hundred years, our proliferating technologies have been selected on the criteria of marketability and profitability, and by and large the market has furthered usefulness and efficiency. (But not invariably. Moral economists like Ned Ludd and Coleridge, Ruskin and Ebenezer Howard have been critical for the same two centuries.) In the past fifty years, however, new conditions have developed that are unambiguously baneful. There has been systematic corruption of the public notion of what *is* useful. (An early typical example was the campaign that put across bleached flour as tastier and more "refined," since it spoiled less in the grain elevators.) The growing public ineptitude and ignorance, and a growing mystique of technical experts, have made rational restraint difficult. And finally, by an inevitable reflex, the stream of science itself is channeled and hampered by the too abundant technology that it has created.

This, I submit, is the context of the current debate about what should be taught and how it should be taught. Then it is dismaying to read arguments, like Sir Charles Snow's, from the "scientific point of view," that completely disregard it. Sir Charles is so puffed up with the importance of science in its technical applications that he fails to ask any scientific questions, or to have any qualms of scientific conscience. Apparently some scientists feel so grand about being on the governing board that they are stone-blind to the evident fact that they are not the makers of policy. Do they choose as scientists to have scientific knowledge kept secret? Are they satisfied as scientists that space exploration has so speedily become a means of spying that Russians and Americans cannot co-operate? (It is said that at present our instruments for gathering information are superior, but the Russian rockets can carry more payload: now, what would be logical? who is proposing it?) "The sciences," wrote Jenner—to Paris in 1803!—"are never at war." This follows from the essence of science as a consensus of observers.

But perhaps this is the kind of wisdom to be got from the humanities.

The fact that just now scientific technology is controlling, abusing, and threatening to devastate mankind is neither here nor there as an argument for how we should educate our youth to make a better world.

There were long periods when priests had power, other periods when soldiers had it, and even periods when literary mandarins had it. All of them did useful things and all of them made a mess. So I would propose that scientists think twice about what kind of power they have, what they are co-operating with, and with whom, and try a little harder to know themselves. There is a well-known humanistic technique for this chastening enterprise, the method of Socrates. (Psychotherapy is one of its modern branches.) A little history, too, should be a required course.

4

(Before proceeding to a deeper consideration, allow me to explain that I myself have never been able to distinguish between "science" and the "humanities"— perhaps this is *my* blind spot. The reasons for the absolute autonomy and indeed pre-eminence of science that I listed above are all humanistic reasons, they are what belong to a whole, free, risky human existence. The moral criteria for selecting and refining an industrial society that were listed above are common to scientists and humanists, they are philosophic. If scientists do not think in these terms about technology, it is that they have lost touch with common sense; if humanists do not think about technology at all, it is that they have become withdrawn and therefore stupid. But further—and this is a point that scientists and many modern literary critics are singularly unaware of—the chief content of literature is itself scientific, it is the worldly wisdom and "criticism of life" of good observers who, *in the field of human relations*, had plenty of empirical experience and some pretty hard experiment. If the classics of literature do not much state summary propositions like those in sociology and psychology, but rather have the complex density of poems and plays, it is because the subject matter of human conduct requires this density of statement; it is notoriously missed and distorted by less concrete and moving language. The interpretation of literary statements is the job of humanists, using the tools of historical criticism, linguistics, poetics. Certainly it is a subtle, difficult, and often vague business; but I don't suppose that anybody in his right mind ever thought that the science of man would be less complex than physics or biology. Just consider how the idiomatic use of a language, so judged by the consensus of millions of users of the language, must give us far more experiential evidence for what is the human case than could possibly be gathered by the trivial samplings of sociologists and psychologists. I take it that this was the great rediscovery made by Wittgenstein in his old age, and since developed by the new school of linguistic philosophy.)

5

A hundred years ago, when Matthew Arnold was debating with T. H. Huxley about the merits of literature and science, there was a different cultural climate. Not only had scientific technology not yet spread so triumphantly over the globe, but England was still somewhat a "Christian country." Arnold could rely heavily on tradition and sentiment and arguments about conduct and character. In our times it is "Science" that has become the dominant belief, replacing Christianity and many other faiths. It is now the scientists who rely on assumptions of tradition, sentiment, and right conduct. I think it is necessary to explore this profound change in order to explain the present uncritical acceptance of the technical fruits of science. Radically new ways of behavior require profound changes in popular belief. A system of thinking spreads unlimitedly when it no longer meets serious opponents.

In my opinion, science has become a superstition for both the mass of the people and scientists themselves. For the mass it has the power of magic. For the scientists it has the exclusive virtue of an orthodox theology.

Roughly defined, magic is the power of affecting material nature, including men's souls and bodies, by occult means known to a caste of specialists. Let us recall that from deep in the Middle Ages, and earlier, the practice of experimental science was popularly linked with magic rather than with the philosophic quest for truth or the immediate utility of industrial arts. The typical figure is Roger Bacon. For the savant or contemplative natural philosopher, gazing at the stars, people have always had a rational respect, sometimes good-humored; but experimental science is dangerous in its nature. If the systematic observation and manipulation of matter can elicit truth, the discovered truth can be used to manipulate matter. And indeed, the early experimentalists were afraid of themselves. For instance, the great alchemists did not fail to insist that pure motives and religious life were essential to the work; and, in the same moral climate, there was a history and literature of charlatans, sorcerers' apprentices, and mad scientists.

We have poor memories and perhaps no longer keep in mind that Christianity, at least, once thrived greatly by its sacramental magic, its relics, and its miracle workers; and its present lapse is owing to the brute fact that, over several centuries, it has been defeated by experimental science in a frank and fair contest of miracles and wonders. Science has worked better against plagues and it has proved to be immensely better at flying and distant communication. As late as the Russian Revolution, a means of defeating Christianity was to take a moujik up in an airplane and prove to him that God wasn't in the sky after all. On the other hand, Christianity still does have something to say about conversion and peace and mind, for here it has a few fumbling techniques, like revivalism and prayer. Western science knows nothing about such matters and resists learning anything. But the Eastern technologists have invented brain washing.

Our hope was, during the Enlightenment, to dissolve all such magical fears. Tyrannies and castes were undermined; religion was refuted; progressive education began to be invented; and the claims of science, too, became modest (I think that this was the chief contribution of Hume). The climax of this effort against superstition was the amazing synthesis of Kant, who managed to combine Hume and Rousseau with his own background of astronomer and pietist. But the history has turned out otherwise. For political, economic, and technological reasons, magical fears have not been dissolved. The specialist caste of wonder workers has grown more specialist (and recently less modest), and the rest of the people more out of touch and inept. And inevitably, given the actual disasters that scientific technology has produced, superstitious respect for the wizards has become tinged with a lust to tear them limb from limb. Calling this antiscientific bent Luddite, machine-breaking, is to miss the public tone, which is rather a murderousness toward the scientists as persons, more like anti-Semitism. Wiser scientists, like Huxley or Helmholtz or Einstein, have been sensitive to the danger of scientific estrangement, but their efforts of a hundred years to enlighten the people have not succeeded.

In one respect the popular superstition of science is more desperate than the medieval superstition of the Church. In the past, as counterevidence to what the priest said, there was the tradition of scientific experience and natural philosophy, and especially every man's experience in industry and agriculture; but now it is just this kind of counterevidence that is pre-empted by the specialists. For instance, our learned physicians are much better than the ancients, but when they happen to be off on a wrong tangent, a patient cannot escape to his common prudence, veterinary wisdom, or old-wives' folklore. If a man does not trust in Science, in what shall he trust? It was to address just this problem that Kant, again, insisted that in the university the faculty of philosophy must stand apart as a critical "loyal opposition from the left" (the phrase is Kant's), in order to purge of superstition and extravagant claims the other faculties: of theology, law, and medicine—and he would now surely have included engineering.

6

The majority of our modern scientists are certainly not magically afraid of their own powerful experiments, whose operations they understand better, and which they have the illusion of controlling. Indeed, the religious benevolence anxiously demanded of the experimenter by a Paracelsus is neglected even beyond the limits of prudence and common morals. First-rate scientists are today working, apparently indifferently, on fantastically harmful projects that ordinary mortals would shy away from; and, with no signs of extraordinary moral suffering, skilled mathematicians estimate that fifty million sudden American corpses would not set back the "economy" more than ten years. This is an odd frame of mind for natural philosophers to have arrived at. (I assume that we must take their "indifference" and lack of a position as a profound unconscious dissociation: they are warding off feelings of involvement, whether of fear, guilt, or power.)

To understand our scientists, let us contrast what might be called their "official" modern scientific ethics with a more traditional scientific attitude that has come down from the heroic age of the seventeenth century, and which many *also* hold.

The official modern position is that *scientists are dedicated to science.* Let us spell this out. (1) Science is a self-contained, infinitely self-accumulating and self-improving system of consensus, corrigible only by further science. Scientists are committed to this system and get their satisfaction in its service. (2) They do not get their satisfaction from the truth of nature, but from fitting that truth into the system of science. As such, nature is valueless (neutral); they do not love nature. (3) Truths of nature can, however, be usefully applied to human desires, but scientists do not properly have these either; so it is not the scientists who care about the applications of scientific discoveries. (4) Scientists are not responsible for the use made of their work. They may have sentimental biases, but these do not exert much force on them. The important thing is the chance to work, and all problems provide the chance for equally excellent service. (This does not, of course, preclude feelings of pride when use is made of one's work.)

What shall we make of this astonishing theological position, maintained with considerable dogmatism, that began to flower, I guess, in the German universities of the nineteenth century? It establishes a caste serving an abstract entity, the self-developing system of scientific consensus. The form of service is adherence to the "scientific method" and it is strict, sometimes obsessionally so, as when, in a particular case, no matter how results are really attained, e.g., by luck, insight, or philosophical appraisal, they do not enter into Science until they are ritually checked and put in proper form. The method is the only sure way. With this goes a detachment from any other immediately human or divine commitments.

The dogmatism is pretty absolute. The fact that certain areas of experience have proved stubbornly *un*-fruitful for the scientific method as we practice it, is not taken as problematic. Rather, sometimes such areas are slighted as absurd or nonexistent. (This is when, as C. D. Broad said on psychical phenomena, "The editor of *Nature* seems to think he is the Author of nature.") Sometimes, as with morals, fine arts, and letters, the areas are compartmentalized off as "subjective" and "emotional," although quite important—on this view, the emotions are denied any value as a means of knowledge (a view, by the way, that is biologically absurd on Darwinian grounds). And very often, as in social studies, problems are piously swamped with busy-work scientific approaches that yield little, but, being in proper form, preserve the seamless robe of science. It is frankly puzzling to me that the historians and philosophers of science do not systematically and empirically explore the failures of scientific method and the blank areas recalcitrant to scientific method. Finally, with regard to the applications of science, it is confidently promised that the fruits of scientific methods will produce happiness. Evidences to the contrary are not given much weight, and anyway they will be nullified by the further advance of science. For instance, "sin" is now experienced, by laymen and scientists both, as physical and mental disease, corrigible only by further modern science. Understand, my point is not that these prejudices and claims of modern science are necessarily false, but that we are obviously dealing with a rigid orthodoxy and plenty of superstition.

In ideal structure, the self-improving objective system of science that one serves is simply a theodicy, the working out of a gradually revealed plan; but it is a theodicy of a rather low grade, compared, say, with

Augustine's, for it is too caste and obsessional and does not allow for personal and historical storm and stress. How, for instance, does our scientific theory account for the present facts of warring scientists? Is that part of the self-improving system? If so, how? If not, why do we not hear charges of lack of dedication?

Contrast with all this the more traditional view of science as natural philosophy, which goes back to the Renaissance and is still the abiding strength of many scientists. There is no doubt that from the beginning, and still today, the natural philosophers have regarded themselves as in rebellion against ecclesiastical dogma and popular prejudice and (as is common with banded rebels) they conceive themselves as devoted to a kind of personified Nature, from whom they get primary satisfactions. They would not say that "nature is neutral," though of course "she" is beyond men's petty concerns. They love nature, or are curious, or surprised, or awe-struck at finding Cosmos in Chaos. Sometimes they are fearful, like Job confronted with Warhorse and Leviathan, for nature is "red in tooth and claw." Correspondingly, nature provides principles, and often goals, of ethics. This is different from the excitement of a "modern scientist" in his confrontation of nature, which is rather that of solving a hard puzzle and getting on with the work of the self-contained system of science.

The contrast I am trying to draw can be expressed formally in terms of linguistic philosophy. The "modern scientist" has as a program a Unified Language of Science—the movement pushed by Neurath, Carnap, and other logical positivists and operationalists; because the unity of science *is* the communication and consensus of the scientists, and there is only one method. Natural philosophers, however, seem content to let language and method follow the various subject matters as they always have, with the faith that there will always prove to be coherence and mutual understanding, since Nature coheres. Historically, the movement for a Unified Language was premature; each separate science has continued to use its own vocabulary. But perhaps the present craze to program everything for computers will produce a unified language.

"Objectivity" can mean different things. For a natural philosopher it is nonattachment, keeping oneself out of it, in order not to disturb or contaminate the object of absorbed attention—though the philosopher may experimentally intervene to put the object in the proper frame. The fruition of this absorbed reflection is an insight or theory that unites him with the object. (The type is Darwin gazing long hours at the bee and the flower.) To the "modern scientist," objectivity is the detachment, necessary for accuracy, of the good reporter or scout, whose satisfaction comes from bringing home the true account to headquarters. Essentially it is the experiment that is reported and not the "object," for the natural object is what is indifferently whirled and banged.

Mostly, of course, there is no such sharp classification among our scientists as I have been describing; but I have been trying to make precise certain "modern" characteristics of the scientific attitude, as they seem to me, because they explain something important about "applied science" and "scientific technology."

7

"Applied science" is a peculiar notion, and I think a recent one, though it already seems commonplace. Normally we would conceive of a man's scientific thinking as a worth-while action in itself and as, besides, operating in the whole of life in either of two ways: His curiosity and experimenting might find out something exciting or practical, a new phenomenon, a new force, and he would then repeat the experience and regularize it for his own and other people's use. Thus he might give us a way to boil water or see great distances through a telescope. Or conversely, a man might have an important life problem, a virus or an enemy to destroy, or a great wish to fly; then he would concentrate his resources, including his science, to destroy the enemy, or to get off the ground. These are the familiar classical senses in which science is useful (of course mistakes may occur and a produced force get out of hand). In this context we would not come to say that "scientific knowledge may be well or badly used," for the scientist is precisely concerned in the product and consequences, either adding something of his own style to the world, or solving problems meaningful to mankind. The only danger would be the one feared by the alchemists, that the experimenter himself might be a devil.

But the case is very different when scientific knowledge is "applied," or when a scientist works, for money, etc., to solve problems that do *not* concern him or that may even be trivial or distasteful to him. Now, an immense amount of our technology is of this kind, and this affects the quality of products and their consequences. For, instead of the human environment being illuminated and probably simplified by scientific intellect —made comprehensible, efficient, elegant, modest, etc. —it is rather flooded by technological products of science that have the following characteristics: they have been worked up in a spirit that is detached from ordinary uses, and yet they mix into ordinary uses; they are used in a way irrelevant to the scientist's human concerns and often contrary to his concerns; they embody knowledge increasingly far removed from ordinary experience; and therefore they are imposed on society and compel people to move and work in ways increasingly strange to them. The machines that people use are, effectually, canned rituals. The structure of a scientific world is a simple one: inquiry and intellect coping with problems. This has a lovely style, a kind of paradisal style, for the character of Paradise is to be practical. But the world we have is not a simple one. It consists of an isolated system of scientific knowledge with an esoteric style, a vast system of technological "applications" with venal and faddish purposes and no style, a confused populace, and no direct approach to glaring problems.

Perhaps it is necessary for most scientists to continue to regard themselves as unconcerned priests of the system of science, supported and exploited by various dictators and brigands; but if so, their detachment and their puzzle solving will continue to saddle society with life-complicating, indirect, obsessional, and essentially irrelevant and boring products. Naturally, human beings are adaptable and malleable; and they manage fairly well to go through the song and dance of our industrial and other technological systems. But this is undesirable. People can be socialized to scientific technology, but they are not at present adequate to it. (If the present arrangements continue, they will become less so—it is estimated that only 15 per cent of the youth is academically talented enough to study the sciences; and many of the 15 per cent are merely test-passers and symbol-manipulators, without feeling for the causes of things; they are not scientists.) Therefore people are conformist and superstitious. And much of the technology is worthless anyway! If *this* is what is meant by a scientific society, the world of "the new scientific revolution," as Sir Charles Snow calls it, I cannot see the advantage of it, either for mankind *or* for science.

Pornography and the sexual revolution

One kind of "utopian thinking" that rouses anxiety in people is the suggestion simply to stop doing something hard and useless; for instance, to stop repressive efforts that do not work and that indeed increase the evil that they are supposed to prevent. "I am unimpressed," says William Sloane of Rutgers, "with the record of repressive legislation in this country. The laws against narcotics, for example, are supporting a large criminal class and leading to large-scale corruption of our youth. The laws against off-track betting are supporting a large criminal class and leading directly to police corruption. No set of laws will prevent the bootlegging of pornography." Yet the bother with this good sense is that, in these cases, people apparently cannot simply leave off, for these laws and prosecutions are psychological means of keeping down their own confused panic.

The case of pornography, however, is peculiarly interesting, for here both sides of the public ambivalance are now on the surface. It is not the case any longer that the pornographic is "obscene," shocking to society's conception of itself. The sexual is now, in an important sense, quite acceptable; yet at the same time the sexual is guilty. This puts the courts in an embarrassing position. Not only to protect vital liberties, but also to express existing public sentiment, the higher, more intellectual courts stand out against censorious police, postmasters, and popular prejudice; yet since they don't dare tell the whole truth, the issues are never settled. And worse, the courts lend themselves to the sexual prejudice which, at this moment in our history, creates the very "hard-core" pornography that is objected to. That is, the court corrupts, it helps the censors to corrupt. Nevertheless, perhaps precisely in this issue of pornography and censorship, "utopian thinking" *can* avail, since instead of simply "stopping" and becoming panicky, people can busy themselves with something practical, namely, the real problems of the sexual revolution.

We are faced with the dilemmas of a society in transition. In discussing censorship, it is impossible to make good sense and good law without sociological and psychological analysis; rehashing the statutes and precedents will not do. But it is no secret that in this field earnest authorities angrily clash on the most material issues (this is a sign of transition). Take the most undoubted sadistic pornography, socially worthless and sold at a criminal profit: one psychologist will say that its effects are disastrous, it causes "sex crimes" and juvenile delinquency; yet another psychologist will flatly assert that no such connection has ever been proved, there is no clear and present danger to warrant legal action. Now, in this particular difficulty the courts seem to have a convenient out: since admittedly the dubious object has no social merit, since its associations are unsavory and the purveyor is a racketeer, why shouldn't the court go along with the censorship? No real freedom is impugned. But here is a dilemma: what if the censorship itself is part of a general repressive antisexuality, which creates the need for sadistic pornography sold at a criminal profit? We must remember that the tone of the censorship, *and* of the usual court decisions, is vindictive and anxious; it is not the tone of a simple prudential choice in terms of broad social policy. The censoring is a dynamic and emotional act, with novel and perhaps unthought-of effects. The social question is not the freedom of a venal purveyor, though the case is always argued in his terms since he is the one brought to court; the question is whether the sexual climate of the community is perverted by the censorship.

The censorship justifies itself as protection of children and adolescents. But consider this issue in terms of an accepted commonplace of contemporary pedagogy, that we must provide the child a "structured permissiveness" to grow in: permissiveness so that he can act without fear, shame, and resentment, and learn by his mistakes; and a structure of firm *parental* morals and culture—"how we behave," not, "how you must behave"—with which he can identify when, in his anxiety and confusion, he needs security and guidance. A good parent rarely sees a situation as a clear and present danger (of the level of swallowing poison or being hit by a car). Most dubious associations and behaviors of a child outgrow themselves in his ongoing career in a moral and cultural environment. And indeed, this ongoing career is the only real solution for him; whereas a "protective" parental attitude will almost surely communicate the parents' anxieties and complicate things further.

If this is a correct analysis, then the recent "liberal" decision on *Lady Chatterley's Lover* is inadequate. It is not permissive in the right way and it does not provide a firm moral and cultural support. Therefore I am urging the court to re-examine its anxieties, decide that the pornographic is not in fact, in our times, obscene, and give light and moral leadership.

1

Judge Bryan's exoneration of *Lady Chatterley* takes its doctrine from Woolsey on *Ulysses* (1933) and Brennan in *Roth vs. United States* (1957). Let us consider these in turn.

In clearing *Ulysses*, Judge Woolsey's method is first to equate the obscene with the pornographic, as "tending to stir the sex impulses or to lead to sexually impure and lustful thoughts," and then to show that the book does neither, but "is a sincere and serious attempt to devise a new literary method for the observation and description of mankind." Let us postpone the literary criticism till the next section, but here stop short at the definition of obscenity.

The notion that sexual impulse or stirring sexual impulse is a bad thing comes from an emotional climate in which it was generally agreed that it would be better if sexuality did not overtly exist, at a time when people bathed and slept fully clothed, and a bull was called a he-cow. Then anything which was sexual in public—as the publication of "detailed representation in words and pictures"—violated society's self-image and was certainly obscene. In our times such a notion is absurd. The pornographic is not as such obscene. As Judge Jerome Frank pointed out in 1949, "No sane man thinks that the arousing of normal sexual desires is socially dangerous." We live in a culture where all High Thought insists on the beauty and indeed hygienic indispensability of sexual desires, and where a vast part of commerce is busy in their stimulation. Nevertheless, Judge Bryan on *Chatterley* finds himself compelled to repeat the precedent of *Ulysses*, in 1960! This leaves us in utter confusion. For consider: Bryan goes on to define the "prurient . . . that is to say, shameful or morbid interest in sex"; but if the stirring of desire is defined, and therefore treated as, obscene, how can a normal person's interest in sex be anything else *but* shameful? This is what shame is, the blush at finding that one's impulse is unacceptable. Only a brazen person would not be ashamed. So the court corrupts. It is a miserable social policy. I would rather have Lawrence condemned than defended by such reasoning.

But it is Woolsey's second clause, "leading to lustful thoughts," that is the more interesting, for this is the likely and immediate effect of literary or pictorial stimulation. Bluntly, "lustful thoughts" means incitement to masturbate. I guess that in the overwhelming majority of cases this is the chief use of pornography. Let us again look to history. In the nineteenth century, all sexual facts were suspect, but masturbation was a mortal sin and the prelude to insanity. Let me quote from a great, good-natured, and liberal man, the prince of the Enlightenment: "Nothing weakens the mind as well as the body so much as the kind of lust directed toward oneself. It is entirely at variance with the nature of man. We must place it before the youth in all its horribleness," etc., etc. (Immanuel Kant, *On Education*.) Now contrast with this a philosopher of our own day: "Left to itself, infantile masturbation has, apparently, no bad effect upon health and no discoverable bad effect upon character; the bad effects which have been observed in both respects, are, it seems, wholly attributable to attempts to stop it." (Bertrand Russell, *Education and the Good Life*.) And this is pretty nearly the identical opinion of Benjamin Spock, M.D., in his book on *Child Care*, which is, I suppose, in every middle-class home in America (more than twelve million copies of the paperback have been sold). Also, since the connection between pornography and juvenile delinquency is much touted, let me quote the identical opinion of a revered criminologist: "Masturbation is a habit without deleterious effect in itself, yet a source of behavior difficulties because of strong social disapproval." (Donald Taft.)

My point is not that this habit is good; it is morally otiose. But when the court says that stirring to masturbate is obscene, certainly the court corrupts. Let me specify the damage. According to sexologists, the dangers in masturbation come from (1) inhibited performance, holding the body rigid, holding the breath, keeping silent; (2) guilt and shame of performing the act; and (3) guilt about the accompanying images. Our public policy obviously worsens the first two conditions, but it is also importantly responsible for the guilt-inducing images, for it associates lust with punishment and degradation and so creates sado-masochistic thoughts.

It is claimed that the court must judge according to public sentiment; but there is plenty of better public sentiment. Why must the police and the courts follow the worst part of the population instead of leading with the best? A more enlightened court would not solve these problems any more than it has created integration in the South; but by the same example, a good decision is not irrelevant.

This brings us to the doctrine of *Roth vs. United States.* The standards to be applied in determining obscenity, Bryan quotes Judge Brennan, are "whether to the average person, applying contemporary standards, the dominant theme of the material taken as a whole appeals to prurient interest." Bryan then uses part of this sentence, "the dominant theme taken as a whole," to exonerate *Lady Chatterley* by proving that it is a "serious" work, following the tactics of Woolsey. Again let us defer the literary criticism, and here stop at "applying contemporary standards," which is an attempt on the part of the court to cope with the changes in emotional climate that we have just been discussing. As Judge Bryan puts it, "Much of what is now accepted would have shocked the community to the core a generation ago." But I do not think this is a sufficient account of the sexual history of recent times.

As one reviews the many cases, one is struck by how, year after year, this theme of changing standards recurs in the decisions. "What was regarded as indecent in the days of the Floradora Sextette, is decent in the days of the fan dance." But what is most striking is that in the long chain of decisions over two generations, the standard becomes increasingly broader in almost every respect: the bathing suits more scanty, the four-letter words more tolerable, the descriptions of the sexual act more realistic, the "unnatural" themes more mentionable. It is just this tendency through time that the courts fail to take into account as they judge each case. Therefore they are always behind, they miss the essential nature of the phenomenon they are judging, and this has consequences.

The essence is that our generations are living through a general breakdown of repressive defenses, increasingly accelerating, and therefore a deepening social neurosis. Freud's doctrine, let us remember, is that it is not repression (total amnesia) that causes neurosis, but the failure of repression, so that repressed contents return in distorted guise. This process is irreversible. Our culture has experienced too much of the emerging content to ban it, or will it, or frighten it, out of mind. Therefore the only recourse is to try to get, as methodically and safely as possible, to the end of the line, to undo the repressive attitude itself, so that the drives can reappear as themselves and come to their own equilibrium, according to organism self-regulation. It is in just this that our high courts, like the Lords in England, could be excellent social counselors. With expert advisers they could try to forecast, and guide toward, a sane sexual policy. Instead, they cling to an outmoded concept of obscenity and they prevent outmoded statutes from becoming dead letters. Yet at the same time they are forced to cede to changing public taste and to relax standards. Now, this must lead to social chaos—the pornography is only an example—for so long as the attempted repressing continues, the repressed contents must continually emerge in more and more distorted forms. And of course we also get legal chaos, as the court twists and turns to avoid the outmoded statutes.

For a writer like myself, there is a bitter irony in Bryan's statement that the previously shocking is now acceptable. Yes it is—because Flaubert, Ibsen, and Wedekind, and Dreiser, O'Neill, and Joyce paid their pound of flesh to the censor. They opened the ever new sensibility and were punished for it. Probably this is inevitable, and any advance worth having is worth suffering for; but it is a bitter proceeding. And now *Lady Chatterley* is accepted as a community art-work just when it has ceased to be a living art-work. Lawrence has explicitly told us that he wrote it "in defiance of convention"; that defiance and the awkward rusticity of the book were its life. Now we are left merely with a rather neurotic fantasy of a frigid woman and a class-resentful "dominating" man. The court's lagging acceptance of bygone classics for the wrong reasons makes it difficult for a living classic to be accepted and exert an influence in the living community.

In the breakdown of repression, the artists do their part by first dreaming the forbidden thoughts, assuming the forbidden stances, and struggling to make sense. They cannot do otherwise, for they bring the social conflicts in their souls to public expression. But the court does not do its duty; and the critics (I will mention no names) go along with the court's convenience, and lie and lie.

The court's duty, as I see it, is to set aside the definition of pornography as obscenity—just as it set aside the doctrine of separate but equal facilities—and to clarify and further the best tendency of the sexual revolution. In my opinion, as I shall argue later, such a policy would indeed tend to diminish pornography, make it not a big deal.

As it is, for well-known historical reasons, we live in a stimulating, unsatisfying society midway in transition; and while the liberal court hedges in embarrassment and the critics lie, the police and the administrators lurk to get convictions on any grounds. The police make wholesale raids against girlie magazines, they entrap a harmless old man for collecting postcards, the postmaster bars Lawrence from the mails, and the Drug Administrator burns the books of Wilhelm Reich as "labels" for a contraband commodity. Only a wiser policy can restore order.

2

Let me proceed to a philosophical question raised by these decisions, which is, in my opinion, even more important for our society than the sexual matter: What is the nature of speech and art? To protect their "serious" books, the courts attempt to distinguish speech as communication of an idea or even as talking *about* a subject, from speech as an action that does something to its speaker, subject, and hearer. This is the tactic of Woolsey when he devotes most of his opinion to Joyce's "new method for the observation and description of mankind" and of Bryan when he says that the plot of *Lady Chatterley's Lover* "serves as a vehicle through which Lawrence develops his basic . . . philosophy

Most of the characters are prototypes." The judges reason that if something like this can be established, a book can be protected under the Bill of Rights' guarantee of freedom to communicate opinion. Yet, although this is a useful distinction for some kinds of speech—e.g., scientific reporting and conscientious journalism—it simply does not apply to common speech, and it is necessarily irrelevant to art, for one essential function of art is to move the audience. If Joyce and Lawrence felt that all they had done was to convey ideas, they would have considered themselves failures.

Naturally the decisions themselves, based on an unphilosophical distinction, have been notoriously inconsistent. For example, *The Well of Loneliness* was banned because "it seeks to justify the right of a pervert . . . it does not argue for repression of insidious impulses . . . it seeks to justify and idealize perverted ideas." Yet these are merely the ideas of the author. But contrariwise, Justice Stewart defended the film of *Lady Chatterley* by saying, "The picture advocates an idea—that adultery under certain circumstances may be proper behavior. The First Amendment guarantee is freedom to advocate ideas." Jerome Frank has wryly commented that if an "idea" is eloquently argued, it is in danger; if it is dully argued, it is safe.

Here is an example of the legal doctrine at work. At Marble Arch in London, crowds gather to listen to popular orators vent their grievances and longings on every topic under the sun: freedom for Nigeria, a subscription for the Irish Republican Army, the ethics of deceiving one's wife, the nearest way to salvation. Like Bernard Shaw, the orators test their repartee against a powerfully insolent audience. All is strictly legal. But if a man comes within twenty-four inches of the speaker, he is at once hauled off by a guardian bobby! A man can say anything, but he mustn't do anything; he can listen to anything, but he mustn't let himself be aroused. Freedom of speech means freedom to talk about. Speech is not saying-as-an-action. The limitations are clear. If there were incitement to riot, the freedom would cease. "Fighting words" are forbidden because they lead to fights. Pornography is forbidden because it is in the nature of detailed sexual reporting that it leads to physiological reactions and likely acts. Blasphemy and obscenity are forbidden because they are acts as such, they break a taboo in their very utterance, as well as presumably undamming what is held in repression by the taboo. Also, there are even particular topics, like the subject of *Lolita*, where merely to treat them at all in some public way is tantamount to sanctioning their existence in the universe. Here speech becomes magic, to name the Name creates the thing.

Jefferson and other revolutionaries who insisted on the Bill of Rights probably had a more risky notion of freedom of speech than our courts, as they did of political action in general. But if to them freedom of speech meant merely freedom to communicate opinions, they could not have intended the First Amendment to apply to belles-lettres at all, for the neoclassical esthetic doctrine of their time held that the function of art was to move and instruct, to instruct by moving. In our modern esthetics, the legal embarrassment is extreme; we pay less attention to imitating reality and lay all the more emphasis on speech as action. To Freud, the art-act alleviates a repressed conflict by daring to express and publish it (this is Lawrence's "defying convention"). In advance-guard art, where the artist is reacting to and vomiting up something intolerable in society, the art-act cannot help being offensive. Since the nineteenth century, the naturalists have meant to defy and shame when they stripped away the mask of hypocrisy. The primary aim of Dada is to shock. In his *Theater of Violence*, Antonin Artaud declares that theater is precisely not communicating ideas but acting on the community, and he praises the Balinese village dance that works on dancers and audience till they fall down in a trance. (For that matter, the shrieking and wailing that was the specialty of Greek tragedy would among us cause a breach of the peace. The nearest we come are adolescent jazz sessions that create a public nuisance.) The "poetry readings" of the Beats try to give us their "existent situation," usually drunken, and the audience copes with it as best it can. I could continue a long list.

To these facts of modern art, the doctrine of Woolsey, Brennan, and van Pelt Bryan is not adequate. Such art cannot be defended as communicating ideas, and anything objectionable in it (there is much) must condemn it. Indeed, the arguments of the censoring customs officer or postmaster betoken a more genuine art-response, for they have been directly moved, although in an ignorant way, by the excitement and inner conflict of Joyce and Lawrence. Their experience is ignorant and low-grade because they are unwilling to let the sexual excitement belong to a larger world of experience, and this is why they excerpt passages. But at least they have been made to feel that the world is threateningly sexual. As the British Magistrate Mead said, on paintings by Lawrence, "Art is immaterial . . . Obscene pictures should be put an end to like any wild animal which may be dangerous." And so Justice Manton, in his dissent on *Ulysses*, "Obscenity is not rendered less by the statement of truthful fact," for it is precisely the fact, the nature of things, that is obscene to the censor.

Woolsey's doctrine is insulting to the artist. He says that the book did "not tend to excite lustful thoughts, *but* the net effect was a tragic and powerful commentary" (italics mine). Surely the author wants to say, "It is lustful among other things, and *therefore* its net effect is tragic."

In our culture an artist is expected to move the reader; he is supposed to move him to tears, to laughter, to indignation, to compassion, even to hatred; but he may not move him to have an erection or to mockery of public figures making a spectacle of themselves. Why not? By these restrictions we doom ourselves to a passionless and conformist community. Instead of bracketing off the "classics," as especially the British courts do—indeed, the legal definition of a classic seems to be a "nonactionable obscenity"—let us pay attention to the classical pornography and we shall see that it is not the case, as the court feels obliged to prove, that a work has a "net" social use despite its sexual effect, but rather that the pornography in a great context and spoken by a great soul, *is* the social use. Aristophanic comedy was still close enough to a seasonal ritual to encourage rebelliousness and lead to procreation. Rabelais is disgraceful, like a giant baby, and this *is* the Renaissance. Catullus teaches us the callous innocence of high-born youth, free of timidity and pettiness; and Tom Jones is a similar type, with a dash of English sentimentality. If we may believe their preludes, both the *Arabian Nights* and the *Decameron* are cries of life in the face of death; and in our times Jean Genet, one of our few fine writers, is pornographic and psychopathic because only so, he tells us, can he feel that he exists in our inhuman world. But apart from these lofty uses, there are also famous pornographic books made just for fun, since sex is a jolly subject.

To explore the nature of speech as action, consider the other forbidden topic, the mockery of sacred public figures. In our country we suffer from a gentleman's agreement that is politically and artistically disastrous. For instance, our recent President could not frame an English sentence, and according to some observers his career as the head of a great university was dismally

hilarious. "Dwight Eisenhower at Columbia" is a title
to rouse an Aristophanes. In the eighteenth century
Ike would have been richly mauled. But our satirists on
stage and TV avoid such subjects. Then there cannot
be great comedy, for if you dare not mock the pink
elephant looming in the foreground, you can't mock
anything. Instead, our satire consists of isolated gags
that do not add up to an explosion. But satire is an
essential of democracy, for how can we expect our
leaders to be anything but front-figures if they do not
take any personal risk and cannot be stung?

The court is not philosophical. It does not see that
lively speech is active speech. Sexual action is a proper
action of art. The question is not *whether* pornography,
but the grade of the pornography. To sting powerful
figures into personal engagement is a proper action of
art, otherwise we sink in a faceless swamp. What the
more intellectual court does do is to protect exceptional cases against vulgar prejudices and police busy-
work. (But often, as in the astounding case of the rev-
ocation on moral grounds of Bertrand Russell's ap-
pointment at New York's City College, the matter
never gets to a better court.) This is not enough to
improve the cultural climate. In principle, the living
writers are not exceptional and famous cases. Rather,
it works out as follows: publishers will not publish
what will get them into trouble; authors cease to write
what will not be published, or what the lawyer censors
the heart out of; soon the public has lost the authors
at their best, and the authors have lost the common
touch. The actual situation is that there is little that is
published, and perhaps not much that is written, that
does or would get into trouble with the censorship,
except precisely the hard-core pornography. Why is
there so little? If the publishers and authors were
doing their duty, the courts would be battlegrounds.
Instead, the void is soon filled with safe entertainers,

gag men, pap journalists. Advertising is the chief public art. The community hears no ideas.

3

It has become the fashion to say that the esthetic and libertarian matters we have been discussing have no relation to the actual police problem of hard-core pornography; let the police be careful not to encroach on serious writers, and let the writers leave the police to their raids and entrapment. This schizophrenic theory is false. We are one community, and the kind of high culture we have and the kind of low culture we have are opposite faces of the same lead quarter. But let us look at the hard-core pornography in itself.

I have been arguing that not only is there innocent and useful pornography that ought not to be censored, but the method of censorship helps to create the very kind of harmful pornography that we should like to see checked. The case is similar—and not causally unrelated—to the social creation of juvenile delinquency by social efforts to control it. When excellent human power is inhibited and condemned, it will reappear ugly and dangerous. The censorious attitude toward the magazines and pictures is part of the general censorious attitude that hampers ordinary sexuality and thereby heightens the need for satisfaction by means of the magazines and pictures. It is said that the pornography artificially stimulates, and no doubt this is true—though there is no evidence that there can be such a thing as "too much" sex—but it is not so importantly true as that the pornography is indulged in because of a prior imbalance of excessive stimulation and inadequate discharge. Given such an imbalance, if the pornography heightens satisfaction, as it probably does in many cases, it is insofar therapeutic. This is an unpleasant picture of our country, but there is no help for it except to remedy antisexuality. I have argued that the revolution is irreversible, and the attempt to re-establish total amnesia must lead to more virulent expressions, e.g., still less desirable pornography.

Let us consider two aspects of poor pornography, its mere sexuality or "lust," devoid of any further human contact, drama, or meaning; and its very frequent sado-masochism.

The experience of mere "lust" in isolation is a neurotic artifact. Normally, affection increases lust, and pleasure leads to gratitude and affection. The type neurotic case is the sailor ashore, who seeks out a "pig" and works very hard *not* to get emotionally involved. Why should he behave so strangely? An explanation is that his promiscuity is approved by his peers but, more deeply and morally, it is disapproved by himself. If he regarded the woman as a person, he would feel guilty and hate her, and sometimes he manifests this as brutal violence, really meant for himself. More decently, he restricts his experience to bare lust, though this is not much of a *sexual* experience. I choose the example because it is a fair analogy of the attitude of a large population in America, not unknown in middle-class suburbs. We accept the naturalness of sexuality in an abstract and permissive way, but we have by no means come to terms with its moral, family, and pedagogic dilemmas during a hard period of transition. There then occurs an isolated "sexuality" which at its best is hygienic and at its worst comes to mate-swapping, disowning the sexuality of those we love. Finally, I would suggest that this is the style of much of what the court elegantly calls "dirt for dirt's sake," the sexually stimulating without dramatic, plastic, or other artistic value. Necessarily this must be limited to a few stereotyped anecdotes and a few naked poses; and it must soon become boring.

The sado-masochistic pornography, however, that

combines lust and punishment, torture, or humiliation, is the darker effect of a more restrictive and guilty-making training, for example, certain kinds of religious upbringing. There are comparatively few real-life sado-masochists, but all the more do the smash hits of popular culture cultivate fantasies that proceed in guilt and end in punishment, genre of Tennessee Williams. This calamitous requirement, that the lust be punished, used to be a standard of legality employed by learned judges. How stupid can grown men be! For the consumer, such fantasies have a dual advantage: they satisfy both the need for righteousness (sadistic super-ego) and the "weakness" of giving in to pleasure; they embody an exciting conflict. But the bother with such images when used privately as pornography is that they are socially disapproved and enhance individual guilt; the excitement proceeds against strong resistance, and mounting fear, and often dies; and there is a tendency to raise the ante. It is said that this kind of pornography creates juvenile delinquents; the likelihood is rather that the type of delinquent who has a need to prove his potency has a hankering for such pornography, all the better if it can be combined with cerebral know-how, as in hipster literature. Nevertheless, it doesn't do him any good, for, on balance, it increases tension.

From even so rudimentary an analysis, it is clear that we can differentiate the moral quality of various pornography and make a rough rating of useful, indifferent, damaging. The social question would be how to improve the first and eliminate the last. But police courts and administrative officers, and even jury courts and high courts, are not the right forum for important and subtle moral debates. Expert opinion doesn't agree either—I could quote a crashing dissent to most of the propositions I have been making. Still, I am even less impressed by the bellow of J. Edgar Hoover that the police cannot wait for the experts to make up their minds; for one of the few things that *is* demonstrable is that ignorant suppression is wrong.

Yet I do not think that moral problems are private problems and can be left alone. Here I must dissent from my bold and honest classmate, Judge Murtagh, who wants to leave most such issues to a person's conscience before God. On the contrary, it is because moral problems are so publicly important—sexual practice is crucial for family, courting, friendship, education, and culture—that they must be ongoingly decided by all groups, as well as individuals; and they are so subtle that only the manifold mind of all the institutions of society, skirmishing and experimenting, can figure them out and invent right solutions. In this essay, I have been proposing to the judges a particular public experiment, a "firm morals and culture" and "permissiveness" in which there might be both the progressive solution of social evils and, more important, a growth into a more living culture. Let us speculate about it. Suppose that the courts altered their previous doctrine, as I have suggested, and now decided that it was not obscene to stir sexual desires and thoughts. What might occur?

An immediate effect of this drastic change would be to open to the legal public media a very large, and I think soon preponderant, part of the traffic that is now subterranean and culturally uncontrolled. This is an advantage, for the traffic can now meet open evaluation, the appraisal of critics, the storm of angry letters that frightens advertisers.

In principle anything might now be shown, from the hero beginning to have an erection when he sees the heroine across the street, to the drama of the sexual act itself. Since the change-over would be so drastic, the court might aim at a deliberate slowness, and the mass media would wisely want to meet and agree on a prudent rate of change. The test of proper deliberateness would be that, *regarded as mere isolated and excerpted pornography,* there would be little difference of effect on the audience between showing the hint and showing the coition. (In between these extremes, it is hoped that there would develop the habit of treating sexual facts as the common part of life which they are.)

Artistically, of course, there is a vast difference between a hint and the showing of a sexual act. It requires a setting of powerful passion and beauty, or ugliness, to make artistically workable so vivid a scene as a couple copulating. And indeed, one of the most salutary and hoped-for effects of the proposed change would be the radical diminution in sheer quantity, and the improvement in variety and quality, of the hundreds of shows that a person exposes himself to every year. Since at present the stimulation is low-grade, the repetition is chronic; perhaps if the experience were fuller, there would be less need to repeat. Perhaps we could have something other than the endless westerns, crime stories, and romances, if there were more animal satisfaction and not merely the symbolic stereotyped satisfactions that these genres offer, with the sex climaxing in shooting, which for some reason can be shown. As it is, the public never gets beyond sex and violence. Culturally, the greatest curse of censorship is that it produces too many and too trivial art works, all of them inhibitedly pornographic.

The aim is to establish a principled general policy. The states and localities could continue to enforce whatever censorship they please, so long as they do not risk a national suit and are content to do without some of the national culture. The situation, as I envisage it, is somewhat the opposite of the school-integration decision; for the federal court is not intervening in any region, but is insisting that national policy must provide intellectual and historical leadership unhampered

by local prejudices; yet as far as possible it will keep
hands off to allow for regional experimentation. This
is not the effect of the court's present policy—e.g., in
opening the mail to *Chatterley*—for that does violence to local sensibilities, necessarily, in order to give
some scope for mature experience. But if there were a
more principled general policy and the courts were
not continually obliged to fight, a generation too late, a
rear-guard action against morons, the nation could allow the localities to be even more restrictive and self-
defensive; in order to protect local option they could
even uphold the postmaster. In a federal system, it is
possible to decentralize the cultural climate. This allows for experiment and for citizens to have a freer
choice of the life that suits their needs; but there must
be freedom to experiment here and there. Now we
have the worst of the contrary situation: a degenerate
centralism, a conformist mass made of the lowest
common denominator of the narrow provincial multiplied by the venality of Hollywood and Madison
Avenue.

Legalized pornography would, naturally, deplete the
criminal market. (As Morris Ernst has speculated, the
price of dirty postcards would drop from three for a
dollar to three for a nickel.) In my critical opinion, a
first effect would be that the great publishers, newspapers, networks, and film producers that now righteously keep their skirts clean and censor the prose and
poetry of their moral and intellectual betters, would
eagerly cash in. But a fairly quick effect, one hopes,
would be that as a genre such isolated pornography
would simply become boring and diminish, just as
women's short skirts today create not a flurry.

Finally, there would be immense cultural advantages.
Less embarrassment, a franker language, and a more
sensual feeling would magnify and ennoble all our art
and perhaps bring some life to the popular culture; and

conversely, the exposure to such art would help to humanize sexuality and break down the neurotic compartment of "mere lust." In the difficulties of our modern sexual transition—where we do not know the best form of the family, the proper attitude toward premarital and extramarital sex, nor even what physical behavior is "normal"—we certainly can profit from the treatment of these subjects in lyric and tragic art. And not least, any social change in the direction of permissiveness and practical approval, which integrates sexual expression with other ordinary or esteemed activities of life, must diminish the need to combine sex with punishment and degradation. To increase the possibility of satisfaction in real situations is to make unnecessary the hipster struggle for violent and apocalyptic experiences.

My argument is a simple one: a more principled high-level policy on obscenity, which realistically takes into account the tendency of our mores, would facilitate the moral and cultural structuring that can alone solve the problems of hard-core pornography; and it would also have beautiful cultural advantages. Whereas the present attempted repression by the police, administrators, and lower courts not only must continue to fail, but in itself keeps creating the evil it combats. I suggest a remedy that many earnest people might consider worse than the disease. They would perhaps prefer to muddle along. But I doubt that we can.

Designing pacifist films

I am asked for my thoughts about the content and style of anti-war films, and how to make such a film.

First of all, such a film must at least not do positive harm by predisposing its audience toward war. The images of senseless violence, horror, and waste that are usually employed in the commercially successful "anti-war" films do have a titillating effect and remain in the soul as excitants and further incitements. Let me show how this works.

(1) In cinematic conditions of bright screen and dark theater, lasting for many minutes and tending to fascination and hypnosis, images of horror easily detach themselves from the kind of intellectual and ethical framework in which they are usually presented, and they attach themselves to quite different subliminal ideas. We must bear in mind how a child wakes up screaming with his nightmare of the animated cartoon he has seen, the nightmare now expressing a kind of wish.

(2) Also the response of a theatrical mass audience is different from the more intellectual and ethical re-

sponse of a small company or an individual reading. (Perhaps TV is a special case.) What a theater audience experiences most vividly is how it has, anonymously, shared in breaking a taboo, in witnessing with accomplices the forbidden and shocking. The "message" of the spectacle is then employed as a rationalization. Of course it is only the rationalization that is mentioned outside the theater or in the reviews, though the advertising hints at the shocking.

(3) This dual process is specific for the heightening of guilt: a forbidden stimulation with one's censorship lowered by crowd feeling, disapproved by one's ethical and social self. Now, the effect of guilt is not reform or, finally, deterrence; but inevitably resentment for having been made guilty, and perhaps then clandestinely or unconsciously choosing more congenial buddies. (Pacificist propaganda in general, let me say, is prone to arouse guilt just because it is irrefutable and on the side of the angels. This is an important reason why accompanying persuasion some immediate *action* must be available—just as a loving sexual seduction must lead to acts or it does harm.)

(4) The arousing of lust and self-disapproval leads to the specific pornographic effect of wished-for punishment (the hallmark of popular sexual art). The image of punishment is often provided in the film itself, as its poetic justice. Such self-punishment is evil in itself; but worse is that usually it is projected far and wide as vindictive hatred of scapegoats. And alternatively, it seeks for allies in mass suicide, as if to say, "We are not worthy to live."

(5) Especially in cinema, the conditions of fantasy and the habits of the audience are so discontinuous with behavior in the waking public world that the shock of strong images is sentimentalized: the rationalizing sorrow and regret is used to *insulate* the experience from any possible action. The energy of revulsion

turns into pity, a pornographic emotion, rather than active compassion or political indignation—not otherwise than with Christians who exhaust their neighbor-love in the sentimentality of the Cross. The next step is for the sentimentalized horror to be taken as matter-of-course in the public world, just as for those Christians the poor *must* always be with us, so Christians can be charitable.

(6) Finally, bad audiences cannot be relied on to respond to a whole work of art; they will select from it what suits their own repressions, and interpret according to their own prejudices the very fact that they have been moved despite themselves. The lovely is taken as dirty, the horrible as sadistically thrilling. This derogation is partly revenge against the artist. Bad audiences follow the plot as a story; they do not identify with the whole work as the soul of the poet, but they identify with the actors of the story and take sides. Given a film about capital punishment, for instance, a Camus will notice, and be steeled in revulsion by, the mechanism of execution: he will deny the whole thing the right to exist because it is not *like* us (this is the reaction-formation, denial, that is characteristic of active compassion); but a vulgar audience will identify with the victim, get involved in the suspense, thrill to the horror, and weep with pity. The effect is entertainment, not teaching or therapy; and to be entertained by such a theme is itself damaging.

2

By a good audience, of course, a work of genuine art cannot be easily taken amiss and abused in this way. By definition, the images of genuine art do not allow themselves to be detached from its idea, for the whole is solidly fused in the artistic activity. But this standard of excellence is useless for our present purposes, since such works are not conveniently had for the asking. And when they do occur, they are just as likely to be embarrassing to our rhetorical purposes. For example— I choose classics of literature that are beyond debate —both Homer's *Iliad* and Tolstoy's *War and Peace* are infused by, and teach us, a profound pacifism, a lofty and compassionate dismay at the infatuated violence of men in their armies. Yet they certainly also express, and even celebrate, the demonic in war, the abysmal excitement of mankind gone mad. This was interesting to these artists and it *might* be to any contemporary artist —how could one know? The counter to such demonism in a great artist would have to be a kind of saintliness. We are here clearly outside the context of planning pacifist films.

Again by definition, in a work of genuine art the images of horror, etc., do not have a pornographic effect and do not incite to repetitions, for the experience is finished and cathartic: the fearful images are purged, transcended, interpreted, or otherwise integrated with the rest of life. An art work leaves its audience with a saner whole philosophy (more congenial to pacifism in so far as pacifism is truth); and it has taken some of the venom from the cruelty and arrogance in the soul. But such a re-creative "finished" experience is precisely not rhetoric; it does not lead directly to action or any *immediate* policy. The Athenians seeing Euripides' *Trojan Women* were no doubt wiser and sadder about the very course of folly that they continued plunging along. (I do believe, however, that great art, forcibly confronting us with a more meaningful universe, does *initiate* conversion, and pacifists do well to perform these achieved monuments of their tradition.)

My guess—I judge from my own art-working—is that a serious modern artist who happens to be a pacifist (and how could he not be, if he once attends to these matters?)—if such an artist begins to move artistically among the scenes of war, his art action will soon lead to the exploration and expression of his *own* horror, rage, pain, and devastation. The vegetarian will disclose his own cannibalism, the pacifist his murderousness. Such works, e.g., *Guernica*, are monuments of how it is with us; they have no leisure for a practical moral, nor even for the luxury of indignation. The eye lamp flamingly thrust forward over Guernica does not light up the deed of Nazi bombers, but the violent soul of Picasso, brought to a salutary pause.

If we consider spurious, *kitsch*, or propagandistic antiwar art, on the other hand, its actual pornographic and provocative effect is equally to be expected, for the fantasy and the art-working convey the disorder of the weak artist and speak to the underlying wishes of the bad audience.

We thus have, by and large, the ironical situation that precisely the best cause, which has irrefutable sense and common humanity, ought to avoid "psychological," "artistic," and mass-rhetorical effects.

3

What, then, are the available resources of pacifist persuasion that can be used for a pacifist film? They can be roughly classified as:

(1) Factual education
(2) Analyses of character-neurotic and social-neurotic war ideology, and the withdrawal of energy from the causes of war spirit
(3) Opportunities for positive action, and pacifist history and exemplars.

(1. a) As a strictly prudential argument, pacifism has an easy case, perhaps too easy a case, so that peo-

ple do not take it seriously, it is too obvious. People have always known that war is a poor expedient, inefficient for any plausible purpose. And "present-day war," not only *our* present-day war, has long been out of the question. It is best if the facts, of the senselessness of it, are allowed to speak for themselves, without admixture of moral or emotional appeal or any grandiose references to saving the human species. The matter is much simpler. War talkers are pretty close to fools or else not a little crazy; their postures and remarks are not proper to normal grown men. This can be simply demonstrated, relying on logic, statistics, and history. The framework must be an irrefragable and unmistakable structure of verbal propositions, even printed subtitles, however "uncinematic"; for we are dealing with a deeply neurotic and even schizophrenic phenomenon, and the *reality of ordinary reasoning, and ordinary dismissal of stupidity*, must be strongly affirmed.

(b) On the other hand, the dangers of pacifist action—e.g., the risks involved in unilateral disarmament —should also be dispassionately and *fully* presented, so far as they can be fairly estimated. *It is not necessary to have an answer for every argument*, even grave arguments, for we cannot do what is senseless and unworthy of men anyway. Pacifism is a decision. The "serious" position is not, as Niebuhr, for instance, seems to think, to choose a lesser evil; it is to realize that we cannot have been so wrong for so long without purgatorial suffering.

(c) The facts or war policy, war makers, and war economy ought to be exposed with unsparing honesty and detail, at the risk of inevitable censorship. E.g., delineating the personalities—a Teller, Kennedy, or J. Edgar Hoover—on whom so much is allowed to depend. But further, the immense network of the power structure must be made clear and diagrammed, so that a person comes to realize how nearly every job, profession, and status is indirectly and directly involved in making war.

(2. a) Psychologically, our "tough" warriors live by a conceit of themselves as strong, to ward off the anguish of their spirits broken by authorities they could not face up to; and a conceit of themselves as hard, to ward off loss of love and fear of impotence. A film might profitably analyze the military posture, pelvis retracted, belly kept hard, exhalation restricted; the military ethos of inhibited feeling; the conceit of superiority by slavish identification with authority symbols. For comparison, analyze the social and family genesis of an underprivileged gang tough. Explain the details of Marine discipline as a means of destroying manliness. The system of griping fostered in armies as a means of maintaining childish dependency and avoiding mutiny. But further, show how in our times the classical sociology of the armed services as a substitute for civilian responsibilities is combined with the use of the services as complements of, and training for, organizational civilian life. The soldier seeks for ratings like a junior executive, while the Organization Man has a tough as his secret ideal. A thorough social and psychological analysis of these types might immunize the young.

(b) Analyze the notion of the Enemy as a projection (scapegoat) and also as a political red herring. Show in detail how Enemies have been manufactured and miraculously reformed by techniques of press and promotion. Show also how foreign nations have thus manufactured the Americans as the Enemy and assigned to us Enemy traits and wishes.

(c) But probably the chief factor of war spirit that must be analyzed is not the military character nor the projection of the Enemy, but the paralysis with which the vast majority of people of all countries accept the war that they oppose both by conviction and feeling. This must betoken an inner, fatalistic attachment to the feared disaster, and it is best explained as "primary masochism" (Reich): the hypothesis that, because of their rigid characters, people are unable to feel their pent-up needs, especially of sexuality and creative growth, and therefore they dream up, seek out, and conspire in an external catastrophe to pierce their numbness and set them free. The prevalent conditions of civilian peace and meaningless jobs tend to heighten this lust for explosion. (My experience, however, is that in analyzing this factor of war, one is opposed precisely by the more moralistic pacifists themselves. Rather than condone normal homosexuality or encourage the sexuality of their children, they would, apparently, accept the brutality of armies and see people blown to bits. One is dubious about the sanity of their pacifism, which seems to be rather a defense against their own hostile fantasies.)

Social and psychological subject matter of this type is sufficiently interesting in itself and is only confused by attempts at drama or case history; a straight classroom approach, the illustrated lecture, is most quietly effective.

(3. a) Factual exposure of the political and corporate operations of war society, and psychological and social analysis of its war ideology and spirit ought to disattach and release the energy that had been bound up in conventional symbols and habits of life. We must then have uses for this energy and opportunities for pacifist action. In principle, any animal satisfaction, personal self-realization, community welfare, or humane culture will draw energy from the structure of conceit, projection, and fatalistic masochism of the war spirit. "Waging peace" is the best means of preventing war, and pacifists do well to invent and support programs

for the use of our wealth and energy freed from the expense, fear, and senselessness of war. In my opinion, let me say, there is also natural violence that diminishes war, e.g., the explosion of passion, the fist fight that clears the air, the gentle forcing of the virginal, the quarrel that breaks down the barriers to interpersonal contact. War feeds on the inhibition of normal aggression. (Of course, many pacifists disagree with this point of view.)

(b) Specifically pacifist action—usually in the form of refusing—is called for when people are required to engage directly in war-making, e.g., by the conscription, the civil defense, working in war science or war factories. The defense of civil liberties, also, seems to be congenial to pacifists, because the libertarian attitude goes contrary to the power state.

(c) Finally, the preferred pacifist means of exerting social force has gotten to be nonviolent direct action, shared in by the group. Any instance of this, even if it fails, is proof of the feasibility of the pacifist position, for it shows that sensible and moral individual and small-group action is possible, and thereby it diminishes our masochistic paralysis in the face of an approaching doom "too big for men to cope with." (The history and the heroes of civil disobedience and nonviolent direct action, achieving or failing to achieve happiness, social welfare, or cultural progress, constitute the mythology of pacifism. They have the heartening exemplarity and the, perhaps, sentimental irrelevance of any mythology.) To my mind, pacifism is like Rilke's unicorn, it *"feeds on the possibility of existing."* For the resistance to modern warfare is natural and universal; the arguments against pacifism are weak; and the spirit of war is reducible by analysis; but what is needed is stories, examples, and opportunities for action concrete in the experience of the audience.

4

Factual and analytic handling of images of war can neutralize their pornographic effect. My bias is that even the exemplary images of pacifist action are best handled in a documentary fashion, avoiding audience identification with their heroes and keeping the real situation in the foreground. The purpose of the film is not so much inspiration as to point to opportunities in the audience's real environment. *It is better to err on the side of dryness. The heart is already enlisted.* Emphasis on the pacifist "movement" with its charismatic symbols and "leaders" betrays us into the field of public relations, where we are swamped. The charismatic excitement that gives courage and solidarity must emerge in each concrete occasion of pacifist action, and it will emerge, if it is really a man's own occasion. We are in the tradition of bearing witness. It was just the genius of Gandhi to notice faultless occasions.

The kinds of theme I have outlined could be the substance of a useful series of documentary pacifist films. Developed forthrightly and in particular detail, they would certainly prove offensive to many audiences, including some pacifist audiences, but they could hardly fail to hit home. They would rouse anxiety both by the character analysis of the audience and by the need for the audience to make decisions in their actions. The shared shock of the truth and of possibility is, in our society at present, equivalent to breaking a taboo. For most, I guess, the effect of such films would be uneasy silence, a dangerous but transitory state of feelings. The hope is that some of this feeling would be mobilized to decisive action, just as some would surely result in ugly reaction. Perhaps most persons would be made deeply thoughtful.

For its makers, such a document would certainly be a pacifist action, a commitment, and a bearing witness.

Post-Christian man

It is evident that the Americans are no longer a Christian society in any important sense. Their vital dogmas, tinged with superstition, are scientific; their ethics, rapidly changing, are the product of economic and urban institutions that are already only distantly related to Christian ideas. We are Post-Christian men. This must be a very important fact, and yet not much attention is paid to it—what more striking proof that people are not Christians than that they don't bother much whether or not they are Christian or Post-Christian! And perhaps this indifference is one of the striking characteristics of being Post-Christian! Ministers of religion in their sermons of alarm usually speak as though they were speaking to Christians, or sometimes, more luridly, as though they were speaking to pagans, backsliders; but their sermons are irrelevant, because they are speaking to Post-Christians.

To delineate this interesting state of being, let us ask what it was to be Christian and what has become of that. The term "Christian" was applied to a complex of attitudes and notions that became signal at various periods and that always formed an uneasy unity which theologians organized in various ways. It was a complex infinitely rich, composed of personalities and social movements, literature and controversy, laws and buildings, etc., etc. But for our purposes let us single out half a dozen important articles of belief, which we might arrange in a rough chronological order as follows: Christianity has held that:

(1) There is a new heavens and new earth. (Mark and Paul.) A Christian is a man reborn in a new flesh, and bearing witness by his presence, his affirming, and his acts of love. He lives by waiting in the last days.

(2) The history of the world is a theodicy unfolding the City of God. (John to Augustine and Erigena.) Jewish history, Roman history, and cosmic history have been parts of this process. A Christian acts in this world in imitation of the patterns of paradise.

(3) Dreading death, man has an immortal soul, and a Christian is personally ransomed to live immortally happy. (Romanesque period and Anselm.)

(4) Through the Church a Christian belongs to a universal community of Christendom, which inspirits and gives meaning to society in all its parts and is destined to embrace the world. This involves converting the heathen abroad, and the interpenetration of sacred and secular at home. (Period of the "medieval synthesis.")

(5) An individual man, by his resolute will against sin, demonstrates himself to be a Christian and a member of the Church. (Later Reformation and Counter-Reformation.)

(6) Besides these, Christianity has importantly mediated into Western civilization such attitudes of the old Roman Law and the Hebrew prophets as universalism, philanthropy, and the tempering of personal violence. A Christian is the loving brother of all mankind.

Through the centuries of Christianity these almost incompatible notions have managed to cohere, uneasily but always recognized and respected. They have been theologized as if they were all implicit from the beginning; and sometimes they have been as if miraculously united in saintly persons.

In recent times, however, there has been a change. Some of these properties of Christianity have so strongly and universally established themselves in our culture that there is no point in attributing them to a special group of believers—the Church is no longer militant—and indeed they have come to look strangely un-Christian. Other properties, however, now seem archaic, eccentric, and even to be dis-values, so that the expression "a Christian" almost connotes, as Dostoevski foresaw, an idiot. I think that this parting of the ways increasingly characterizes the past century. By "Post-Christian" I mean *the falling apart of the complex of Christian notions*, so that they no longer balance, limit, and inspirit one another. Some Christian attitudes have historically fulfilled themselves and have begun to seem anti-Christian. Others have begun to seem irrelevant. Nevertheless it is assumed, without inquiry, that the old global unity still exists. It is the tensions and the paradoxes of this situation, rather than any new idea or image, that we experience as Post-Christian.

2

Consider first some Christian tendencies that have fulfilled themselves in anti-Christian form.

The conception of Modern Science which I have described in a previous essay, as an infinitely self-accumulating and self-improving system, is, I think, a Christian one. It is like the old Augustinian theodicy, the notion that the history of the world is a process unfolding the City of God, and it is the part of a Christian to inhibit or otherwise detach himself from natural satisfactions and to imitate the abstract patterns. God's purpose is replaced by the consensus of scientists, but this does not make their activity any more humanly pragmatic, for scientists are interested in solving the problems of Science. The psychology of both scientist and priest is objective and obsessional, frowning on spontaneous responses and rejecting other methods than the proper ritual discipline as essentially irrelevant if not wicked. Both nobly propose Truth and Beauty as absolute aims and models, and promise happiness for mankind; but these goods are attainable only through strict observance. Among the folk, modern science has replaced Christianity as the chief object of superstition. The transformation from "idealism" to "materialism," in which the revolutionists of the eighteenth and nineteenth centuries had such high hopes, has not mattered much for true believers; for our empiricism is detached from ordinary experience and its products are imposed on ignorant people. We can say that both priest and scientist give forth matter sacramentally improved; the Church, having a religious background, has given psychological techniques for well-being, whereas Science, with a background of industrial arts, abundantly produces scientific technology.

In the heroic age of science, in the sixteenth and seventeenth centuries, the scientists, as natural philosophers, were in rebellion against the ritual order and turned, as a band of rebels, to personal contact with personified Nature who provided them a new ethic. But when the enterprises of science combined with the "Protestant ethic" and became bureaucratized, and then became the dominant system of ideas, the theodicy and its service again came to the fore. It would be absurd, of course, to call modern science Christian—indeed, the scientific miracles have beat out the Christian miracles and have destroyed Christianity—but the present attitude of both scientist and folk is comprehensible only on a firm foundation established by one successful tendency of Christianity: belief in the progress of an objective abstract entity.

Another closely related example of anti-Christianity established by the fruition of Christianity is our economic relations of production and consumption, in the line of development famously traced by Max Weber as the Protestant Ethic and the Spirit of Capitalism. I do not think that Weber gives enough weight to the psychological factor of the individual anxiety felt by the pre-Lutheran and early Lutheran saints when reduced to a simply personal relation to God, unmediated by old institutions, and therefore to their need to internalize a new abstract system. Losing their community organs and their local intercessors in heaven, men fall back on Augustinian, imperial, Christianity to cushion the new individualism.

But when we extend the line of economic development further than Weber did, to the present system of semimonopolies and state collectives, and when we find that the Calvinist virtues of asceticism, rationality, individual self-help, etc., have been transformed precisely into their opposites—a high standard of living, various kinds of boondoggling and feather-bedding, and the morality of Organization Man and bureaucrat —nevertheless the underlying moral demands of attending to business, righteously one-upping one's fellows, and disciplining one's animal and communal self, are the same as when it was the Lord's work that was to be done. At least from Adam Smith on, the system of rational business accommodations has again been seen to be a theodicy working itself out independently of any human wishes. And outside the strictly business world, we can go back a century earlier and see the lineaments of our mature corporate system and its mores. Pascal's satire on the Jesuits sounds exactly like a description of the techniques of Madison Avenue. He rightly called this system anti-Christian, but it certainly grew out of Christianity.

Still another example of anti-Christian results of significantly Christian tendencies is the development of modern national and world-wide conformity. Nationally, the modern style of conformity began in the sectarian exclusiveness of Protestant or Counter-Reformation small towns, with their stern disciplining of animal expression. In the course of time, this Christian norm has become the national norm of behavior —as men's business suits seem to carry on a clerical cut; but of course on a national scale it has become non-Christian and nonascetic, simply a respectable coloration, without sacramental community meaning. On a world-wide scale, the European conformity has spread also by the proselytizing and crusading zeal endemic in Christianity from its early days. The spreading empires of Christendom have been different from the other empires of history, which either let be and taxed or wiped out and resettled or forcibly enslaved; but the Christians have had to convert by various means. Under modern conditions of economy and communications, however, this Christian universalism has sloughed off its other Christian content as irrelevant, and what we export is our machine tools, mass culture, and other secular goods. (Faiths we tend rather to import.)

The contrast is striking when it is a subordinated minority that promotes Christian universalism, as in the sit-ins of the Southern Negroes and their friends. Then nearly the full spectrum of Christian attitudes is carried along, including brotherly love, singing of hymns, militant pacifism, personal purity of motive, and almost millennial expectations.

It is worth mentioning that in the very long run Christian pacifism has not had the effect, as Nietzsche claimed, of shackling the strong in the interests of the resentful weak. Rather, it has subordinated all persons and local communities to the concentrated power of the constituted authorities that alone bear arms. We have little personal violence, but only big wars with plenty of slaughter of noncombatants. Correspondingly, philanthropy, grounded in Christian charity for the sick and poor, has in modern conditions been taken over by social welfare, which precisely insulates the giver from the creaturely facts of life.

So Christian universalism, Christian pacifism, and Christian charity have ironically fulfilled themselves in Antichrist.

3

Perhaps superficially, perhaps essentially—it is hard to know—mankind seems to be galloping toward the condition of a social beehive or termitary, in which individual uniqueness, creaturely contact, neighborly charity, the satisfactions of local community, and the high culture of real cities, are all increasingly irrelevant. In this process the tendencies of Christianity have certainly been influential. A conformist and universal population, working to keep running a busy economic machine, and controlled by an abstract and normative science: this is socialized human nature. One cannot help thinking of Auguste Comte's remarkable simulacrum of Christianity in his Positive Religion.

Yet such a religion of socialization is, of course, also the very contrary of Christianity; for Christianity is a personal relation of the creature and his creator, it is individual saintliness and neighbor love, existential commitment, the folly of the Cross, spontaneous illumination. In its history Christianity has known love feasts, speaking with tongues, martyrdoms, chivalric honor, and militant conscience.

To be sure, whether man *can* be essentially socialized or not, forming almost a new species from anything we have known, is a question for future history. If essential socialization is impossible, what will become of our present gallop toward such an absurd state? There seem to be two alternatives: either the unbearable heightening of anxiety, total apathy and anomie, and catastrophic violence; or the revolt of nature, existential disgust, conflict, and new religion.

4

Let us consider, now, a couple of important Christian notions that have become eccentric or archaic, and no longer belong to Post-Christian man.

For the first time in nearly two thousand years Western people are losing their belief in the personal immortality of their souls. It is astonishing how little this extraordinary change of opinion is mentioned by the writers, as if there were a tacit agreement to overlook it. In the Old Testament there is not much belief in such immortality, nor evidence of longing for it—the Resurrection in Ezekiel is a different matter; but from Rabbinic times it has been a fundamental article, and the apocalyptic resurrection of Jesus was rapidly transformed into a theory of after-life in heaven. In some periods, as during the building of the great Romanesque crypts, the dread of death, the cultivation of relics, and the longing for immortal personal salvation seemed to be the chief business of Christian society; as again during the waning of the Middle Ages, with greater emphasis on black spirits and damnation. These wishful thoughts of survival and the intercession of dead saints were an important cause of the immense efflorescence of Christian plastic art; and our Western poetry, from medieval times deep into the Romantic movement, is marked by the fear of dying and the esthetic triumph over death. I doubt that love-death would have been so sought if it did not promise immortal bliss. So, too, Augustinian theodicy and modern both, imitating their abstract patterns, have been vivified by the sense that the thinker, the image of the Creator, is also a creator of images and in them proves his immortality. Among religions, Christianity has most cultivated the Holy Spirit, infuser of life into the dead. It could be said that Christianity extended to all folk the immortality of Fame and Muse that in antiquity had been reserved to heroes, emperors, and poets.

What can it mean that in recent times this energy of despair, and of reaction by denial, is waning? One does *not* have the impression that it is because of animal satisfaction and self-fulfillment in meaningful action, which would be the normal means for draining energy from impossible wishes. On the contrary, one has the strong impression that death is being kept out of mind and out of feeling. This appears clearly in our urban arrangements and entertainment, our hospitals, our funerary institutions, our popular optimistic philosophy. We seem to have here a character-neurotic repression of a psychoneurotic fantasy; this may be regarded as a technique of socialization, and perhaps also our peculiar American socialization is needed to make this repression stick.

But even more absent from contemporary ideas is the primary notion of Gospel Christianity, that there has *already* occurred, in the incarnation and resurrection, the transformation of the physical and psychical worlds into a pneumatic new heavens and new earth. This psychotic belief bloomed in an apocalyptic climate. (I say "psychotic" technically, without valuation, to mean contrary to the evidence of the senses. Whatever else it is, religion is, as Freud said, a socially acceptable psychosis; but I need hardly point out that the deliveries of some psychotic states are pragmatically truer and better than usual "reality" and "prudence.") As early as John, this material belief began to be toned down to the psychological reality of love or the metaphysics of otherworldliness plus allegories; nevertheless, through two millennia it has always revived in evangelical and millennial movements, especially in the face of vast natural and man-made calamities, and has been attended by miracles with their peculiar pneumatic physics. Now, here again, it is astonishing how in the face of our recent and threatening calamities, there have been so few and tiny millenarian impulses. The mass-evangelism of Graham or Buchman is entirely moral and sentimental; it is uncosmological, no miracles are reported. The psychological Christianity of confident living and positive thinking is even less messianic. So total, apparently, has been the victory of the rival scientific superstition, thin as it is! To my mind, *this present failure of millenarian nerve is an irrefutable proof that Christianity has ceased to exist as a living world faith*. If a Christian has not been reborn, he is nothing at all. But the religiously lifeless institutions of Christianity still do plenty of emotional damage to children and adolescents.

In our Post-Christian times, we have a vacuum of religious expectation; one would assume that in this vacuum people would be frantically busy about political changes toward a satisfactory reality to replace the vanished dream; or at least that the institutions of modern science had accomplished something, or promised something, in that direction. But no such thing. It is amazing. Can it be that the standard of happiness has fallen so low that the present-day "reality" seems better than a flight from reality? I prefer to believe that people are simply temporarily too confused by the complicated technology and social changes in which they are wandering, to be able to dream awake. Also, we have not yet recovered from the shell shock of the wars and the continuing colonial upheavals that have taken away the traditional world.

5

In America, the vacuum left by Christianity is perhaps a new and promising factor. Especially among Protestants there is dismay at how the establishment of Christian notions has resulted precisely in anti-Christian life. Since the Reformers were more progressive theologians to begin with, their doctrines have come to the abyss sooner; being less relevant, the Catholics are now smug, and the editor of *America* has recently proclaimed that we are in "Post-Protestant" times and can enthusiastically share "in this fascinating thing we call America."

Conversely, the best of the Protestants are willing to conclude that the Christian notions most dear to them might be better served if they are no longer thought of as Christian, though nobody knows *how* to think about them. This is not a new story. Kierkegaard was saying it in the time of Hegel and Pastor Moeller. But Kierkegaard is first being heeded in the past thirty years, and Nietzsche, Gide, Wilhelm Reich, and other voices of Antichrist, including even Communists, have come to sound like truer Christians.

If I may judge from my not-extensive experience, there has been also a marked change of personnel. When I was young, a minister of religion was likely to be an ass, and seminarians were little better than morons, comparable to the military. Nowadays, many clergymen are brighter than average, and the theological students are among the salt of the earth. Rival secular careers, in law, science, teaching, politics, no longer seem more enlightened nor eminently relevant to an earnest and honest lad who consults his feelings about the world we live in. The ministry makes as much sense as psychiatry.

And often on issues like pacifism, racial and social justice, or even attacking censorship or bad narcotics or sexual laws, the churches are the *only* traditional groups to speak up for common reason. This does not follow from their orthodox Christian tradition, but simply because, as Christians, they are more serious and therefore less afraid to be unconventional.

Indeed, some honest pastors can be said to be carrying on a holding operation. Rather than giving over their valuable real estate to secular hands that will use it worse, they are holding onto it, hoping that they will learn *what* to do with it. Creator Spirit come.

On the intellectual inhibition of explosive grief and anger

For the explosive release of strong feelings, such as anger and grief, a person must have the object of passion concretely present, even tangibly present in some way. The object of one kind of anger is a present obstacle; grief is for an object present by its felt absence. To blaze with anger and be ready to strike, a person must first be approaching what he desires, he must be actively committed to the approach; and he must believe that the obstacle in his way is the real cause of his frustration. To bawl for loss, he must first have been attached to something, and then he must believe that its absence is the real cause of the misery he feels.

We see that children easily have these beliefs and often flare up and often cry. Faced with even a temporary delay or absence, children pound and scream and bawl; but as soon as the situation changes, they are bafflingly sunny, and take their gratification with relish, or feel secure again when mother returns. It is said that "children cannot wait," but just the contrary is true. It is children who *can* wait, by making dramatic scenes (not otherwise than religious people get through hours of stress by singing hymns). They have a spontaneous mechanism to cushion even minor troubles. Rather it is the adults who have inhibited their spontaneous expression, who cannot wait; we swallow our disappointment and always taste what we have swallowed. For where the occasions of passion occur, where there is actual frustration and misery, and yet anger and grief are not explosively released, then the disposition itself is soured, and such happiness as follows is never full and unclouded.

Especially among intellectual and sensitive persons, there is an inevitable abuse of intelligence and understanding that keeps them from the conviction that there is a real, present object of anger and grief; and thus they cannot purge these passions. This is their philosophic or scientific insight that the tangible obstacles or losses are not the "real" ones; for the "real" causes of trouble are seen to be remote, general, intangible; they may be social, technological, even cosmological. Behind the immediate frustration or loss, is the understood cause of it. But the thought of such general or distant causes is not able to bring on an explosive release in the physical particular person. There is no doubt that such a flight to the abstract—and indeed, most "thinking" altogether—is a neurotic method of avoiding strong feelings, of substituting "knowing about" for awareness; yet it seems to me that this use of intelligence is inevitable, because indeed such insights are true. The dilemma is this: that desire aims at something tangible, at a present change in ourselves and our physical environment; but when desire is thwarted or love lost, the passional feelings that have been physically roused find no tangible object on which to be vented.

The classical solution of this dilemma has been to equalize matters by turning desire itself toward what is theoretical or ideal: "intellectual love." This has several immensely important variants. One is to achieve stoical *apatheia*, the dissociation of emotion altogether. Another is to achieve Buddhist compassion, the secure response to inevitable misery (in psychoanalysis, this great and constructive frame of mind is a reaction-formation). Neither of these—*apatheia* or compassion—has any relation to animal happiness, so we need not discuss them here. But Intellectual Love can be embarked on also with full risk and, soon enough, somatic commitment; and there then emerge the following interesting possibilities. Suppose intellectual love is frustrated—e.g., by the problem of evil or the problem of infinity—then one comes to a kind of anguish or terror that marks precisely the "return" of the alienated tangible world, perhaps fraught with menace. The particulars of the world will then be regarded not as indifferent to the intellect, but as symbols. A more amiable possibility is that intellectual love is gratified, e.g., by finding proofs of grace and cosmos; then there is said to be a kind of serene ecstasy in which precisely the tangible world is recreated in love; the saint returns to us and performs miracles, the scientist orgastically achieves his theory, and so forth.

Let us ask, however, what occurs with the intellectual and sensitive person who does not leave behind the tangible objects of desire to devote himself to ideal objects. Superficially considered, such a man has a good thing: he enjoys, or at least tries for, animal satisfaction, yet he avoids the worst pains of frustration and failure. It is only when the going gets rough, when he meets too much opposition, that he finds that he cannot take the tangible obstacles seriously, he knows better. Nevertheless, as every intellectual knows, this hedging bet is a desperate disease. He would give anything, he says, to experience frank bawling and hot wrath.

We are not speaking of those who repress grief and anger altogether—as when a child is made to fear the consequences of his anger and is shamed out of crying, and grows into a smiling insensitive adult. This is the inhibition of appetite itself, and must be treated by character analysis. In this essay I want to speak of a well-defined group: persons who have appetites, who show initiative in approaching and possessing their objects and are therefore subject to frustration and loss, but who cannot give way to anger and grief because they know too much. The character neurotics who repress appetite and passion altogether, before they arise, seem to have been intimidated, for example, by harsh parents. Our sensitive intelligent persons, on the contrary, seem to be anxious about blind passion itself: when things do not work out, the self is threatened with confusion, and so the intensity of appetite, grief, anger is controlled and made to *dribble away*, partly in reasoning. The mechanism of dribbling away makes us think of the last-minute inhibition of orgastic surrender and ejaculation. Correspondingly, at the last minute he withdraws from contact. Contrast him as a child with a less intelligent child forced to repress. If a child is intelligent and intuitive, he can avoid dire consequences so long as he takes care of himself; he learns to keep within his safety zone. Here is he lonely but he is also protected from terrible disappointments and punishments. He feels, too, that if he ventured outside his zone, his anger might become uncontrollable and he might murder somebody. He does not repress but he learns to "know better."

In this essay my interest is not in interpreting these misfortunes of the past, but in the problem of coping with this tried and proved defense in the present.

2. GRIEF AND WEEPING

The intellectual person feels his deprivation but he does not weep because, as he says, "My feelings are not hurt, I am not hurt." Since he sees that the causes of his loss are objective and general, he knows that they are not aimed especially at him. He is not insulted. (If he were insulted, his ego-protecting anger would flare and this would bring on grief.) Quite the contrary, by his intelligent understanding of causes, he is able to identify himself with the depriving power, he is even somewhat magnified.

Suppose he is in love. So long as pleasure is forthcoming, he cautiously but progressively opens out to it and enjoys his beloved. But as soon as there is threat of loss, he rises above the situation. He at once sees that the loss is inevitable: it is inevitable in the character of the beloved and in his own character, and these cannot be changed; indeed, he might understand that the very increase of their pleasure has created their anxiety, for they have begun to risk confusion, so they withdraw. All this is because of something that happened long ago; it is in the nature of our institutions; it is objective, he himself being one of the objects. It does not touch him at present; he does not feel himself, subjectively, as lost. So he is not softened to bawl.

Nevertheless he feels he is deprived and he is miserable. Being miserable, he characteristically draws back from the feeling of loss and explains it, and he lets his grief dribble away. He is ennobled by understanding. He is now wiser still. The experience was worth it. But he is not purged, and he is henceforth less open to love. He has not mourned enough to be able to live again.

We could say that what is lacking is *surprise*. If he were surprised, he would not have the opportunity to rise above the situation and survey it and let his feeling dribble away. But he is intelligent and foreseeing, not easily surprisable. He is quick to judge by portentous signs and he is always ready. (When such a person becomes more cynical and callous, he even begins to rehearse the outcome beforehand, the more efficiently to prevent any anxiety—or novelty—from occurring.)

Of course he is perfectly right. His lost love is not for him a real object of grief, for, protecting himself, he did not spontaneously engage himself, but only deliberately and cautiously. It is certainly his own character that is the real object at least of anger, for it is a frustrating obstacle to him. If he could feel this, he would weep in pity for himself hemmed in by his character. But it is just one's own character that one does not feel. It is the character of an intelligent sensitive person to understand itself in principle, but not to feel engaged in the struggle between happiness and character, and break down. As an object of observation, a man's character is no surprise to him; he has long known its ways. Does he ask himself the question, "Have I been happy for thirty-forty-fifty years?"

Nevertheless, it is not the case that an intelligent sensitive man who cannot weep for his misery cannot weep at all. We find, to our surprise, that he weeps in two interesting situations, and these give us useful clues how to help him.

First, he weeps when he attends to something of pure and simple beauty that suddenly surprises him. It may be a phrase of melody or words, a flower, a graceful or noble gesture or behavior. Such things, when they occur surprisingly, bring tears to his eyes, and he may even softly weep. The sequence is as follows: because the object is beautiful, promissory of pleasure and giving pleasure, he allows it to come close to himself and then, at the surprising turn to something still simpler and more resolving, he has had neither the time nor the inclination to guard against it; he *is* surprised and touched. Feeling rises, and the feeling that rises is—unexpectedly—weeping. Why is this?

Such beauties are the signs of paradise; experiencing them is an activity of paradise. But paradise is lost. So the tears are, after all, tears not of joy but of loss. It is his own hurt self that he is weeping for, because now, in these special circumstances, *his persistent misery is confronted with an actual loss that he believes in.* On reflection, we can understand why it is precisely an object of beauty that can get behind, or under, the habitual defenses of intelligence. The experience of beauty is preconceptual; it moves between sensory presentness and a meaning coming into being, not yet rigidly defined. Experience of beauty is prior to the separation that a man makes between his present pleasure—which is meaningless, because he does not fully give himself to it—and his general conception of what would "really" satisfy him, which he does not believe, because it is merely a thought. But the tangible present object stands, as part for whole, for a tangible lost object, and he weeps. But it is only an object of beauty, whose meaning he again gathers and interprets, and his soft weeping dries before it deepens to orgastic sobbing.

It is not by accident that the intelligent sensitive person often turns out to be an artist, to create this experience that is alone meaningful to him.

The social situation that brings our man to tears is still more curious; it is relenting, the relaxation of unnecessary torture. Note that, again, it is precisely not a deprivation but a kind of gift that is the prelude to weeping. Thus, suppose a judge sympathizes with a condemned man and says he is sorry. He holds out his relenting hand to shake yours, perhaps remarking that justice is not perfect. He expresses his relenting in order to save your feelings, not, of course, to suspend the sentence. And so, because your feelings *are* saved, you take that reptilian hand and choke up. One's intellectual defenses were strongly marshaled against the oppressor, but now the tension is relaxed. The tears are for oneself, but not because the self has been saved but because, in so far saved, it can afford to feel what it has lost. The relenting is a sign that the oppression, with which one identified in part simply by standing trial, has not after all been inevitable; one *could have been* happy, but it is lost. In this soft mood one then accedes to the present unhappiness. Naturally one does not frankly bawl for it, but chokes back the crying and dries the eyes.

Tragic poets relent and win the audience's tears at just the worst moment, as when Mrs. Alving in *Ghosts* suddenly recognizes that her husband had perhaps had a hard time of it himself, and was somewhat justified. In tragedies, the pity is for the protagonist as he approaches his catastrophe; the fear is for him and oneself at the catastrophe; but the tears are for oneself when, after the catastrophe, there is a relenting of the judgment. The poet sympathizes—I quote from Genet's *Les Pompes Funèbres*—"*T'as été malheureux, hein?*" *T'as été malheureux, hein?*

That is, identifying with the depriving and condemning causes that now relent, our man allows himself a certain self-pity. This is already a great step, for especially the intelligent sensitive man is likely to be harsh and implacable toward himself, to make the highest demands on himself. Often, because he understands, he is kindly to others and makes no demands on them. For others he is kindly and he feels sorry, but he does not love them; himself he loves, but he is not kindly to himself. He knows enough to regard his hurt self as a small insignificant object; he has grown beyond identifying with himself, he understands the causes. But in the special case of relenting, he can pity his small self.

Nevertheless, the small self is not the whole self. The one who is pitying is not himself suffering a present loss.

So we see that our man weeps—and therefore provides us with clues—for beauty and the remnants of self-security. Both are present gifts that revive the memory of old losses, but it is only present losing that one can frankly bawl for.

3. SOLUTION

The intellectual sensitive man does not presently lose because he does not presently stake himself. Our clues makes us see that two things are necessary for frank bawling. First, instead of looking for reminders of paradise, which lead to weeping softly, *he must engage in the present hope and effort for paradise.* In such a pursuit he cannot passively identify with the existing causes of things, for paradise does not exist. So, second, he must identify with paradise by actively *making* the causes of his reality. Then, instead of relenting pity for himself, which leads to choking up, he will be vulnerable to present tangible loss. For in the pursuit and creation of paradise, a man is surprisingly confronted with obstacles and present loss, and he is angry and bawls.

Usually, a man plays it safe by engaging only in what he knows he is more than adequate to. For an intelligent man this is not a small area, and he can respectably exist in it a long time. But if he wants to be surprisingly miserable, he need only raise the stakes, move where it is no longer safe for him, and aim at what he might or might not be adequate to. Precisely because one is able to cope with what is usual, one must therefore hunger also for paradise. Such an aim cannot be evaluated by a psychologist, for he is a man in the same situation and knows no more about it than his patient. We may now define "paradise" relative to the working of intelligence adequate to the usual. Paradise is practical activity among improbabilities, it is what is "fool-

ishly hoped for." Engaged there in a struggle for life
—for such activity is not safe—a man will have plenty
of occasion for explosive passion.

Let us pause a moment and consider the usual existing condition of our intellectual sensitive man. He is
likely tired, and he is too intelligent to hope and try
foolishly. Assume that he has made an adequate adjustment in personal and social life; even his painful
reactions are not unbearable; his personality does not
break down. This is probable if he is intelligent and
sensitive, can learn the maze, and intuit when to let
his strong feelings dribble away. (An insensitive man
runs more risk of breaking down.) He sees that the life
that is practical is not paradisal. He feels the persistent
misery involved in the loss of paradise, but he does not
confront this as his present loss, because he is not
turned to it practically. Where he happens to be practically engaged, he is not unsuccessful; he is perhaps
more than adequate to such problems as arise; and just
understanding his own and the world's troubles is a
steady comfort. As the *New York Times* explained in a
recent advertisement for itself, "You'll be delighted at
the satisfaction you get every morning by knowing
what's going on in the world." And what is the use of
arguing? One protested enough as a child. The man
employs his intelligence to protect himself from his
misery, and this is as it should be. He uses his intelligence to calculate what is feasible and to understand
what is lost. For intelligence has these two functions: to
help complete unfinished situations by solving problems and coming to practical responses; or, where problems are insoluble, to circle and dissipate energy in
fantasy and idea.

Why would such a man want to be surprisingly
miserable? He is tired, miserable but not dissatisfied,
enjoying the satisfactions of the usual standards. Why
should he willfully encourage the hunger that will re-

create his, and our, misery, when we have "gotten over" our misery, and things are well enough? In brief, what is his symptom?

He is unused and bored. Being intellectual and sensitive, he has grown to a considerable size and, unawares, continues to grow, but his pattern of "adequate" activity does not realize his powers, and this restiveness is interpreted by him as boredom.

Let us distinguish acute and chronic boredom. In general, boredom is fixing the present attention on what cannot be interesting because eros is attached to something outside of attention. In acute boredom, the unconscious attraction is definite, claims attention, and must be actively repressed—e.g., being somewhere and really wishing to be elsewhere. But habitual or chronic boredom is boredom with the pattern of activity as a whole, with oneself. It is being adequate where in fact one is more than adequate; failing to exercise powers, because they are dangerous or destructive; failing to hunger after impossibilities, because one will be disappointed; failing to deepen misery, until one is surprisingly miserable.

It is not with impunity that one exists with impunity.

In boredom one senses a constraining force that fixes the attention on what cannot be interesting enough. In acute boredom this is some present duty, for instance, that could, with more courage, be abrogated; it is often the reactive opposite of a guilty attraction actively repressed. The condition is therefore one of lively pain. But chronic boredom is spiritless. The constraint is both peculiarly relentless and peculiarly anonymous. There is nothing to oppose and it is omnipresent.

It is the self that must relent. The self, its theory and picture of itself and its habitual reasonableness, is the chief constraining force. As we say, "It takes two people to make a bore," and oneself is always one of them.

Typical standards of the relentless self are: the need to be always right; to be consistent; unwillingness to be a fool; satisfaction with the situation as it is when it is well enough. The bother is that these standards are irrefutable. Our rationalizations are usually true.

So long as paradise is regarded as "lost" or again as "not yet," we are not able to cry, for our losing is not tangibly present. In the present it is not possible to know the laws of paradise, but only to make them.

4. ANGER

> Let us treat the men and women well, treat
> them as if they were real—perhaps they are.
> —EMERSON

We may sketch more briefly the plight of the intellectual sensitive person who cannot give way to anger and strike a blow. His case is more familiar.

Self-pity and utopianism are disesteemed among us —they are, for instance, damning criticisms of novels and poetry; but the capacity for wrath and indignation is valued precisely among intellectuals; it is considered strong, manly, and serious; its lack is strongly felt.

But what to be angry with, and where to strike? Every man feels frustrated; a man is, for instance, frustrated by poverty that uses his time and hampers his enterprise; but the intelligent man understands that the obstacle is not really the employer or nonemployer in front of him, but it is the economic institutions. Sexually frustrated, he realizes that the obstacle is not his tangible partner but the moral code, religion, upbringing, working in himself and his partner. How to strike at these? They are not things.

An expedient that used to be much recommended was to identify oneself with a group or movement dedicated to striking at the real obstacles; because of its size and power, the group is more commensurate with the vast obstacles. This is perhaps a practical mode of action but I doubt that it solves our dilemma. Instead of bringing oneself into the tangible presence of the frustrating obstacles, it confronts one with symbols or agents of the obstacles, e.g., the policeman or the school board; and if one is sensitive, his feeling toward these mere agents cannot be anger. But suppose that a man hardens his sensitivity and learns to feel and act as if these symbols and agents were his tangible enemies; then he even rather easily works himself into habitual wrath, a condition that we used to observe in many Communists, when there were Communists around. But it is not *oneself* that is wrathful, so the discharge is not deep-going. Rather, one strikes at an agent, using oneself as an agent. One is not angry, but has worked oneself into the role of being angry.

Let us again seek for clues in the opposite direction, in situations that are not particularly frustrating in any way but make our man flare up. First, let me mention a curious reaction that I should not believe if I had not observed it in myself and others. Someone is displaying, perhaps in a parlor conversation, a bumptious overbearing stupidity. Suddenly, quite beyond any expectation of his own behavior, the intelligent man strikes the stupid one in the face. He was not being immediately frustrated at all, but it is as if his frustration of all the hope of the world has arisen and caught him by the throat. If *this* object exists, he feels himself frustrated of everything, of paradise, of any possibility of making sense. The stupidity before him makes him feel that he is in a morass; his nausea rises; he blindly strikes. But of course the blow is itself senseless and the next moment he is apologetic and tries to make amends. The blow has no direction—"I didn't mean *you*"; it is blind, has no relation to one's practical concern—"I don't know what got into *me*."

A second occasion for flaring up is extremely familiar to myself. The intelligent man is earnestly giving his best opinion or advice, without trying to persuade, for he is disinterested in the affair and is just trying to be helpful; but the other smiles smugly and says, "Hm." The intelligent man then flares in anger and shouts, "Who do you think you are!" His affect is strong, but he does not strike. The affect is strong because his best "whole" self has been actively committed to its best activity, of earnest intelligent opinion. So committed, he ventures outside his safety zone toward a tangible contact. But he has been betrayed, not so much by the other's indifference as by his own engagement.

Let us look more deeply at this same occasion and mention a usual sequence of which it is a part. The intellectual sensitive man makes a sexual advance and is rebuffed; but he does not yet feel the anger of frustration, for he understands that it is in the nature of things, etc. Instead, he is merely sad. Retreating to the security of his own best strength, he then begins to offer good general advice, friendly, but tinged with an hostility unknown to himself. The other, noticing the hostility, withdraws into indifference. Now I flare in anger. For it is just in acting among generalities that, having given up the tangible, I am really trying to appropriate the world. I was not committed to the tangible sexual advance, but to the good advice I am deeply committed. Now I am really frustrated. My anger is strong, but I cannot discharge it by striking the tangible person before me—for I *am* disinterested, I have not been trying to persuade.

Just as he is always on the brink of tears, so our intellectual sensitive man is always on the verge of anger. He is angry with himself, with precisely his intelligence and its abuse in generalities, rather than its achieving tangible goods. The stupidity that enrages him is his own stupidity, for he is shrewd everywhere but in getting what he wants. There he is disarmed and stupid. He is angry with the world because it does not allow his earnest intellectual concern to become concrete in tangible effects; and he is angry with himself because his tangible desires do not really enlist his intellectual concern.

What he lacks is patience. Just as he is chronically bored because unused, so he is chronically impatient because greedy. This is why his aggressive initiative does not meet with a tangible object.

Impatience in general is desire without its object, going forward with desire to meet an object that is not tangible through properties of time, appropriateness, availability. Let us distinguish acute and chronic impatience. Acute impatience is the interruption or delay of a particular desire that is already on its way. But chronic impatience desires to desire, it abstractly anticipates its object, it exhausts itself in an idea, whereas desire would normally rise in the actual or imminent presence of its object. Inevitably the premature desire of chronic impatience is a cause of present frustration; it takes the object not as it is but as it is imagined— and also as it is feared, for to fail, except within one's own narrow conditions, is an important purpose of chronic impatience. The frustrated intelligent man is especially prone to anticipate in this way. He gathers his unfinished desires in one perfect bundle of satisfaction that he desires, and the coming object must, somehow, be such as to fulfill all this recipe. He makes a demand on it according to his preconception. And meantime *he disregards the new possibilities in the actual object.* The presence of the object is necessarily disappointing to him; it is unworthy to enlist his intellectual concern. Also, the way he takes it does not fit it, so he acts, with regard to it, like a fool.

Chronically impatient, the intellectual sensitive man does not regard what is present as possibly interesting as it is, and as it is available; thus he is chronically bored.

5. SOLUTION

But supposing he waits patiently for the object before him to rouse his desire: and patiently uses his best intelligence on it as a possible object and exercises his best discrimination and other powers. Then, as the world goes, he will usually find himself really frustrated anyway, and, without reproaching himself for his stupidity, he will have occasion to flame with anger.

For let us bring together our two prescriptions: (1) to cease longing for lost paradise and make a present effort for paradise; and (2) to cease aggressively anticipating the paradise not yet, but to wait patiently for felt desire. These are the present: the present effort, the felt desire. It is necessary for a person to have a sphere in which he can, actually, in the present, exercise his best powers. This he will not easily find. In the kinds of occasions that generally offer, he will have plenty of tangible objects that are the real causes of his grief and anger.

We have thus characterized the intellectual sensitive person nowadays as letting his passions dribble away; his grief dribbles away in consoling explanations; his anger dribbles away in impatient approaches. He is always sad and on the verge of anger. He is chronically bored and chronically impatient; unrelenting toward himself; stupid with regard to the others. If he would relent and pity himself, he would bring himself near to tears; and if he would then aim at a condition worthy of a man, he would come to orgastic sobbing. If he would be patient and let his concern rise in the presence of desirable objects, he would use his intelligence incisively and objectively, and would soon flame with anger and—probably not strike—but *shake* the object in rage.

But he lets his feelings dribble away in order to avoid the excitement of explosive release that is too strong for him to bear. It is to avoid a terrible darkness, whether black or red, that he becomes wary and characteristically intellectual and sensitive. The available world being what it is—for he is not, for the most part, in error—he marshals his energy against these mounting excitements, and therefore in the present he **is** tired, impatient, bored.

My psychology as a "Utopian sociologist"

When I think of what I know and the books I have studied, I am astonishingly blank in modern sociology; I hardly know the names of the authors, e.g., Parsons or Merton. This is perhaps partly their blame; they are too methodological, not enough involved. Comte, Marx, Durkheim, Veblen, etc.—whom I know as much as I tend to know things—were more political and moral. But clearly it is mainly a psychological problem of my own, since I am convinced that intelligent doctors do not waste their talents on nothing. The case is that I do not grasp their subject matter, it does not interest me. How is this?

I *am* interested, I am even one of the authors, in social psychology. I take this to be the extension—by projection, identification, and other mechanisms—of primary interpersonal relations into the wider secondary environment. Thus, a man's attitude on the job may be like his pre-adolescent family life; or behind the charismatic leader is the infantile father; or the public feeling about war and the bomb is importantly grounded in primary masochism and creative block. These are propositions in social psychology.

Sociology is something different; let us try to derive it. Men are inherently social, share action and sentiment, and affect one another: this is the subject matter of psychology and social psychology. But suppose that the accumulation and interplay of these group relations come to existing facts that overshadow personal and group psychology and strongly determine the behavior of their members just as members of groups, whether riding on a bus or in the institutions of society. Such behavior is the main substance of the social scene, of history, politics, and economics. We can analyze such group behavior, make models of it, treat it statistically, make predictions. We have a science of sociology.

Where in this subject matter, and in the science of this subject matter, do I sign off? I strongly experience shared activity; but it is at the second proposition, the overshadowing of the social psychology by group relations in which the persons are structured, that I lose touch with what is going on. In my own primary relations as son, father, friend, and lover, I have been so little satisfied, I have so many unfinished situations, that I resist becoming further involved in events that would reduce me to a unit that may be counted in or out without being able to react on the total and its laws. I fail to experience myself in groups that I cannot immediately try to alter by personal decision and effort.

I understand, of course, that my primary dissatisfaction is our average human condition. But whereas most people seem to respond by inhibiting their unsatisfied needs and throwing themselves all the more into conformity and mass action, for comfort and for abreaction, it is just this that I resist. Rather, I keep alive my close needs and withdraw from group interplay that for me would be superficial.

The result of what I do is disastrous in both my life and thought. By living all contacts too personally, I lose the advantages and the accepted techniques of simply belonging. My thinking, therefore, has a certain radical irrelevance and insubstantiality. Since I resist existing in the usual areas of history and society, I am not serious about most people's *actual* plight in the world; but I am a good teacher, because I seriously address each individual's potentialities.

No doubt my failure in these things is appropriate to me as a creative artist, for we artists do personally and idiosyncratically initiate, and we stay with, our close conflicts. Artists are difficult to summate or manipulate sociologically. There is likely no possible sociology of creative action. But there is plenty of social psychology, if this allows, as it should, for novelty as a crucial principle of behavior. Indeed, in *Gestalt Therapy* I define psychology as the study of creative adjustments.

At the same time, when I do not matter-of-factly confront the "big" realities as limiting conditions for others, I become conceited and a coward in myself, and for the others I am a bore who expects the impossible. Paradoxically, my withdrawal from being a sociological unit as if in the interests of maintaining my creative integrity—though I do not need to rationalize it in this way, for I am secure in my integrity—becomes in me an evident lack of personal dignity. Since I fail to take the others in their actual plight, with the corresponding techniques, I do not, I do not know how to, assert myself as an equal in the social milieu, whether at the corner tavern or in the elections. Being above it, I cower beneath it. I doubt that this is a general dilemma of artists; it is my own problem. An artist can have the dignity of his art and speak as an equal from that position. I have the grandeur and responsibility of art, but I get from it no dignity—and little joy.

Most people seem to be in a neurotic situation the

contrary of mine. They are not enough in touch with their personal inventiveness, so they conform like sheep, for one must structure one's experience somehow. But they have more humility, courage, and dignity in their secondary group dealings. May I say that this same amalgam seems to me to characterize modern sociology: it combines natural historical and group situations and neurotic inhibitions and errors, and treats them as one social reality.

I must, however, make the obvious and now much repeated observation: that at present the major group relations—whether we look at the standard of living, the job-holding in organizations, or the front politics that has no place for rational persuasion—are uniquely empty of human meaning to the point of metaphysical absurdity; so that the common man, the healthier artist, or myself, all are equally out of contact with "society," for one cannot touch nothing or share in nothing.

Then, to sum up these reflections on my coldness to modern sociology, let me mention three factors:

(1) My own unfinished interpersonal situations, keeping me from group belonging.

(2) The unsociological nature of all original creative behavior.

(3) The unique emptiness of the major group activities in America at present.

2

Nevertheless, I am political beyond the average man in the sense of having a lively concern, and engaging in action, for the common welfare as such. How is this? Let us examine the details of my concern—my patriotic concern, for I feel it as such. They are such as belong to a man with the relation to sociological groups that I have been describing.

(1) They are isolated and desperate, therefore quix-

otic, attempts to impose on people something better, about which they couldn't care less. This follows from my not taking seriously their actual plight and limitations.

(2) I am concerned not for material improvement or safety, but for conservation or innovation in our culture and humane ideals. I feel myself and my colleagues to be in special touch with the holy spirit.

(3) In the face of the general absurdity, I consider it reasonable to propose things "gratuitously," by arbitrary voluntary decision, without needing party or historical warrant; or, what comes to the same thing, using all human existence as a warrant.

Of these points, the first is merely personal to me and of no literary interest. But I think that points two and three do give a useful and relevant motivation for action in our times. Again let me offer my meaning concretely.

Recently I tried to stir up some protest in the university and the publishing world on the issue that the wave length of our Discoverer satellite "has been withheld for unexplained reasons of military security." (*New York Times*, March 6, 1959.) Now, the tack I took in this was that it was a shame that the grand and ingenuous enthusiasm of people, of my own children, for the adventure of space, should be thus debased to the level of the cold war and business as usual. I was not moved by the horror of war as such—though I am a pacifist. Rather, that we must not lose the ideal feelings that make life worth living; and the ideal of science is tainted by secrecy.

Similarly, I waxed indignant enough to speak publicly against a statement of Dr. William Kvaraceus (*New York Times*, Feb. 10, 1959) that the teaching of geometry should be curtailed because it is too hard for most kids and so it increases delinquency. Again, my tack was that we owe a duty to *geometry as such*, to Euclid, Archimedes, Newton, and we must promote it no matter what the consequences. Though indeed, I would argue, the social consequences of the doctor's proposition are also calamitous, for the root of delinquency is in the kids' dumb but accurate perception that our present society is not worthy of a man's effort, and the doctor would strip it still further of the lovely sciences that are worthy of a man's effort.

I turn the same attitude against my political friends. At the height of the protest against the Russian censoring of Pasternak, a usual group of us held a meeting on the issue. I insisted that any attempt to discuss it in itself was effectually a cold-war maneuver, so I proposed—and had so written the press—that the censorship of Pasternak, the recent collapse of the Dublin An Tostal because of opposition to O'Casey and Joyce by the Catholic hierarchy, and the suppression of some early Chaplin slapstick by the village of Hicksville should be treated as equally significant and blameworthy. This would raise our protest to the proper philosophical plane. My proposal managed to sabotage the meeting. (Let me say that William Phillips and Mary McCarthy supported me.)

3

The existential absurdity of our society appears as increasing means and increasing impracticality, increasing communication and information and increasing superstition and ignorance, increasing socialization and increasing communal anomie, etc.; but however we consider it, it invites "arbitrary" utopian intervention, for there is no doubt that the usual procedures are self-contradictory. My own experience, however, makes me dissent from the French existentialists; I do not find myself personally or religiously in an "extreme situation." Both my animal and spiritual values are unquestionably worth while and justified. (Incidentally, the French psychologizing seems to me to be primitive and melodramatic. They do not have the technique to stay closely in contact with everyday emergencies and anxiety—a contact which yields hard but managable expedients; therefore they believe that life can be touched only by catastrophes.)

Positively, the content of my own "arbitrary" proposals is determined by my own justified concerns. I propose what I know to be my business. These are definite and fairly modest aims; whether or not they are practicable remains to be seen. For instance, in 1958, inspired by reading some documents of the American Revolution, I resolved to "do something for my country," just to be more proud of her, and I conceived the following little program of tasks to work at as much as I can.

(1) I want to transform the physical training and play periods in the public schools according to the principles of character analysis and eurhythmics. The aim is to unblock and animate, so that school becomes a place of excitement and growth. Such techniques must be directed at the repressions in each child, they cannot be stereotyped; and they require cultural invention by the group. The chief obstacle seems to be the anxiety in the teachers and administration. My concern is natural to anyone who has been maimed in his own upbringing, as I have. My hope is to get on some local school board and effect the change.

(2) To my heart the most dismaying object in American life is the eighteen-year-old who says that he has no ambition to work at anything in particular. This is a problem of vocational guidance, but precisely not the kind we usually get. The task is not to fit the youth into some useful place in the economy, but to find

what work will bring him out, be his vocation. If there is no such job, then do something about *that*, not him. My concern in this springs from my erotic urgency toward these youths, which is to have them as ideals fulfilling my own unused youth; that is, to be productive citizens in a practical community.

(3) I want to do something for the man-made landscape, especially of the country towns. Traveling in Europe, I have been struck with dismay at how ugly, shapeless, and neglected our own small places usually are; whereas in Ireland, England, France, Italy, every small place has a shape and often a uniqueness. I am not sure of the grounds of my concern about this. As an artist I believe that the sensuous scene is, of course, important for its people. But besides, I am a regionalist, even a local regionalist. The centralizing uniformity of America seems to me to be insulting to all of its people, depriving every place of its own fancy and spirit.

(4) I want to restore the reality of our freedom of speech. The merely legal freedom has come to mean little. The Russians have their commissars and we have our feudal lords of the networks and the mass press. Our system is such that a wise, eccentric, or minority voice is deafeningly drowned out by sheer quantity, there is no need for "censorship." The letter columns of the *New York Times*, for instance, carefully screen out anything controversial; the very news, e.g., about Cuba, is withheld—from us—till it is safe for "security," and long hours of the few TV channels are stamped with corporate images, though they are public property. Naturally, this has me by the throat as a man of letters.

I have reported these incidents and this little program in order to illustrate a kind of political attitude, with obvious weaknesses and strengths. The weaknesses seem to me to be: irrelevance to the issues that are in fact agitating people; a frigid emphasis on ideal values and profound aspirations, by-passing immediate needs and dangers; and a certain fastidiousness that makes solidarity difficult. Yet by and large I am not impressed that those who are better socialized to our present society are wise and brave or, indeed, altogether sane. On balance I do not think it would be an advantage to identify with them more than I do. It is better to follow my own genitals, heart, and head, family and friends.

On a writer's block

There are productive authors who cannot imagine a story to tell. This is not an inhibition of writing as such. They may be productive, able to finish whole works that have a beginning, middle, and end. By writing, they can disengage themselves from "inner problems" and get them outside, in public. They can act through a lyrical work that includes conflict, surprise, climax (ambivalences, ironies, resolutions); or again they can carry through a dialectical argument and write criticism, sociology, and so forth. But the inhibition sets in when they try to invent a dramatic plot with characters. Nothing seems interesting enough to engage them in beginning; or they cannot make the action move, or the action loses its direction and dwindles away. Such writers "resign themselves" to being lyric poets and theorists, but they feel unfulfilled as authors. What is the block?

The specific property of dramatic stories seems to be the imitating of interpersonal contacts and conflicts. We may then say right off: (1) *our authors are inhibited from freely imagining interpersonal relations.*

Now, if we go deeper into this difficulty, we come on material of more general interest.

In the first place, we see that most persons, not authors at all, are able to tell stories of the contact and conflict of persons. People are continually daydreaming them, remembering them, telling them as gossip, retelling the stories of plays and movies. The daily newspapers are full of stories. The bother with most such primitive dreaming, recollection, repetition, or reportage is that it is not dramatically interesting, it is not "probable or necessary," as Aristotle would have said. The account of the interpersonal action does not penetrate the personalities of the actors, the story does not spring from their characters, thoughts, and passions. We are presented with nothing but "people" in different situations. Unless we fill out the internal relations from our own experience, the account does not move us and certainly it cannot instruct us. The dramatic author, on the contrary, draws out the internal relations of the characters for us and so unifies and explains the external situation; and he presents this internal-external complex as a work of the imagination.

In my opinion, it is at this last point, in projecting the interpersonal conflict as *imagined*, that our inhibited authors bog down. Like anyone else, they can tell a straight story, or daydream, or report an incident. And being sensitive, intelligent, and experienced, they can at once internalize the story, find its meanings, relate it to their own feelings and ideas. But then they find it to be too close to their own reality; they are frozen in the actuality of the story; they are unable to project it as a fiction. That is, (2) *their difficulty is in dissociating the events from their own actuality, in imagining that the events might be otherwise or that there might be others*. Then they cannot use their technique of authorship, of handling the medium and ordering the incidents, to disengage themselves.

2

Let us briefly consider just the opposite condition: great ease in imagining interesting dramatic fictions. Two contrary exemplary types at once suggest themselves.

First, there is the person who has a lively interest in actual personal relations and feels them deeply, but is prevented from following them through to their conclusions because of situation, status, disease, or some such reason. Then, if he is a productive author, he can complete his arrested real impulses in fictions, and so work out the various alternatives. The actuality is imagined to be otherwise. This is classically the type of the "lady novelist" in a man's world; her fictions are the continuation of the actual gossip of letter writing. In the history of the modern novel, we can easily trace this series, from the dramatized actual letter to the fictional letter to the imagined story. The author starts with her actuality and completes it in a fiction.

On the other hand, there is the person who seems to live out his contacts as they exist, but on close inspection it is found that he is always experimenting with abstract possibilities. In his relations, the other people are always playing roles, they "stand for" something; and he himself is playing a role, trying it out. He does not have a very definite grasp of his own actuality; his desires are not *his*. They occur, for instance, in incompatible directions that force him eventually to disengage himself altogether; or he is suggestible to random forces. In a warring family he might consciously identify now with mama, now with papa, now with sister. Such a person, if he is a productive artist, might employ fictions as a means of discovering, fixing, and structuring his own actuality; or perhaps of identifying in all directions at once. This is, I think, the "novelist" par excellence. He can imagine other actualities; his problem is to bring them home to his own actuality.

In both these types it is clear where the need is: thwarted in life, fulfilled in fiction as a technique of life. On the one hand, the "lady novelist" does not *live* her life; on the other, the life that the "novelist" lives is not *his*. And from these different needs, there follow different problems of the art. The first must try more for the realism of the scene; the direction of the plot is given to begin with. The second must study the theme and construction; the experiences are real to begin with.

3

But our author, inhibited in imagining stories, cannot imagine other actualities than his own, nor can he imagine his own actuality to be otherwise. What occurs is that his need seems to him to be so rigidly bound with his actual interpersonal situation that he feels himself existentially at stake; then he cannot play in the medium.

Consider, if he starts to write the story, he finds himself at once confronted with autobiography or case history, and these are socially taboo. One may not present the conflicts of actual persons, or attribute motives to them. Nor is this a merely external difficulty, avoidable by not publishing, for we must bear in mind that an author will regard his central act, authorship, as central in his interpersonal relations: to him, to write is to betray, to confess, to deal a blow, to woo. Further, if he presses on anyway, he soon finds it impossible to limit the plot and characters in order to tell a definite story, for in the actuality every detail is relevant; it is only the perspective of imagination that enables one to abstract and simplify. Then his story becomes inextricably complicated and wanders into a morass.

In the anxiety of confronting his actual interpersonal situation and still trying to complete his act of authorship, he may do one of two things (or, alternately, both of them). He may shut his eyes and give in to less externally defined feelings: so he carries through the action as a lyric poem. Or he may open his eyes and coldly scrutinize the external situation, dissociating it from himself; then he will theorize it.

The bother is that he cannot tell a lie. I mean, of course, a literal lie, the statement of a nonactuality. (I do not mean an artistic lie, an omission or inclusion for some nonartistic purpose, for no artist can lie in this sense.) Among poets, the inability to lie is far more common than is realized. Since they themselves rely largely on unsought feelings, they superstitiously regard every factual association as necessary for the effect. In a love poem, it is the beloved's factual name that must be employed, later to be replaced by some metrical equivalent that always jars on the poet himself as a lie. Thus, many of the obscurities of Mallarmé are simply due to his need to copy off the precise actuality—and the effect of such precise naturalism is, wonderfully, the *un*reality of an unexpected snapshot. Unable to falsify, poets avoid the embarrassments of the interpersonal story by telling only their feelings, without the events: the one who knows them personally reads between the lines, the public cannot guess. Yet we notice that poets are concrete and discursive in writing about the weather, landscape, plants, and animals.

Or, suppose the author opens his eyes and becomes a theorist: then he cannot lie because he has a noble superstition of objective truth. He avoids his interpersonal story by speaking in generalities. A celebrated instance of such avoidance is Kierkegaard. Or again, at a further remove from the personal, but recapturing some of the urgency of practical contact, the theorist may turn to sociology, politics, or psychiatry.

4

Let us compare and contrast our author who cannot imagine away from his own life story with an important type of novelist. This is the "first novelist," the young writer whose book is about a young writer with family and sexual problems remarkably similar to the author's, who expresses the thoughts of the author, and who is writing a first novel on a subject not much delineated for us. Obviously such a "first novel" plays in its artist's life a unique role. It is his act of rebellion against his family, and his act of self-appointment as an independent author. It is a kind of revenge against his past personal relations and it is a turning toward quite a new life with new relations. For instance, the completion of the story may inaugurate a change in the author's loves. The "first novel" is not embarrassed by the difficulties of telling the actual story. Rather it makes capital of them: it *means* to strike a blow. Afterward— the writer, assuming he is a productive artist, is either freed in imagination and becomes some other type of novelist; or, often enough, he turns out to be just the poet, critic, or theorist that we are here talking about. According to the critics, he "does not fulfill his promise."

(However, we must distinguish between this "first novelist" and the "man with one book," for these are frequently confused. The "one book" is not a work of art at all; for, in general, the artistic strategy of living is ineradicably deep, and the one who has it will produce numerous works. The one book is rather a confession or exposition of the man's life as a whole: it is in principle a biography; it is to be correlated with his other nonliterary expressions, like the memoirs or apologiae of statesmen. It may be, of course, that the one book is written in youth, and is then mistaken by the writer and others as the beginning of an authorship. It is confused with a "first novel.")

5

So far we have been raising a problem of art. But unfortunately the inability to imagine away from the actual interpersonal situation is calamitous also to personal happiness; it is an effect of unhappiness and a cause of unhappiness.

All creative adjustment requires the flexible interplay of imagination, perception, and proprioception. (I have discussed these ongoing relations—of hallucinations, sensation, and appetite—in *Gestalt Therapy*, Vol. II, ch. 12, iii-v.) Now suppose a man's imagination tenaciously clings to the actuality. The actuality will be overdramatized and overinterpreted: and finally sensation itself is obscured, because it is too fixedly and narrowly selective. On the other hand, bound down to dogged hour-by-hour commentary of the actual, the imagination loses the free flight that is its glory; and then it cannot make the great over-all interpretations —of hope and despair, anticipation of pleasure and loss, making plans—that give salt to actuality by touching off deeper eros or dread. A man who cannot imagine away from the actual soon cannot move, because he is like Zeno's arrow, which cannot move where it is and cannot move where it is not. He is doomed to boredom. He is doomed also to loneliness, for he cannot dissociate himself enough from his own plight to take an interest in the stories of others. The situation has a sad irony: for just because he takes his relation to others too seriously and dramatically, he soon ceases to know the others at all, and his own action is therefore sure to be stupid and unsuccessful.

When the imagination is free, even a constricted world affords scope and opportunity. But conversely, where the imagination is bound to the actuality, the world is a prison even without bars. It seems to our man that he is not imagining at all, he is seeing things as they are, and what he sees is dull and hopeless; but largely what he sees is what he is imagining.

To dare to feel, he shuts his eyes. To dare to see, he withdraws his feelings. He cannot imagine that the actual situation were different, because that would arouse an unbearable excitement of unknown grief, anger, or even pleasure; but he cannot learn to tolerate those excitements because he will not imagine them. So the imagination is hobbled to the banal sequence of fact.

His productive art is also infected. We saw that he can invent poems or theories, or both, because these avoid the one possible dramatic story. Yet these are likely to be clouded, burdened, overparticularized by details of the oppressive actuality. The lyric song is marred by prosy fragments of story. (Indeed, it is good advice for poets to write prose stories, to keep their poems from incorporating the stories.) The theory, on the other hand, tends to rationalize only his personal situation.

6

In this impasse, for the purpose of therapy of this writer's block, we must return to the possibility that we previously brushed aside. (3) *Since the imagination cannot take wing away from the actual interpersonal events, the author must deliberately experiment telling the actuality as a story.* (Let me emphasize that this is a recourse of therapy, not of art.)

Surprisingly, the experiment turns out to require two

separate decisions. The first decision is hard but rational. To tell the true story, to forgo publication, to hurt the others and oneself, to embark on an inartistically detailed and perhaps endless enterprise. These difficulties we have mentioned above.

Very soon, however, there arises a quite different decision that takes one by the throat, namely to dare to tell the story *as it comes up*, without withholding. This might occur as a series of decisions, but likely it is one terrible decision, to be taken once for all, at one moment, and that moment is the following: The author is embarked on telling the actual story, when suddenly he says to himself, "Oh, but—I see, I remember—if I tell *this* and try to unify it dramatically, I shall have to mention—*that*. But I didn't foresee that!" For obviously it is *not* the actuality that takes one by the throat! We do not observe that people ordinarily act as though they were in such extremity. It is something *unnoticed* in the actuality, that has been brushed aside, avoided.

(4) *The imagination is inhibited, and fixed to the actuality, because something is avoided in the actuality*. It is fixed to the *actuality* because the something is present there; but it is *fixed and cannot play* because the something is avoided.

It is my experience that once this decision to be frank is made, the other difficulties vanish. And it can be made unhesitatingly, though with suffering: for once they are handling their medium, free artists are characterized by reckless courage. The author is now on his mettle; he is freely engaged in his central act of authorship, to formulate what would otherwise escape. And at once the social taboo against disclosure and the fear of hurting are seen as usual things, for every author is long accustomed to saying precisely what no one, including himself, wishes to hear. It is on this edge, indeed, that he habitually moves. But further, he soon discovers that the actuality has been not the ongoing reality at all, but his fixed image of it. It is truly *only* a story that he is telling. The great hurt that he does is not to the others at all; it is a hurt done to himself, and done to him by others, namely his embarrassment and shame.

He is now interested in the story as a story; and once he is interested in it, it does not disperse indefinitely like the banal actuality; rather it organizes itself. *The principle of organization is the something that was secret in the actuality.* Previously the actuality was indefinite and wandering because the organizing figure was unnoticed; now that it is allowed to claim attention, the rest falls into place. Here then is the difference between the actual story and the first novel. The first novel is made definite mainly by the paucity of experience of the author, marshaled to the nonartistic purpose of rebelling against the past and affirming his authorship. The actual story is made definite by some hidden but now accepted need that appears in the foreground. Traditionally, such "actual stories" are finally published as "educational romances." By telling the story, the author frees himself from a certain phase of his life.

The inhibition of imagining stories is now freed. The apparent actuality is seen to be nothing but a set of stories; the overdramatizing that hampered an ongoing creative adjustment now serves as the drama of story. As a structure of actuality, the "educational romance" tends to have the following form: the "I" character of the novel maintains a certain identity with the author, but the "others" are found to bear only a superficial resemblance to actual persons; the "others" were formed in accordance with the plot, and the plot was formed in the author's imagination. This is a difference from the so-called *roman à clef*, for in the *roman à clef* the superficial resemblances and the actual situations are avoided, but the actual persons are reported; whereas in the educational romance the actual situations are often reported, but the internal plot is imagined, and the characters are imagos.

The obstacles to the activity vanish. But the activity itself is carried on in shame, recognition of error, retroflected anger or outward indignation, and grief. The art need that becomes evident is not so much a thwarted life that the work fulfills, nor a scattered self that the work reintegrates, but a phase of life wrecked that the work mourns for and memorializes.

So, in following the therapy of a literary inhibition of telling stories, we have become aware of four stages:

(1) The inhibition of freely imagining interpersonal relations.

(2) The fixing of the imagination on the actuality.

(3) Experimenting in making the actuality into a story.

(4) Finding something avoided in the actuality, to which the imagination has been fixed.

Obviously the malfunction of the flexible interplay of imagination and actuality has a general importance far beyond cases of a specific inhibition of writing. Conversely, the analysis of this specific problem casts light, in literature, on the production of several major genres of novels.

Notes on a remark of Seami

"If there is a celebrated place or ancient monument in the neighborhood, [mention of it] is inserted with the best effect somewhere near the end of the third part of the Development." (Seami Motokiyo, *ap*. Waley.)

Seami is prescribing the construction of a Noh play. The Development or middle section he has divided into three parts, of which the last is to be heightened by animated dance motions or "simple chant," and it will lead into the ending, the climactic dance and full lyric song in which the Noh spirit reveals itself undisguised—that is, in gorgeous costume—to our awareness. The action of Noh as a whole is a progressive seeking, explaining, hinting at, adumbrating such a revelation. By the end of the Development, the preliminaries have been animated to the emotionally warm esthetic surface of dance and chant; and the climax is the present dancing-out of the thing that is made aware. Let us then ask: Why is the celebrated place in the neighborhood brought in just at the end of the Development, as if it is *this* that precipitates the climax?

It is because pointing to the place or monument in the neighborhood arouses belief. It is the evidence that what might be, what has been presented as a meaningful and interesting possibility, is indeed a fact and compels the assent of our senses. (It is the real reference that changes emotional excitement into full emotion, for an emotion, as I shall try to show, is a kind of cognition.)

As if a poet said, "I have been telling you a story of the olden times, exploring its allusions, explaining its moral, collecting the associated ideas and images. But this story is true, it is history." By true he means that it exists in some way in your environment too—you live with it. Go there and you too will see the very cherry grove whence he took the sprig and put it in his hat before the battle; or the churchyard where they buried the Boy who used to whistle in the valley; or the cliff overlooking the Hudson where the general stood peering hopelessly through his spyglass.

There are other ways, and stronger ways, than pointing to an historical marker, by which a poet compels us to take his fiction as not merely an entertaining fiction, but as important to us, as making a difference, as something we must henceforth put up with because it is real. (And I suddenly remember that terrifying anecdote about Goethe bursting into tears when Beethoven was improvizing; the composer leapt up and shouted at him, "Admit that it's important!"— that is, that it *means* something.) There are other ways than the historical marker; nevertheless, it is a great ease and comfort to a poet to be able, just before his climax, to astound us with this particular trump card of factual demonstration, because he can then, at the very moment he is performing his risky and socially dubious deed of giving us the strange, feel the security of a common home from which he cannot be excluded. He has a Public Occasion, as if he were to say, "The occasion for my poem is our one and only world; you cannot deny me the right."

2

Seami's prescription for the right use of the historical place is natural; it is a correct reading of, and reconstruction of, the process of comprehension and awareness. Let me illustrate this by briefly analyzing this single aspect of one of our own occasional poems, Emerson's *Concord Hymn*.

Emerson begins:

> By the rude bridge that arched the flood,
>   Their flag to April's breeze unfurled,
> Here once the embattled farmers stood
>   And fired the shot heard round the world.

We know it is a dedicatory occasion and that the poet and his audience are at the very scene, yet he begins as if he is telling them a story, for there is no bridge. "Here" then is ambiguous; it might, but faintly, refer to the present place; more strongly it means simply, "and it happened to be in that place that they took their stand." A particular and undistinguished place, an astonishingly loud report.

> The foe long since in silence slept;
>   Alike the conquerer silent sleeps;
> And Time the ruined bridge has swept
>   Down the dark stream which seaward creeps.

The use of the definite past in the first of these lines gives one a curious wrench. It is as if he is *merely* telling us an old story, that has no relation to any present. And the present-tense "sleeps" in the next line is in its strongest sense even more estranged, for it is the eternal present. At the same time it is a present tense, and the poet will use it as a transition. Eternity makes us think of Time, and the next verb is "has swept," a past indefinite that therefore has reference to our present. Even so, it is such a reference as proves that the whole affair is dead and gone: "You see, there is no bridge any longer, and as for the stream, all streams flow on forever to the sea."

But no—

On this green bank, by this soft stream,
    We set today a votive stone;
That memory may their deed redeem,
    When, like our sires, our sons are gone.

It was *here* (where *we* are), in *this* place. Here is the factual demonstration of the history. The reciter must quietly emphasize the "this" (the first of them; I think it is more delicate and musical to let the second emphasis fall on "soft"). What he means to show is not that streams flow forever to the sea and are therefore "dark," but that we are now standing looking at the very stream, and therefore it is "soft." We are dedicating the marker. (Let me say that the third and fourth lines of the stanza are, to my taste, academic and pretty frigid, although good enough for the rhetorical occasion—they do not ruin the poem. They introduce a solemnity different in tone from the simplicity of the rest; the rhythm too doggerelizes. The word "memory" is excellent, but the thought ought, I think, to be more like the following: "How strange, *I* suddenly remember something; I mean, I *really* remember it, as I look at this place.")

Spirit! that made those heroes dare
    To die, and leave their children free,
Bid Time and Nature gently spare
    The shaft we raise to them and thee.

We must certainly punctuate "Spirit!" with an exclamation point, as a sudden recognition and apostrophe. The direct address to something that has suddenly revealed itself. And this revelation has been precipitated by the moment of presentness, by the feeling that this is the very place, by pointing to the votive marker. (One can imagine the same climax treated dramatically: the Noh warrior himself appears.) The appearance of this Spirit is apt and thrilling, but such an ideal creature could quickly freeze us. Emerson, however, admirably restrains him to the same theme of time and change as the rest of the poem. The hymn is touchingly brief. And certainly the modest wish of the last two lines rings truer than the grander boast of the ending of the third stanza. The thought that a memorial, *any* memorial, is always also dedicated to Time and Nature, is good. And I personally do not find anything objectionable in the indicated sociable goings-on among the Ideals of the Transcendentalist pantheon.

3

Again, let me illustrate Seami's remark by a point from the psychology of the emotions. The case is that an emotion is not merely a state of the organism but is an awareness of a relation between the state of the organism and something in the environment.

This can be shown experimentally in psychotherapy, when the problem is to bring a man to feel emotions that he has ceased to be able to feel. By body concentration and muscular exercises to loosen tension, it is possible to remobilize the particular combinations of body behavior that embody the emotion: e.g., for anger, tightening and loosening the jaw, grinding the teeth, clenching the fists, gasping with the upper chest, and so forth. All this will rouse a kind of restless excitation: a feeling of the inhibited anger. But if to this proprioception is added perception or memory (but ultimately present perception) of something in the environment that one can be angry *with*, at once the emotion flares in full force and clarity, with flushed or white face, ringing or dark voice, and menace about to act. (Conversely, of course, it does not matter how emotional the "real" situation is; a man will not feel unless he accepts the corresponding behavior of his organism.)

A moment's reflection will show that there must be such immediate and urgent awareness of one's relation to the world. For an animal in a difficult field must know immediately and truly what the relations of the field are, and must act. Therefore, as Aristotle pointed out long ago, to explain an emotion we must give its material cause (the body state), its formal cause (the relation to the object in the field), and its purpose (as action). For instance, longing is the heightening of appetite confronted with a distant object, in order to overcome distance or other obstacles; grief is the breaking of the tension of loss or lack in accepting the absence of the object, in order to withdraw and recuperate; anger is the destroying of an obstacle to appetite; spite is an attack on an unavoidable overpowering enemy in order not altogether to capitulate.

That is, "the emotions are means of cognition. Far from being obstacles to thought, they are unique deliveries of the state of the organism/environment field and have no substitute; they are the way we become aware of the appropriateness of our concerns: the way the world is for us. As cognitions they are fallible, but are corrigible not by putting them out of court but by trying out whether they can develop into the more settled feelings accompanying deliberate orientation—

e.g., to proceed from the enthusiasm of discovery to conviction, or lust to love." (*Gestalt Therapy*, by F. S. Perls, R. Hefferline, and P. Goodman, vol. II, xii, 6.)

4

The historical place helps to induce belief, to make the emotion flower. This is what Seami is saying, and it is very well as a prescription for reconstructing the world, in poetics; or for removing hindrances, in psychotherapy. But more philosophically considered, all this is quite upside down. The historical place or other existing thing is not something that can be simply added on to an art-work or an excitement; for the existing is certainly something prior to the other devices and structures of experience which are, indeed, only aspects of the existing. There is no art without the real, and there is no excitement without the real. To have Occasional Poetry, they must give you an occasion. Take this very instance of the historical place that is our theme. Salomon Reinach showed that when there is a myth of the origin of some sacred place or sacred stone ("here he leapt into heaven leaving behind this footprint"), we must assume that the place or stone was sacred from a more remote antiquity than the myth; it was sacred and one did not know why—so that the same shrine serves many a creed. The myth is invented later as a confabulation to explain or otherwise domesticate the unknown and probably maleficent power latent in the thing that is present.

Perhaps it is best to speak as follows: Quite apart from any local taboos, or from the fact that a meteorite unaccountably fell from heaven and frightened everybody, or that some grove or fountain seems to have a peculiar investment of mana, we must say that any existent thing that confronts us, any historical place where we know we are, anything that is present, has power. It has the power by which a possibility has broken the barrier into being a fact; the pouring, inexhaustible power by which a present thing maintains itself as a present thing. If we ask what is this power, it is incomprehensible, for, as Kant said, any explanation will again establish only a possibility and will never show the difference between the imaginary Hundred Dollars and the real Hundred Dollars. But fortunately, it is *just* in this case that we do not come to ask, for the present is given with perfect evidence, shaping us with its power. And one of its beautiful properties is to be an inexhaustible reservoir of explanations.

The audience, however, happens not to be confronting its present. The poet, by his language and construction, turns them toward it; and then we are aware of the existent place and feel ("remember") its power.

As we are, the present does always seem to be dangerous and taboo, and we hedge it with avoidances and superstitious explainings-away. Doing so, we indeed make it impractical and therefore dangerous. It is the role of poetry and other humane philosophy to eradicate our superstitions and make us stop avoiding, skirting, shutting our eyes. To open our eyes. And then we see our celebrated place and ancient monument patiently burning up in the day and not consumed.

Dr. Reich's banned books

We are here concerned with the fate of Dr. Reich's books, banned by the Food and Drug Administration. The relation of theory and practice, of a scientific theory and its applications, is a thorny one; but it *must* in every case be decided in the direction of absolute freedom of speculation and publication, otherwise it is impossible to live and breathe. The practical policing of therapies is not an author's responsibility. The Administrator's reasoning in Section 5 of his injunction is intolerable; if it cannot be struck down, it must be flouted—we must applaud the republication (by Farrar, Straus) of some of the banned passages, and the forthcoming publication of *The Function of the Orgasm*.

The forbidding of "statements pertaining to the *existence* of orgone energy" is simply ludicrous. The Administrator of the drug law is not the Creator of the heavens and the earth; he is not even the Pope in Rome. Is he quite sane, to write such a proposition?

His notion of the books as "constituting labeling" is more interesting; for no one can candidly read *The Function of the Orgasm; The Cancer Biopathy; The*

*Sexual Revolution; The Mass-Psychology of Fascism;
Listen, Little Man;* or *Character Analysis* in any edition, and regard them as labels or advertisements. In
the first place, the very vulgarity of such a conception
makes one smile—and wince. The Administrator has
been moving too much in the racketeering circles of
the drug companies, the medical journals, and certain
members of the A.M.A. who were recently under Con-
gressional investigation for their plugging and pricing.
But my guess is that the Administrator's lack of candor
betrays a different intent. The real objection to Dr.
Reich's work has little to do with orgone energy, but is
to its whole drift as pedagogy, social science, and perhaps medical science; and *therefore* his books are
banned and any convenient pretext is seized on to im-
pede their circulation. Dealing with strong universal
drives and terrible real situations, Dr. Reich's theories
cannot easily be disregarded or explained away. They
generate their own propaganda. Therefore it has been
convenient to try to silence them altogether by treating
them as commercial plugs for a contraband commodity.
How American!

2

Consider a fair analogy to the Administrator's high-
handed procedure in banning the books with the box.
Let us compare Reich and Volta. At the end of the
eighteenth century, Volta was able to make available
electrical energy of any potential by wrapping some
metal sticks in wet rags, a device as primitive as Reich's
box. Now suppose that—inspired by his colleague Gal-
vani's jumping dead frogs, and perhaps by Mesmer's
"animal magnetism" (which we here analogize to
Freud's "libido")—Volta or somebody else hit on the
electro-shock therapy for "lunacy." (This therapy was
highly esteemed among us ten years ago, is still in use,

and has certainly done more damage than all the orgone accumulators, though nobody has gone to jail.) And suppose again that, like mesmerism in France, this electro-shock therapy was banned:

According to the logic of the Administrator of the drug law, all traces of Volta's battery, his equipment, his reports, his theory of differential potentials, should then be expunged from the face of the earth. They are labels for the illegal therapy. And the *existence* of flowing electricity must henceforth never be mentioned.

Whether or not Reich was a Volta, I don't know; but how in the devil is a bureaucrat to decide the question? It is the kind of thing that must be determined by generations of scholars and their experiments, with free publication and no holds barred. Naturally, as a human being, I hope that Reich was right and that we have discovered something new and wonderful, whatever the applications.

3

Let me say something about a few of these banned books. (I am writing from memory, if the reader will pardon me.)

The Function of the Orgasm is a classic almost by definition, from its title. For here Reich seized on a phenomenon of universal occurrence and obvious importance, definite, observable, and experimentable, which had nevertheless never been seriously studied. Simply making the obvious metabolic, electrical, and muscular observations and experiments, and fitting the findings into standard modern psychology and his own character-analytic methods, the doctor produced a great book. Why should not such a book exist? To answer this question I submit to the philosophical reader the following puzzle: How is it possible that this subject had to wait until the second quarter of the twentieth century to get a halfway adequate treatment? Indeed, the puzzle is still with us. E.g., in the Kinsey reports, although Reich's relevant studies are mentioned in the bibliography, the statistics are nevertheless collected by counting undifferentiated and unstructured "climaxes," as though Reich's careful anatomy and physiology did not exist. Naturally Kinsey says many absurd things.

Quite apart from its ingenious cancer theory, *The Cancer Biopathy* is a remarkable work. For what Reich does again is to seize on problems and approaches that are important but are precisely swept under the rug or frowned on by modern medical orthodoxy: e.g., abiogenesis, the frequent embarrassments of the germ-infection hypothesis, and especially the factors of susceptibility and resistence of various patients to various diseases. It is the hallmark of genius to pay attention to such dark and *suppressed* areas, and to find connections among entities that tend to be neglected. But it is not to be expected that the orthodox will shout for joy about it; nor that they will much respect the simple-mindedness and dumb-bunny apparatus of a primary researcher. At the same time, Reich's work is full in the stream of important cancer problems, e.g., the virus or nonvirus etiology, and the puzzling relevance of sexual organs and sexual types. It is a pity that the research reported never seems to be informed about Reich's hypotheses. It is not a field in which we can afford to burn books.

Listen, Little Man I remember as the anguished and somewhat frenzied outcry of a high-aspiring and inwardly oppressed strong soul caught in a petty and apathetic world. Not unlike a chapter out of Dostoevski, and exactly the kind of thing that should be reprinted in anthologies like the recent *Identity and Anxiety: Survival of the Person in Mass Society*. Why it should be banned and burned is beyond me, unless with the spiteful aim of blotting out a man's memory.

Character Analysis is a universally admired text, powerfully influential in modern clinical practice; and I am told that it is now legal "for professional use." It deals with character resistance, the muscular defensive "armor," and methods of active therapy.

The Sexual Revolution and *The Mass-Psychology of Fascism*, finally, are excellent studies in the application of psychoanalysis to politics and history, in the wake of Freud's *Mass-Psychology and the Analysis of the Ego* and *Totem and Taboo*, and no more exceptionable than the similar attempts of Fromm, Kardiner, etc. Like the others, Reich is concerned with the authoritarian character and especially, as an ex-Marxist, with the psychology of cultural lag. *The Sexual Revolution* contains a beautiful history of the reaction in the Soviet Union under Stalin and is, to my mind, invaluable for the understanding of that country. Both books, however, are practical in intent and prescribe, among other things, the sexual freedom of children and adolescents as absolutely essential for the restoration of social health. I am convinced that this is the explanation of the antagonism to them. (E.g., the liberal *New Republic* commissioned and then banned as scandalous a review of them that summarized their arguments.)

Such, roughly, are the actual contents of the books which have been banned and burned as "labels" for orgone accumulators! All six books are interesting; a couple are perhaps great. (I am not acquainted with the other, shorter, pamphlets on the banned list.)

4

I feel impelled to make a further remark to the Americans on this issue. We are living in a precarious time. Let me mention two aspects of it.

During the last months before the execution of Caryl

Chessman, there were several polls of public opinion. By and large throughout the country, opinion ran more than 70 per cent against him. (The pacifist *Catholic Worker* reported with astonishment that *its* readers were 75 per cent for immediate execution!) But the significant thing was the tone of this opinion, as expressed in very many letters. It was violently, sickeningly sadistic, pornographic, and vindictive; and this on an issue not of momentary indignation, but after several years of discussion and debate. Now, the justice meted out to one individual is important; the question of capital punishment is important; but the tone of such a majority was, to my mind, the frightening and portentous fact about that case. It means that when I walk down the street, I am not safe, for these are the thoughts and feelings that seethe just beneath the civil surface in the majority of my fellow citizens. My friends and I, who want to live productively and sexually, must live here; and it is in this insane asylum that I have to bring up my children.

It was to the terrible reality of this "emotional plague," as he called it, that Dr. Reich directed his efforts, according to his lights. I do not know if he had the cure for it; but he accurately named the disease; and certainly no less radical prescription than his can possibly be of any avail. Our government jailed him and burned his books; but if he is not allowed to speak out, none of us will be allowed.

Secondly, on a world-wide scale many human beings are manufacturing bombs that can blow up the world; they are poisoning the atmosphere testing them; they are impressing the best brains of mankind in the study of how to develop them and best launch them. Meantime, the rest of the human beings, in the "advanced" nations, are acquiescing in this, paying for it, and de facto approving it. All this may explode any day. Such lunatic behavior and catatonic paralysis are not new things among us, but there has never been a time when the behavior was so dangerous and so universally admitted to be universally catastrophic, and when, therefore, the paralysis of people was so evidently irrational.

It was against this trend toward mass suicide that Dr. Reich evolved and, rather desperately, tried to apply his theory of primary masochism. Just as Freud spoke in despair of the need for Eros, and others of us are willing to risk other desperate alternatives like anarchy, ahimsa, and wooing the creator spirit. It is not a good time for Administrators to put obstacles in the way of freedom of the spirit. Get them out of the way.

Banning cars from Manhattan
(with Percival Goodman)

We propose banning private cars from Manhattan Island. Permitted motor vehicles would be buses, small taxis, vehicles for essential services (doctor, police, sanitation, vans, etc.), and the trucking used in light industry.

Present congestion and parking are unworkable, and other proposed solutions are uneconomic, disruptive, unhealthy, nonurban, or impractical.

It is hardly necessary to prove that the actual situation is intolerable. "Motor trucks average less than six miles per hour in traffic, as against eleven miles per hour for horse drawn vehicles in 1911." "During the ban on nonessential vehicles during the heavy snowstorm of February 1961, air pollution dropped 66 per cent." (*New York Times,* March 13, 1961.) The street widths of Manhattan were designed, in 1811, for buildings of one to four stories.

By banning private cars and reducing traffic, we can, in most areas, close off nearly nine out of ten crosstown streets and every second north-south avenue. These closed roads plus the space now used for off-street parking will give us a handsome fund of land for neighborhood relocation. At present over 35 per cent of the area of Manhattan is occupied by roads. Instead of the present grid, we can aim at various kinds of enclosed neighborhoods, in approximately 1200-foot to 1600-foot superblocks. It would be convenient, however, to leave the existing street-pattern in the main midtown shopping and business areas, in the financial district, and wherever the access for trucks and service cars is imperative. Our aim is to enhance the quality of our city life with the minimum of disruption of the existing pattern.

The disadvantages of this radical proposal are small. The private cars are simply not worth the nuisance they cause. Less than 15 per cent of the people daily entering Manhattan below Sixty-first Street come by private car. Traffic is congested, speed is slow, parking is difficult or impossible and increasingly expensive. It is estimated that the cost of building new garaging is $20,000 per car; parking lots are a poor use of land in the heart of a metropolis, and also break the urban style of the cityscape.

The advantages of our proposal are very great. Important and immediate are the relief of tension, noise, and anxiety; purifying the air of fumes and smog; alleviating the crowding of pedestrians; providing safety for children. Subsequently, and not less importantly, we gain the opportunity of diversifying the gridiron, beautifying the city, and designing a more integrated community life.

The problem and our solution to it are probably unique to Manhattan Island, though the experiment would provide valuable lessons elsewhere. Manhattan is a world center of business, buying, style, entertainment, publishing, politics, and light manufacture. It is daily visited in throngs by commuters to work, seekers of pleasure, shoppers, tourists, and visitors on business.

We have, and need, a dense population; and the area is small and strictly limited. Manhattan does not sprawl. It can easily be a place as leisurely as Venice, a lovely pedestrian city. But the cars must then go.

In the first appendix to *Communitas* we developed a scheme for Manhattan, paying especial attention to improving the rivers and developing riverside neighborhoods—routing traffic up through the center, and even sacrificing Central Park for the over-all improvement; but we now believe that a much simpler first step toward achieving that livable city would be the elimination of a large part of the traffic altogether.

Manhattan has been losing population to the suburbs and near countryside, with a vast increase of daily commutation. A more desirable center would reduce and perhaps eliminate this trend. Indeed, within the city itself, it is possible to decrease commutation. The I.L.G.W.U. housing near the garment district points the way. It would be useful, also, to establish a municipal agency to facilitate people's living near their work if they so choose, by arranging exchanges of residence advantageous to all parties. This should be possible in many thousands of cases and is certainly worth trying.

(The neglect of this kind of simple expedient in our society is the result of lack of attention to community. There is no agency in our city to attend to the multipurpose problems of community, the integration of the functions of life. Cf., *Communitas*, Appendix C.)

2. PERIPHERAL PARKING

The banned private cars can be accommodated by various kinds of peripheral parking, as studied by Louis Kahn, Victor Gruen, the present authors, and others.

At present many thousands of commuters' cars are left at suburban railway stops and at more or less convenient subway stations in Queens, Brooklyn, and the Bronx. This is because of the obvious undesirability, from the motorists' point of view, of driving them into Manhattan. We propose simply to generalize this common-sense decision in order to use it as a basis for important further advantages.

In addition, we propose the construction of multi-purpose parking piers in the Hudson and East Rivers for cars entering by the main bridges and tunnels. These piers could be developed for promenade, recreational, and even residential use, and might be treated as part of the river development recommended in Appendix A of *Communitas*.

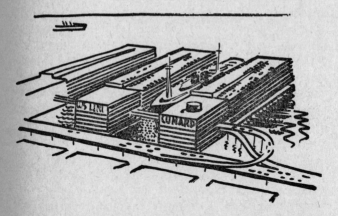

The piers would be served by bus and taxi. Consider a particular case. A large emporium, e.g., Macy's, could provide pier-limousines for commuting shoppers, including the service of delivering packages to the parked cars.

3. ROADS

We keep the broad commercial cross streets—Greenwich Avenue, Fourteenth Street, Twenty-third, Forty-

second, Fifty-seventh, Fifty-ninth, etc.—as two-way bus
and taxi arteries; and also First, Third, Fifth, Seventh,
Broadway, Ninth, and Eleventh Avenues. These should
provide adequate circulation for the residual traffic
(but this would have to be experimented). As indicated above, we would keep the existent street pattern
in midtown—from Twenty-third to Fifty-ninth Streets
—to serve the shops, theaters, etc.; and also wherever
there is a special case. (Every street would have to be
studied individually.)

All other streets become pedestrian walks broad
enough to serve as one-way roads for servicing: fire,
garbage, mail, and so forth.

The proposed grid of through arteries is such that
the maximum walk to the nearest bus stop would always be less than one-fifth of a mile. Subway entrances
exist as at present. In general, bus service throughout Manhattan is expanded, and the two-deck buses
are brought back. We must bear in mind that with the
ending of congestion and the immense diminishing of
pedestrian cross-overs, the speed limit for taxis and express buses could be raised to twenty-five or even
thirty miles an hour. Since there is less need to cross, it
is possible to eliminate jay walking, and perhaps provide pedestrian bridges and tunnels. By and large,
*given the improvement of the bus service, most travel
about town would be swifter and more convenient
than it is at present with private cars.*

There would be more taxis. We conceive of these as
small, half the present length. They might well be
electrics. It is absurd for taxis in a limited-speed metropolis to be the same cars designed for family travel on
super highways.

If opened out and if its blocks are enlarged, the
gridiron plan is practical and has a sort of grandeur.
To avoid the boredom of endless vistas, however, we
should recommend bridging certain streets with build-

ings and creating other spatial effects. Every street and avenue should be studied as an individual artistic problem.

4. NEIGHBORHOOD AND COMMUNITY

The ideal for New York or any other vast city is to become a large collection of integral neighborhoods sharing a metropolitan center and metropolitan amenities. The neighborhoods differ since they comprise a wide variety of inhabitants and community functions, which could be administered with relative independence by each neighborhood. There is no reason for them to look alike. A basically family-residential neighborhood, for instance, might have nearly autonomous control of its local school, with much of the school-tax administered by the local Parent-Teacher Association. The central Board of Education could dictate minimum standards and see to it that underprivileged neighborhoods get a fair share of the total revenue; but it need not stand in the way, as it does at present, of variation and experimentation. The hope is to diminish sharply the amount of "administration"—at present there are more school administrators in the New York City system than in all of France. Our idea, too, is that local exercise of political initiative on local problems like schooling, housing, and planning would educate the electorate and make real democracy possible. A neighborhood should be planned to increase mutual acquaintance of the neighbors and to increase their responsibility for school, market, playground, zoning, and so forth. Such a complex could well serve as the primary municipal electoral unit. Meantime, all the integral neighborhoods share in the great city of the big shops, theaters, hotels, museums, and national enterprises. *The aim of integral planning is to create a human-scale community, of manageable associations, intermediary between the individuals and families and the metropolis; it is to counteract the isolation of the individual in the mass society.* Naturally, in a vast region like New York there will be many thousands of persons who choose precisely to be isolated individuals —that might be why they came here—but these too form a distinctive and valuable element in the federal whole, and they can be provided for in the center, perhaps in apartment hotels, or in characteristic neighborhoods of their own. It is curious, on this point, that the "individualistic" persons who came to New York to escape conformist small-town mores found that precisely they themselves had much in common and formed a famous community, the intellectual and artistic stratum of Greenwich Village.

Toward the ideal of a city of federated communities, the simple device of banning the cars and replanning the gridiron is a major step. The new road-pattern allows for superblocks of from six to nine acres. (For comparison, Stuyvesant Town covers sixteen acres.) With plastic invention aiming at the maximum variety of landscaping, land use and building height, there is here an unexampled opportunity for dozens of eventual solutions that could surpass in urbanity and amenity the squares and crescents of eighteenth-century London. There is space for recreation and play. E.g., the length of a tennis court fits across Ninth Avenue; an occasional corner is big enough for a softball field. Given the large fund of newly available land, now wasted on largely unnecessary and always inconvenient traffic and parking, it is possible to develop new neighborhoods in a leisurely fashion, with careful study and without problems of relocation, or dislocation of such neighborhood ties as exist. *We would especially recommend competitions and public referenda, in order to avoid bureaucratic imposition and to educate the community to concern for its proper business.*

5. MEANS, ETC.

The legal execution of the proposed ban should not be difficult. Streets are at present closed off for play and other purposes. The Mayor banned all traffic in the emergency of snow clearance—though his right to do so has been disputed. We have had a vehicle tax; it could be so pegged as to be prohibitive. A prohibitive entry fee could be charged.

Such a ban should, or course, be leniently interpreted to allow for special cases and emergency use. E.g., a family starting on a trip could use its car to load. Likewise, there must be provision for cars to pass across Manhattan, east and west.

It is likely that the ban on cars could be lifted on weekends, when the truck and bus traffic is much di-

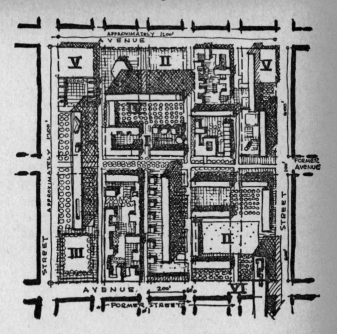

A ten-block area. Density 300-400 to acre. The streets turned into service roads which are also pedestrian walks.

Former traffic area = Avenue: 100' x 1240' = 124,000
4 Streets: 1200' x 240' = 288,000
_____
412,000 sq. ft.

Gross area ten blocks = 1,612,000 sq. ft. We have added 25 per cent to the usable area.

  I. Neighborhood shopping and center.
 II. Play and recreation areas.
III. Swimming pool.
IV. Housing with School in lower floors.
 V. Non-nuisance factories.
VI. Bridge bldg.—office or apartment usage.

Balance is housing for various incomes—some new, some old.

minished. Especially during the warm months this would be convenient for weekend trippers.

6. CONCLUSION

This proposal seems to us to be common sense. The cars have caused many and increasingly severe evils, and the situation is admittedly critical. The proposed solutions, however—new traffic regulations, new highways, multilevels, underground parking—all bear the typical earmark of American planning: to alleviate an evil by remedies that soon increase the evil. But in the special case of Manhattan, the elementary radical remedy, to get rid of the cars, would cause little hardship and have immense and beautiful advantages. (Naturally, in sprawling cities like Los Angeles or Cleveland, one cannot get rid of the cars. Correspondingly, such places lack center and urbanity.)

The chief advantage of this proposal is that it provides opportunity. It does not merely remedy an evil or provide a way to do the same things more efficiently, but it opens the possibility to think about ideal solutions, human values, and new ways to do basic things. Most big-scale planning, however, and most of what passes for Urban Renewal, are humanly indifferent. The quality of life in our cities will not be improved by such planning, but by some elementary social psychiatry and common sense.

Finally, conceive that one of our mayoral candidates were convinced of the advantages of this proposal and made it a part of his program in campaigning for office. This is hard to conceive, for it is just such concrete issues that are never offered to the voters—they are left to special "experts," and indeed to special interests. The voters do not have real choices to think about, therefore they never learn to think. Instead, they vote for personalities and according to ethnic and party groupings. The rival programs are both vague and identical.

If such a plan as this, however, were offered as an important issue, our guess is that the candidate would lose on the first try, because he would be considered radical and irresponsibly adventurous; but he would win the next time around, when people had had the chance to think the matter through and see that it made sense.

Seating arrangements: an elementary lecture in functional planning

Any human function that an architect plans for is rich with cause and shape, with tendency of the organism and adjustment to the environment, with history and cultural meaning. Functional planning is an excellent example of awareness, of creative adjustment, appropriate novelty. In planning, the architect must inquire into the essence of the activity, its purpose, technique, and site; and he must be able to imagine it concretely doing, as part of a whole.

The "functions" that students learn in school, alas, are usually stereotypes; and the act of architecture becomes not reasoned imagination but putting together the pieces of a puzzle. When human functions are taken as generalized stereotypes, it is difficult to distinguish "functional" architecture as a fine art from an inexact branch of engineering. Architecture seems to have become merely an inexact applied science, a way of satisfying a set of pre-fixed purposes called the program. But this fall of architecture from the humanities is not because it has become functional—architecture has by and large always been functional—but because in modern times there is too little and too mindless functionalism. It is man who is chopped up into bits. A closer examination of what it really means to plan for any important human function will show that there is required a kind of culture, philosophical knowledge, and psychological insight that makes architecture an humane, or, if you will, a scientific, inquiry, and not an application of knowledge.

I have here chosen to illustrate a very elementary planning problem, how to arrange the seating for various activities: Eating, Teaching, etc. I shall give many examples, but my single point is to show that there is no stereotype called "Eating," "Teaching," *or* "Seating." It is necessary in every case to understand in a specific way the essence of what is going on, and that is a philosophical act. I do not try, in these examples, to be thorough or nicely accurate, but to say just enough to make my point. And incidentally, when I talk about Seating I am not necessarily talking about Chairs. Those particular machines, devised in the West in the past five hundred years as means of keeping people comfortably attending to business and out of contact with their own or one another's bodies, are usually best dispensed with altogether.

1. PSYCHOTHERAPY

Let us start, somewhat unusually, with arranging the seats for a session of individual psychotherapy. Only two seats are involved, patient's and therapist's, and it would seem there could be little room for variation or refinement. Yet for four important schools of therapy, there are four radically different plans.

(1) In a Freudian session the patient usually lies on a couch and the therapist sits behind, out of sight. This

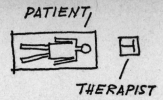

plan is essentially related to the Freudian theory of psychoneurosis, to the treatment, and to the run of patients—hysterics, phobics, etc.—for whom psychoanalysis was devised. In this theory neurosis is caused by certain complexes of repressed ideas, and the aim of treatment is to recover these disturbing contents to consciousness. The patient's deliberate efforts, and the present interpersonal relation of therapist and patient, stand in the way of recovery, and the technique is to by-pass them. So the patient does not see the therapist, does not attend to him; rather, he lies relaxed with his thoughts and "associates" as undeliberately as possible, so that involuntary ideas may emerge. Any social contact with the therapist as though he were a "person" is frowned on. The therapist simply guides the associations with an occasional discreet remark, according to his notion of what is likely important.

In the course of time, however, important unconscious attitudes of the patient begin to attach themselves to the unseen therapist who exists as a disembodied voice insinuating itself at appropriate times into the dream material. The therapist may stand, for instance, for the forgotten parents. There is thus developed the transference, an infantile relation, and treatment is largely management of this transference, in terms of the real present. In principle, the therapist now confronts the patient with the real therapist, saying, "I am *not* your father"; and the seating might change to the following type:

(2)

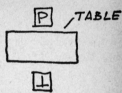

This is the seating, face-to-face across a desk, devised by Harry Stack Sullivan and the Washington School. The Sullivanian treatment was designed, primarily, for schizophrenics rather than psychoneurotics, the distinction, for our purposes here, being that these patients do not have sufficient strength of ego to orient themselves and organize their behavior; they are immature. The purpose of the seating plan is to appeal to that part of the patient's personality that can respond man-to-man and lay problems on the table between the two to be discussed objectively. The table is a protective barrier, e.g., concealing the genitals. Much of the therapy, especially in the beginning, is reassurance, strengthening the patient's self-esteem. One does not seek for his private thoughts or involuntary dreams, but rather to integrate and solidify the attitudes that he can maturely share. And the content discussed tends not to be dreams or early memories, but current events of the day, at the office, with family and friends. Between therapist and patient there is the social contact of professionally talking things over, and transference is precisely avoided rather than encouraged.

(3) Different again is the plan for the method of Character Analysis (Wilhelm Reich). The patient lies exposed on a couch, naked or nearly so; the therapist sits alongside, observes and gives directions, touches him if need be. The theory is that the patient has characteristic "defenses" against his vitality and feeling, and the treatment is to attack them till he gives

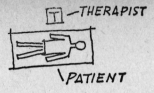

them up. Treatment is importantly physical, for character defenses—sullenness, defiance, impulsiveness, superficial compliance, etc.—are maintained by rigid muscles and other somatic inhibitions. The body lies as for an anatomy, the hope is to reactivate it. The patient is directed to do mimetic and expressive exercises that are often painful, since he is tensed precisely against them. He resists, and the treatment is working this resistance through. The method was devised primarily for recovery of physical energy, especially sexual energy, the best patients being young persons.

(4) Finally, in contrast to any of these, Gestalt therapists insist on a more freely experimental handling of the actual situation, whatever it happens to be. To them, any fixed seating plan overstructures the present, for their aim is to heighten awareness of the changing present and recover possibilities of "creative adjustment" to it. The theory of neurosis is that just the openness to the present is what is inhibited, but the patient repeats archaic habits to avoid anxiety. The very relationship of patient and therapist must not be too strictly adhered to. So the seating is freely altered as occasion arises, and any of the following might occur: The therapist might be unseen. He might have left the room. Patient and therapist might change places. There might be a group.

Obviously this method shades off into a kind of philosophical pedagogy, somewhat akin to Zen. It was devised for persons who have a fairly "normal adjustment"—that is, they can tolerate fairly large amounts

pulpit, and indeed the congregation may turn away
from the altar and toward the pulpit.) The proliferation of symbols, the colored lights, the chanting and
foreign tongue, and the incense create an atmosphere
for the mysterious transformation.

(2) Among Protestants there is also an ordained
minister, but he faces the congregation to address

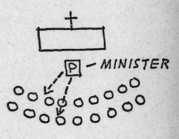

them. (It is an important point of planning as to
whether he addresses each one individually or all
collectively.) Here the objective sacrament of the altar
has been importantly superseded by a different sacred
Act: the preaching of the Word, interpreting a sacred
text. When he ascends to the pulpit, the Holy Spirit
descends on the ministrant, and he confesses the same
to his congregation. The whole congregation is the
choir and there is a great accumulation of chorales—
though, historically, many of these congregational responses have become so elaborate that they have been
taken over by invisible professionals. Besides, the congregation engages in meditation and a kind of communal soliloquizing which facilitate the communication of the inspiring Word. And there is topical
exhortation and moral admonition to correct each one's
personal and conscious will, for all are in direct confrontation with the sacred. There is one space, brightly
lit.

More universalist and unitarian sects, including the
Reformed Jews, seat themselves similarly, the minis-

ter's sacramental Word being more or less transformed into philosophical and ethical instruction.

(3) Since the destruction of the Temple, the Orthodox Jews have no sacramental act and no ordained priest (though there are priestly families). The principal action of the synagogue ritual is the reading of passages from the Torah, including descriptions of the sacrifices *that* would be offered, if there were a Temple. The people are typically grouped around three sides of a reading table. With singing and procession

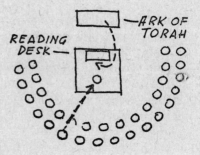

the Torah is brought from a box on the eastern side and laid on the table; and individuals are called from the congregation to take part in readings from the scroll. All (adult males) are called up in rotation through the year. So—omitting the other prayers and the sermon—the service is essentially the literary sharing of a memory and an unfulfillable prescription, and the powerful sense of a present and ongoing congregation. This is an historical people. There is, strictly speaking, no religious leader, but there are scholars who engage in careful exegeses of the law, and a rabbi whose chief functions are juridical and pedagogic. The priestly caste exists in two family lines, but it has few functions when there is no Temple.

(4) The Quakers have a most simple religious meeting. Here there is neither minister nor law, but the

sense of itself of a small congregation expecting direct inspiration if they sit down together and silently com-

ONE INSPIRED —

mune. The Elders, who may sit on one side, have only administrative functions. If inspiration descends on any member, he or she will arise and share it with the rest. In the nature of the case, when there is no hierarchy or other traditional intermediary, the spirit may well be strange, "speaking with tongues," and the response to it ecstatic and trembling. What is sought for is the sense of the meeting.

3. EATING

Let us now, even more sketchily, consider the seating plan for some other major human functions. It is worth while to multiply examples in order to show how significantly different are the plans for what might seem to be fairly simple activities. Eating is eating, yet how we sit down to eat springs from whole systems of moral attitudes and social structure. We ought to expect as much; I am hammering at this point not because it is novel, but because in teaching planning it is just the plain and obvious that is overlooked.

(1) In some primitive societies there is communal preparation of the food, but each one withdraws with his portion to some safe nook and eats privately. The economy is communal, but eating itself is clearly regarded either as a strictly biological function, best

EATING PRIVATELY

COMMON POT

practiced with no table manners or concern for others, so that one may gorge or regurgitate spontaneously; or, more likely, as a dangerous and strictly secret function, ridden with taboos, much as we in the West regard sexual intercourse (and apparently excretion). To some observers, too, the privacy has seemed to indicate a lively suspiciousness, as if each one feared that others were going to snatch the food out of his mouth, or as if, while engaging in this biological indulgence, he were vulnerable to attack and had better sit with his back to a tree.

(2) Civilized people have always regarded eating as a social activity, some common plans being:

NOBLES, KING

COMMONS

Depending on the class structure, those who prepare the food either sit down at the common table or are excluded. The act of eating and drinking together is made to serve as a relaxing and pleasurable background

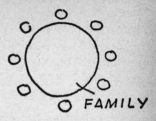

for being together, for family feeling, enlivened conversation, to allay distrust for business deals, etc. To be sure, to socialize the biological activity means also to internalize the eating taboos, and there is developed a system of disgust and, as a safeguard against it, table manners. (Some persons, therefore, who don't wake up and put on their good behavior easily, prefer to have their first cup of coffee in solitude, the way animals eat.) The round dining table of the bourgeois home tends to a tight sense of family and is cement for the Oedipus complex; it is one of the chief schools of inhibition and there may be little conversation. The formal meal at the long table, where the host and hostess sit far apart at either end, takes us back to the table of the king and his nobles, where presence at the king's biological function, his *coucher* or *lever* or dining, is of charismatic advantage. A remarkable American variant of recent times is the Convention Banquet, where the mass may eat in small sociable groups, whereas the im-

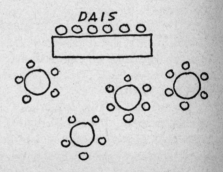

portant people sit at a kingly table on a dais, from which ceremonial speeches will eventually pour forth.

(3) It has also remained for the Americans to arrive at the least plausible of eating plans, seated at a public counter and looking neither to right nor left, like pigs at a trough. The plan is essential to the needs and

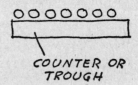

COUNTER OR
TROUGH

mores of our organized society. We eat in company to avoid loneliness, and on an assembly line for efficiency of production, distribution, and consumption. Yet we eat in solitude to avoid surveillance and the anxiety of talking to strangers. Shared solitude is an excellent condition for flights of fantasy that cannot come to overt expression.

4. DEMOCRATIC LEGISLATURES

Even in so specific a field as democratic legislative assemblies, the various chambers that have historically developed are nicely adapted to subtly different notions of the theory and practice of representative government. In different plans, different types of oratory are at a premium, and therefore different personalities among the legislators. Churchill summed this up by remarking, on the reconstruction of the House of Commons, that "Men make buildings and buildings make men."

(1) In the British House of Commons there are a Government Bench and an Opposition Bench, separated widely enough to be out of sword's reach, and there is a Speaker or umpire. The space is kept

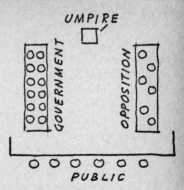

small; the public audience is simply to assure that it is a public function. This is the setup for the lively, short, and often personally acrimonious exchanges that we read in *Hansards*. There are opposed teams—one team is responsible to govern—but each is made of individuals. The legislative theory underlying this is that by the meeting of minds in argument, and the need of the governors to defend themselves against personal attacks and the fire of questions—rather than simply delivering a report or a thesis—there will be reached a new consensus. Naturally, with this clash goes a system of strict politeness to maintain self-respect, and rules of immunity, so that the meeting of minds can go on meeting. The members are representatives of constituencies in only a formal sense; the consensus is not thought of as a compromise of constituent pressures but as a national sense of the House, independently arrived at. The oratorical premium is on ready wit and polemic, thinking on one's feet, being well prepared as to the facts, keeping one's temper; the active members must therefore have a degree of cultivation and somewhat of a common culture, to make them equal and not personally at a disadvantage.

(2) The French Chamber, springing from the revolutionary struggle of heterogeneous interests, has a

very different form and sentiment. There is a spectrum
of opinion from left to right—and during crises very
little common ground between the extremes; and in
the focal place is not an umpire but a tribunal from
which the orator tries to sway the Deputies to his side.

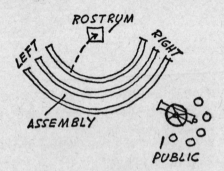

Here the oratorical need is to sweep the whole to a
common, or at least overwhelming, sentiment; therefore, appeals to deep passions that will undercut interest are not amiss. Ups and downs are rapid, and
there is much reshuffling of the spectrum to try for
enough harmony to govern with: it is easy to change
seats. The problem of the sense of the meeting becomes especially interesting when the pressures of the
populace outside the Chamber are strongly felt, as
when during the French Revolution they pointed can-
non. At its best, such an assembly is immediately representative of the General Will; at its worst, of the
fluctuations of the popular will. Its orators are not so
much deliberators as champions.

(3) The various directed or centralized democracies
of recent times tend to have the plan on page 171, top.
Here the Presidium of experts gives out its conclusions
for approval of the representatives. This fits with the
theory that modern technology requires concentration,
central planning, and expert knowledge that the repre-

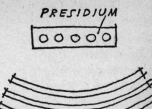

sentatives of the mass cannot really discuss; and with this there is a selection of managerial personalities.

(4) The American Senate, in its idea, embodied a theory of federal regionalism, and the Senators were at first almost as if ambassadors. The characteristic is the wide separation of the desks in a big space, and each

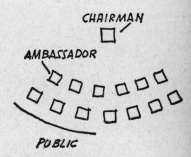

man speaks from his own place. (In the course of time, the gallery for the public becomes increasingly important.) There is not a strong sense of the house as a single mind to be swayed or as having a single best national opinion to be reached. Rather the members are loyal spokesmen of their regional constituencies, and the legislation is any compromise that can win a majority. The oratory in its heyday, correspondingly, was not so much to convince one's peers as it was aimed at the Record and ultimately at the local electorates; it tended to the high-sounding generalities of "public speaking." But of course, the situation has been complicated by a two-party system that was not in the original conception, the members being either for or against the party of the powerful independent Executive; this tension does not exist in the plan. At present the legislative personalities are front figures whose intellectual merit does not much matter. Legislative thought is carried on in small committees.

5. UNIVERSITY

(1) The University is a community of scholars—masters and students. Perhaps we could say that its seating is embodied most typically in the Seminar, a round or

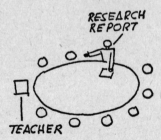

oval table. (Being fancy, we might say that the oval shape has the advantage that its roundness allows the members to be face-to-face for collaborative thought and discussion, whereas the length allows for a head of the table.) Obviously this is not an arrangement for indoctrination or briefing, but for the presentation of fledgling research, reading papers, and hearing criticism from one's peers, under expert guidance.

(2) At one extreme, the Seminar table opens out into the plan for lecture or demonstration. This plan suits the situation when there is in fact a body of authoritative knowledge to be conveyed. The doctor

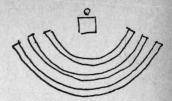

teaches or physically demonstrates a text or experiment
Subsequent questions are directed to him, in the center. But it is best if there is also a strong sense of one's
fellows, and therefore the shape of an amphitheatre.
This differs from the grade-school recitation, where the
pupils sit in rank and the teacher calls on each individual to give an accounting of himself.

(3) At the other extreme, the Seminar table scatters into an informal group, some on chairs, some on
the floor—perhaps with tea, a fire going, etc. This suits
the situation where the subject is imaginative or speculative. The presence of the group encourages, suggests,
criticizes; but each can withdraw into private musing,
exempt from the circle, till he thinks of something.

These plans are all relevant to the University—modified, of course, by the requirements of blackboards,
drawing boards, laboratory equipment, etc. What I
want to emphasize is that the choice of one or the
other depends on the nature of the knowledge involved, and the mode of seeking it.

6. THEATER

Finally, let us remark on the relation of the scene and the seats in theaters. Theatrical Seating is, of course, a vast subject. We cannot here discuss the history of the theater, the class composition of audiences, and so forth. But I want to call attention to a functional relation that is usually overlooked, the essential connection between the seating plan and the kind of play, the kind of plot. This is overlooked in both modern theater-design and modern production, to the jeopardy of the theatrical experience. Advanced theater-architects tend to plan in terms of some putative "modern" theatrical experience that has no plays (nor is it accidental that there are no plays); and advanced directors tend to restyle and cut every kind of play to their own character and convictions, so that there is often a complete loss of the real plot and probability of the play.

(1) The ancient Greek amphitheater was large and in the open air and daylit. The audience sat at a dis-

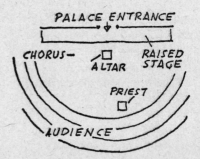

tance from the spectacle, which was enlarged and amplified. The tragic action occurring on the far-off raised stage was performed by sculpturesque more-than-lifesize masks who spoke through megaphones. Their plot was simple, unified, and grand. Not more than three actors appeared at a time. The stories were thrice-familiar national and religious myths. The Greek tragedy presented an important and familiar community symbol. Its audience, seated so as to be conscious of itself as a whole, comprised the entire community, and it was prepared, in this communion, to give vent to the most vocal public expression and abreaction of the fear and grief aroused. There was a presiding priest, and his altar—and the tragic fall of the hero—was still not far removed from a totemic sacrifice. In principle, every play climaxed with the emergence of the hidden through the middle door of the scene on the stage, expressing the return of the repressed and the doom following on a broken taboo. If we consider the relation of the audience to such a spectacle and plot, two contrary things stand out: (a) the audience is at a distance because this is something eerie, bigger than life, not for everyday contact; yet (b) there is one continuous space of audience and scene, lit by one daylight, like a pageant. The play is not a mere fantasy, but a dream emerging into the audience's real world. Such an event is possible only when the entire community is co-present, sharing the guilt. Finally (c), there is an intermediate Chorus, acting *like* the audience but *in* the plot, giving in heightened style the normal responses.

(2) In Shakespeare's stage, everything is otherwise. This is a small theater for an audience bent on enter-

tainment, and actors and poets make a living by pleasing. This is what we today call a "narrative theater," where poet and his spokesmen-actors come close to the audience, on the apron; sometimes adopt a chatty tone with them, abounding in topical allusions, as in vaudeville; and the play is as if "told," rather than presented, illustrated by scenes on the stage and inner stage. The lower-class players are intimate with the groundlings of the pit, and this itself is part of the spectacle for the aristocrats of the balcony. The plots are therefore strikingly devoid of religious or other taboos that must be treated respectfully. Since the story is narrated, there are many episodes and scene changes, but the scenery is not built but consists of mobile properties, suggestive to the fantasy rather than trying to create an illusion of reality. Plots can, then, be drawn from all time and place and conveyed to the audience by the narrator. What occurs when the inner curtain is opened, however, is no longer in the audience's space time; the poet has now taken them to a dimension of dream: often there are faerie masques on the inner stage. Here then is a most complicated relation of audience and spectacle: close-up chatting and soliloquy-to-the-audience, with no curtain; imitated action cut-off and behind a curtain; direct speech and presented dream. But nothing less will suit the complicated Elizabethan plays, with their combination of fable and far-fetched history and contemporary political reference; their realism and fantastic personal rhetoric; their farce, tragedy, and romance.

(3) Most of our present Broadway theaters were planned for a kind of domestic play developed in the eighteenth and nineteenth centuries, and making most sense in the rigid naturalism of Ibsen. The theater is in principle quite simple: the audience is close to the actors, and the unmagnified actors appear

PROSCENIUM
OF VISION

STAGE LIGHTS

the size of life, yet—and this is the most striking feature—the spectacle is absolutely isolated from the
audience by its frame, curtain, and footlights. When
the curtain is up, the system of stagelights illumines
another world than the house lights. Now, such a
close but untouchable scene has always been used to
project ordinary daydreams. (With the addition of
scrim and music, we get the transporting dream world
of the Tchaikovski-Petipa ballet.) Ibsen, however,
chose the opposite possibility: he treated the proscenium opening as simply an absent fourth wall; the
events on the lit stage are *exactly the same* as the day-
to-day reality of the life of the darkened audience, but
now they are presented so that people must look at
them. The spectacle reveals what we in fact do, and
Ibsen turned this mirror to show us what we did but
hypocritically did not admit, or self-deceivingly suppressed. (This school of naturalism, operating exactly
like a nondirective psychotherapy, has proved to be
socially therapeutic and we have inherited a different
world, in some respects franker and cleaner.) The
scenery is built to be very like the actual world, and the
style depends on "maintaining the illusion," that is,
the actor must not break character and the poet must
be concealed.

(4) In the movie theater, finally, the screen is large, its images often huge, so that it is close up to each pair of eyes of the audience. More important, the

screen is brightly lit and everything else is plunged in darkness. This flickering screen is, then, hypnotic and each one experiences the story somewhere in the region of private revery. Others of the audience are vaguely present as a faceless mass. Now, the presentations that have most popularly succeeded in this setting have been psycho-sexual imagos not much individualized; there is little probable plot or hot fantasy. Character types and scenarios are kept fairly like the daily waking experience of the audience (there is little poetic fantasy), but their strong fascination is obviously of a more dreamy kind; they are wishes. Some of the dreamier contents, indeed, are projected onto the "private lives" of the actors who live in a special dimension of their own, e.g., in the "Beverly Hills." The plays are vehicles for these Stars, character types of revery, rather than imitations of action. Almost 100 per cent of these productions have been quite valueless, void of either truth or feeling; but in my opinion it is pointless to try to improve them in the direction of more realism, logic, truth to life, in the simple sense of these terms;

for the relation of audience and hypnotic image is not one of ordinary waking perception. It is better—and this has been the tendency of the few fine films—to dare the logic of dreams and the free association of images, letting emerge a latent plot.

These are four out of a dozen major variations of theater, with different plans. All are, or could be, good; they have been ways in which powerful plays have been presented to receptive audiences. Yet they are also incompatible; a plan suitable for one kind of play will not be equally, or so simply, effective with another. This poses an important and difficult problem in designing an auditorium which might have to be used flexibly for several kinds of plays; or for the director of a particular play who has to use a given theater. The problem must be solved—our living theater cannot be bound to museum-conditions of previous theater; but the solution requires a level of functional thinking beyond sight lines, acoustics, and easy circulation.

CONCLUSION

From this score of examples, from a wide range of human activities, we see that the analysis of a seating plan soon involves us in central considerations of theology, of political and medical theory, of poetics, of community mores. It touches the humane activity itself, with its historical significance.

Now, I want to propose that it is this essential humane reference, rather than problems of esthetics, that makes architecture an art, a ruling or architectonic art, and not a craft or a province of engineering. It is not proportion or decoration that makes architecture one of the Beaux Arts. On the contrary, it is because architecture directly touches the heart of the humanly significant that its esthetic properties, its proportion and decoration, are important. The difference is not between beauty and "mere" utility; but that that utility which is related to such essential and far-reaching meanings of important activities, can be *importantly* beautiful.

I do not mean to suggest that the essential activities we have been discussing cannot be carried on without suitable seating plans. Luckily, architects have no such veto power. One can be sociable even at a lunch counter, and present Shakespeare pretty well on Forty-fourth Street (if only they knew how to speak the verses!). Indeed, an informative study might be made of the expedients by which the essence of an activity realizes itself in spite of ignorant planning. But the planner who can directly and simply facilitate the essential, and thereby enhance the creative adjustment of the function and the environment, is an architect.

This works both ways. The architect who has a broad culture and an esthetic power is himself an important judge of what is humanely essential in an activity; and it is clear that it is valuable for an architect to know something besides "architecture." Naturally this raises a question of architectural practice. Often, indeed almost always, the architect is given a "program" to execute that contains specific requirements that *defeat* the essence of the activity properly understood. If those who made the program had the kind of knowledge of function that an architect has, they would have written a different program. An architect knows the profound meaning, the causes and effects, of architectural functions, of screening or exposing, of sheltering or leaving open, of seating, of zoning, of coming in and going out and circulating, of lighting or leaving dark, of multiplying utilities, of limiting or aggrandizing space, and so forth. The program that is usually given is already full of architectural stereotypes. Certainly the only remedy for this difficulty is to have the architect as a member of the program committee from the beginning; and a valuable training for students is for them to criticize and amend the programs given them as projects.

What is a picture?

There is an important confusion in the present practice of so-called Action Painting, that vitiates the communicative effect of such work. Because of inappropriate framing and the wrong shape of the field of the action, a painting action is irrelevantly seen as a painted picture, and so loses impact and purity. It is essential to have a better psychological analysis of the kind of space involved and the conditions of its perception.

When you can appropriately put a frame around something you have a picture of an object in its special space. An empty frame held up in the air or on a wall is just a frame; but if it surrounds a material different from the wall, a board or a textile, there is potentially a special space and it is presumed that any object appearing on that surface is a picture-object in its special space.

The extreme of this simplest mode of picturing is the Taoist (Zen-imitated) effort to make us attend, by a few marks on the silk, to the silk itself, as a symbol of all the Fertile Void. The silk *was* an actual void inviting the painter's few marks. Before the painter made his marks, we saw raw silk on a scroll; after his work, we see the emptiness of the raw silk in a picture.

The opposite extreme, the fullest possible picturing, is to take the frame as a window looking out on the "real" environment. When we look out a proper window, we presume that the environmental scene is, after all, continuous with our own space in the room. We could go there. But the picture space is special, it is a world we cannot enter; but it "stands for" environment. It is for such a picture-world that the usual frame shape, the flat rectangle, is most apt. The flat rectangle is a compromise between the flat oval of vision, in which we in fact see the world, and the system of horizontals and uprights that we usually see there. When we concentrate on the portrait of a lone man, the frame narrows, as does the oval of vision. For a panorama, the frame elongates. (It is interesting how Griffith and Bitzer study these effects in their early films.)

For this fullest picture, the careful technique of the Dutch realists like De Hooch is useful, particularly in imitating the special lighting of the special space. Yet indeed, those painters were haunted by their *action* as painters and often made pictures just of windows looking out on still other spaces: they were painting self-portraits of the painter thinking a painting.

Most paintings of the past five hundred years, both Oriental and Occidental, make a mutual adjustment of two kinds of special space: the illusory space, and the actual tactile space within the frame. No matter what is illusorily portrayed, the painted marks are *composed* to affirm and bind the actual space within the frame. The "scientific perspective" of the illusory space is generally flattened to adjust to the flatness of the actual surface, to bring the background forward. (The isometric projection of Chinese painting is of course flat to begin with.) Curiously, where the more "scientific" perspective is not altered to the composition of the flat actual surface, the effect is unreal, for indeed the real thing, the feeling of reality, *is* only the flat surface. This unreality may be observed in the ineptly drawn elevations of young architectural draftsmen; but it is powerfully used as an expressive means in Surrealist pictures, that exaggerate the contradictions between the two special spaces and suggest infinite distances.

Broadly speaking, our painting of the last hundred years has turned away from conveying the illusory space and has laid more and more emphasis on composing the actual space, up to the kind of abstraction which is, in program, nothing but composition of the canvas rectangle, and which secondarily reintroduces "nonillusory" effects of depth to heighten the tension and richness, e.g., by values that recede or values that come forward. The watershed of modern painting is universally recognized as Cézanne's philosophic attempt to adjust the two special spaces by reconstructing the illusory world out of compositional bits of actual surface, rather than copying off the scene in the oval of vision.

Picture framing too, is on our side of the watershed. The older deep frame simulated a window looking out on the illusory world; but a tightly composed rectangle itself holds together as a special space on the wall, and does not want much of a frame, if any.

2. EXAMPLES FOR CONTRAST AND COMPARISON

A statue is not a picture because its space is not special, but continuous with ours. There is no frame. This is inevitable when the three-dimensionality invites walking around the object and touching it. Conversely, a picturesque bas-relief—say, a panel from the Doors of Ghiberti—is *more* a picture than a flat painting is, because there is a more complicated special space in the frame.

A strong sculpture *controls* its surrounding space and draws us into it; therefore our space is made continuous with the art-work's, there is *only* special space. Consider a contrast. Imagine a frame around the *Apollo Belvedere* and it easily turns into a picture—it is apt for setting in a pretty rotunda. But imagine a frame around the *Moses* and you at once get colossal Dada. Going further, imagine a frame around the *Captives*, not yet free of the rock, and the effect is abhorrent. The *Moses* strongly seizes on its space and controls ours; but the unfinished *Captives* pervade our ordinary space with courage and melancholy; there is still real rock and these *Captives* are only real.

I take it that this was Jackson Pollock's idea, to control our space and make only one special space, when he said that the onlooker was supposed to be entangled *in* his big canvases, as in a woods. Not dissimilarly, Rothko's big colored stripes have been called backgrounds that make the people look good; the onlookers have entered a special space and actually are in the picture.

A colored wall limits our continuous space rather than being itself limited, so we do not see it as a picture; but when it is painted with figures, like a mural, it is often a matter of choice whether or not it is a picture. The more architectural, the less pictorial.

In general, painted representations of real things tend to be seen as pictures rather than as decorations, emblems, or actions. This is because around the image of the real object we tend to see also an image of some of the space around the object: this puts the representation in a special space and we inchoately frame it. A nonrepresentational design, however, may or may not seem like a picture on the wall, depending on whether or not it makes for itself a limited special space. This provides us a nonevaluative definition of "decorative": designs are "decorative" when they do not make themselves a special space, but are either *on* the wall like shields or emblems, or they are themselves the wall, like patterns that are or could be repeated to form a continuous wall that limits our real space. Many paintings of the Abstract Expressionists, that cover the whole canvas with a kind of pattern, seem to want to continue in this way, as if they were pieces cut from a continuous calico, arabesque, or linoleum, even though only one rectangle has been selected for exhibition. They are not pictures.

Contrariwise, a sublime case of establishing a special space is the bas-relief of the Procession around the Parthenon, which by its rhythm of densities and sparseness, and its climaxes of confrontation, creates for itself a continuous special space, self-enclosing like the Universe. It commences as an architectural decoration, but becomes thrillingly a unique world.

3.   ACTIONS AND THEIR SPACE

Now, a two-dimensional painted representation may, by exception, *not* be a picture. Such is the huge figure that leaps at you from the apse in the Cathedral at Pisa, or Cimabue's crucifix-framed Christ in the Uffizi, Florence. These have the effect of crucifixes that go about in our space. They are means of direct action.

Let us consider a painting as a painting-action. This can mean, not incompatibly, several things. Primitive magical marks are actions. So are paintings like the Cimabue just mentioned. And so the handling of the paint, acting with paint, as by Pollock or Kline. Can we appropriately frame such gestures and get pictures?

The active aspect of painting, the painting of it, has of course been a salient feature of most great art in the past six hundred years, certainly since Giotto and before. We call attention to this aspect when we speak of vitality, freshness, speed, bravura, or, alternately, loving application, meticulous brush strokes, and so forth. The fresco fury of Michelangelo is even his outstanding painterly quality (equal to his poetic and philosophical profundity). In the past, however, this painting-action was mostly used to underscore such picture properties as appropriateness to the subject, atmosphere, composition, and decoration. It has been the genius of our times to isolate painting-action as sometimes sufficient to itself. Such pure gesture sophisticatedly recalls the painting of children or aboriginal petroglyphs, in which what fascinates us is not the painted product but the transmitted action, the sense of the painter painting.

I do not think that such action organizes a special space in any of the ways we have been discussing. There is no illusory space and no composition of the flat surface. Therefore there is nothing to frame. Further, putting a rectangular frame around the action creates wrong assumptions and confuses the direct meaning of the gesture.

Consider, for instance, a real girl skipping down the street or a young chap making a neat double play at second base in a ball game. These are lovely gestures, but to frame them is to kill them: it turns them into cinematographs and destroys their continuity with our space and life.

But perhaps a painting-action might be compared to a dramatic action on a stage, in its specially lit special space framed by the proscenium arch. It seems to me that this is a poor analogy. The proscenium-framed space is much weaker in esthetic texture than the words, acting, and blocking of the drama; it is easily unattended to; we look past the arch. In a painting, however, the negative rectangle surrounding the painting-action is of almost equal textural value with the painted marks; it is colored like them, and extended like them. Therefore it either must be attended to, making a conventional composition, a picture; or it is a dead weight on the action, like an obtrusive set in a play.

The same reasoning holds against those painters who claim that the rectangular canvas is the playground for their action, like the football field for the game. It is again a poor analogy. The spectators of the game do *not* importantly notice that the grass at the fifty-yard line is worn thin and that the corners want cutting, but the spectators of a painting notice the texture, color, and painted or unpainted quality of the background. Also, the spectators of the football game know that, by the rules, the game may at any moment spring into any unoccupied territory, so that the whole field is necessary for the game and is potentially alive; whereas a painting gesture is already achieved and much of the rectangle has become dead past.

I think, however, that the right relation of action and special space is given by the following analogy. When we say that a girl is "pretty as a picture," we mean that she makes *the place of her presence and of her movements* divinely special. She is like a traveling picture. As Harold Rosenberg said in a recent discussion at the (artists') Club, a great gesture, like an historical event, creates a *setting* for itself. But such a setting is not the *a priori* rectangle; it is the place required for the gesture and the aura surrounding that place. This is just what Cimabue gives us in the great crucifix-like painting in Florence, which invades *our* space.

We speak of the space of the object in the picture, but of the place of the gesture in the world.

What I am here saying of action painting has always been said of pure drawing, outlining. In drawing we attend to the line, the signature, of the artist, and not much of the organization of the page or space; therefore it has never been considered important to frame the drawing.

Another way of relating action and space is to think of the painting-action as acting *on* a space, e.g., attacking a surface, caressing a surface, surrounding a territory, entering a void, procession across a field, or even resting in a field. The problem is how to convey, without irrelevance, that *this* is what is being done. If the artist puts his regular frame *around* his achieved gesture, or carries on his action *in* a regular playground, then inevitably we begin to look at his marks as either an object in a frame—usually not a very interesting object; or as an attempt to organize or compose the playground—usually a feeble attempt. Such are the false assumptions created by the rectangle. It is precisely the residual dead space that is *not* the place of the gesture that becomes the framed special space for the onlooker, and this confuses everything.

The correct procedure, therefore, must be to present for exhibition—and why should not great, lovely, or otherwise interesting gestures be exhibited?—just the place required for the gesture and the aura of the gesture. And this is not a picture, but an event.

Advance-guard writing in America:

1900-1950

Se quoque princibus permixtum agnovit Achivis,
Eoasque acies et nigri Memnonis arma.
—VIRGIL, *Aeneid*

An artist does not know that he is advance-guard, he
must be told so or learn it from the reaction of the
audience. *All* original composition—classical, standard,
or advance-guard—occurs at the limits of the artist's
knowledge, feeling, and technique. Being a spontaneous act, it risks, supported by what one has already
grown up to, something unknown. The action of all art
accepts an inner problem and concentrates on a sensuous medium. Obviously if one has an *inner* problem,
one does not know beforehand the coming solution of
it; and concentrating on the medium, one is surprised
beyond oneself. Art-working is always just beyond what
one can control, and the thing "does not turn out the
way I planned." (In the best cases it is *just* beyond what
one can control, and one has indeed learned to control
the previous adventures up to that point, has acquired,
as the ancients used to say, the habit of art that now
again, in act, is in a present and therefore novel urgency.) Thus, whatever the subsequent social evaluation of a work—it may be quite traditional—to the

creative artist as he makes it, it is always new and daring, and he cannot be morally or politically responsible for it. How could he be responsible, if he does not know what it will be? And further, the more powerfully spontaneous the working, the more he himself as a moral being will resist and disclaim it; a poet says what he does not wish to hear said. (Of course he is responsible artistically, to let the coming figure form with the utmost clarity and unity.)

For the most part, the products of such countless acts of artistic daring have been acceptable works, not far-fetched at all, but animating or perhaps troubling. The irresponsible adventure turns out to be another proof of the common sensibility of mankind. The "inner problem" accepted with reluctance by the artist is after all some universal problem that now, thanks to the responsible art-working, has new words, a new image, a new facet. The audience accepts the work as genuine art. Sometimes, to be sure, if the effort has been extremely profound or subtle, or the problem has been new or idiosyncratic, the product does not find a ready or large audience. Nevertheless, it is accepted as genuine, but perhaps "not for us," being too deep, decadent, or so forth.

But now there are also these other works that are indignantly rejected and called not genuine art, but insult, outrage, *blague*, *fumiste*, willfully incomprehensible, or, more favorably, with our childlike American docility, experimental. And what is puzzling is that they are not isolated pieces, but some artists persistently produce such pieces, and there are whole schools of such "not-genuine" artists! What to make of this? In this case, the feeling of the audience is sound—it is always sound—there *is* insult, willful incomprehensibility, experiment; and yet the judgment of the audience is wrong—it is often wrong—for this is genuine art.

This seems to be a contradiction. For we defined the art-act as accepting the inner problem and concentrating on the sensuous medium; yet now we speak of a rhetorical attitude toward the audience, e.g., insult, and of an experimental handling of the medium, as still being genuine art. The explanation of this apparent contradiction gives us the nature of advance-guard and tells us its recent history and present direction.

Within the advance-guard artist, the norms of the audience, of "society," exist as an introjected, unassimilated mass; it is their irk that is his special inner problem. It is his spontaneous attempt to vomit up or destroy and assimilate this irksome material that results in products that, as if willfully, offend, insult, or seek to disintegrate these same social norms. ("Introjects" are other people's standards that one is forced to identify with as one's own.) All creative work occurs at the limits of knowledge and feeling, and the limits here are the risky attack on the unassimilated, and perhaps unassimilable, as if to say, "Until I get rid of this, I cannot breathe."

We may distinguish immature and mature advance-guard. If the undigested mass is indeed digestible to those of experience in society as a whole, then the advance-guard offense is not taken as offensive, but as brash rebelliousness which, if the offender is youthful, is considered hopeful and charming. But if the undigested norms are generally really indigestible, though socially accepted—that is, if the standards of society in fact make everybody unhappy—then the offense is insulting and "dangerous," and is met with social sanctions. Having caused offense and being punished, the artist first knows that he is an advance-guard artist. Secondarily, then, he may as a moral and political act appoint himself to this thankless career and engage programmatically in the offense originally suggested by his creative work. Such a vocation of advance-guard is not only insulting to the audience but a threat to established institutions.

Consider as an example how France has been, up to now, the native home of *avant-garde*. (I presume that the military term comes from the disgusted generation of the Restoration after the Congress of Vienna.) A stable land-rooted bourgeois morality, an official "Cartesian" culture of peculiar uniformity, and a sentimental Catholicism were calculated to impress themselves on a growing mind as the norms of all sense, reason, and charm; one could not help swallowing them whole, without criticism. But therefore, if one had any intellect and spirit, the subsequent inner nausea was bound to be early and total: bohemian, antisyntactical, and social-revolutionary. But therefore again, the French *avant-garde* always turns out to be very "Cartesian," with proofs and manifestoes all in order, and a keenness to proselytize and make uniform in the latest cut. The French way of being a very great writer with world-wide influence has usually been to invent a new method or broach a new subject; writers of other lands have had to write great books.

Whenever the mores are outmoded, anti-instinctual, or otherwise counter to the developing powers of intelligent and sensitive persons, there will be advance-guard work. Yet, to repeat, advance-guard is not a direct attack on the inhibiting mores, except secondarily. On the contrary, it is precisely the intelligent and sensitive who, when they were precocious children, most absorbed and identified themselves with the accepted culture, with whatever value it had. It is only afterward that the nausea and anger set in, inwardly, unknown, pervading the creative work. If advance-guard were a direct attack, it would not be genuine art at all, and it would not ultimately become part of the stream of tradition; but as the response to an inner irk, it corrodes and pulverizes with creative work, it suffers the conflict through, and it prepares the integrated normal style of the next generation. Again, if advance-guard were a direct attack, the response of the audience would be angry defense and counterattack, instead of the peculiar "outrage" which indicates that the members of the audience have the same inner difficulty but are unwilling to recognize it; they are somehow "threatened."

Thus, if we want to retain the concept of "alienation,"—e.g., to speak of artists "alienated" in having no social status and having dissident values—we must be careful not to mean simply that there are rival warring camps between society and the artists—a sociological absurdity. But we must mean (1) that society is "alienated" from itself, from its own natural life and growth, and its persons are estranged from one another; but most members of society do not feel their estrangement; (2) the artists, however, feel it and regard themselves as estranged; and (3) society responds to them not with snobbery and incomprehension, as to foreigners speaking a foreign tongue, but with outrage, embarrassment, and ridicule, as to an inner threat. "Alienation" is primarily self-estrangement—this is, by the way, how Marx used the term—and the advance-guard tries to disgorge the alien culture.

Advance-guard periods are unsuited for the creation of perfect works "exemplary to future generations," as Kant would have said. The unassimilated culture prevents the all-round development of the artist, it prevents him from achieving a habit, and he spends too much energy in merely destroying what is not nourishing. Advance-guard works tend to be impatient, fragmentary, ill tempered, capricious. (Whether they are not thereby nearer to the human truth is another question.) Perfect works are not fostered, either, by periods of "stability," whatever that means. They are fostered by periods of expansion, for these nourish the ongoing adventurous creative powers. If a period of expansion is followed, as Matthew Arnold said, by a period of criticism that standardizes and popularizes the achievement, then, to the creative spirit, such a period is stagnant and will be followed by a disgusted advance-guard. The only healthy stability is an even growth.

2. NATURALISM

I have set down these academic remarks in order to be able to say something about the American advance-guard from 1900 to 1950. During that period there was a deepening cultural crisis, and a deepening literary response, going from an advance-guard of subject matter to an advance-guard of form to an advance-guard questioning the worth of the art itself and its relation to the audience. By the end of the period we can see shaping the lineaments of our present writing. (May I ask the reader's indulgence if, in treating so broad a subject, I speak in terms of decades and mention "styles" and symbolical historical landmarks, instead of individual works and real molecular changes.)

The advance-guard of the beginning of the century introduced offensive subject matter, in novels about the seamy side of accepted morals, economics, and politics. Contemporary with these were direct muckraking exposés of the same subjects—so that advance-guard and reform politics seem very close, but their approach is quite different. In an important sense this advance-guard succeeded, for, just as previously on the Continent, the factual account of sexuality and sexual misery, and poverty, exploitation, and graft has become standard literary content. That is, what was achieved was the destruction not of the institutions but of the hypocrisy and reticence concealing them.

What gave to these early works a peculiar passion,

quite absent from later stories about this same subject matter, was the passionless and precise reportage, the naturalism of the telling. And contrast these creative works with the muckraking journalism (and novels) of the same period. The journalism was indignant with the infamy. If the novels, apparently having the same aim, had adopted the same tone, they would not have outraged, though they might have been banned as dangerous. For the muckraking tone accepts the same moral attitude as the audience's, saying, "We attack what we consider evil, and this is an evil overlooked by you." If the artists had said this, they would have been worthy moral opponents. Instead they offered the detailed image without evaluation and without the selection and arrangement that, according to the taste of that time, implied evaluation. What was the meaning of this naturalism?

The avowed aim of naturalism is familiar; to attack and reform by letting the facts speak for themselves, without style, as if to say, "There you see our world, damn it!" But of course naturalism is a highly artificial style. Its lack of selectivity is an icy selection from the common speech which abounds in evaluation. Naturalism is an icily hostile withdrawal from the audience; it will not share in their moral sense; it says in effect, "There is the world you have made for me, damn you. *I* abjure it. Put up with it if you can." This is an inward reaction to an introjected moral attitude, as if to say, "To be a person at all, to make evaluations, is to be like you, a hypocrite."

We may see the creative, self-curative use of such a response to an inward pathological situation if we bear in mind that naturalism is fundamentally a detailed stream of consciousness without evaluation. This is the means used in psychotherapy to recover a traumatic image; the detail provides associations, the suspension of evaluation prevents censorship. Now, it seems to me that, far from poets' having a conception of the abuse and attacking it, it was only by their method of naturalism that they were able to call up the scene of horror and overcome the hypocrisy in themselves. Secondarily they added on a program of reforms.

We, who have a different acquaintance with the kind of subject matter they broached, might find it hard to conceive their difficulty. Yet, to give a great example, it is hard otherwise to understand how so masterly an intellect as Ibsen could have hamstrung himself with his theatrical naturalism. It was *only* so, by making the scene real before his eyes, that he could believe the magnitude of his dissent from the mores.

In a Mallarmé, the anamnestic naturalism is pure and wonderfully total; he does nothing but notice and he notices, in principle, everything. Our novelists were more limited in what they noticed; and, more important, they at once confused their noticing with muckraking and moralizing. The reason for this confusion was that they made the assumption that a mere institutional change—sexual reform, socialism, etc.— would heal the inner irk, or, what is the same thing, create a society they could breathe in. Hypocrisy overcome, the truth out, everything good would follow. This assumption, which makes them seem close to the political reformers, was an illusion. The irk that brought them to a naturalistic handling of the subject matter could not be healed by merely altering the subject matter. However it was, even before the First World War, the advance-guard was already shifting away from the offensive subject matter to the offensive form and style, a much bolder effort of a much deeper dismay.

The audience reacted to the naturalistic offense with the specific sanction of censorship, on moral and political grounds. Yet this was obviously not a police measure of defense, to protect the children, but a reaction of outraged sensibility. There had to be spectacular trials to affirm the faith of the audience in itself. If there had been an objective danger, e.g., warm-blooded pornography, the sales would have been wider and the police measures more quiet. The naturalistic scenes were socially harmless, the sales were small; but they were insulting, outrageous. That is, the audience felt perfectly well the icy hostility and froze, and rationalized the outrage as best it could.

3. THE REVOLUTION OF THE WORD

The 'twenties, the aftermath of the war, was the golden age of advance-guard, and this kind of art was almost able to transform itself into integrated art. From that time on, the advance-guard has been international. It was an advance-guard of method, form, style.

A golden flowering of advance-guard is a paradox, but the paradox was in the times. People were stunned by the surprising barbarism of the First World War—how far we have come since then! The troubles in Western society, it was clear, were far deeper than could be cured by the intelligent practical reforms of its most social-minded physicians. History had gone beyond the revelations of the naturalists, and an artist could feel that if mankind dared so much, he could justifiably dare much further to solace his inner distress. At the same time, it was period of hope and buoyancy. There was a general conviction that peace would be permanent—the nations outlawed war as "an instrument of national policy." The world became spectacularly international, and there was, after a short interim of reconstruction, an enormous economic production, scientific innovation, and technological application. It was a period of expansion, calculated, if it lasted, to produce modern masterpieces.

To understand the golden age of advance-guard, we

must bear in mind the contrary facets: (1) the profound dismay at the breakdown of "civilization," and the inner disbelief in the previous programs of institutional change; the need to corrode the inner irk with a more thorough destructiveness; but (2) the buoyant hope and material prosperity, and the half-willingness of people in the victorious countries to venture a change—just as the vanquished were driven into a change. The first factor explains the advance-guard; but if we omit the second, we cannot understand the quantity and depth of the experiments, and the almost popularity achieved by the bizarre products. For advance-guard always rouses anxiety, but in conditions of expansion it is possible to tolerate the anxiety and allow the creative excitement to approach an integrated solution.

The advance-guard of the 'twenties was a concentrated attack on the formal attitudes of literature, the vocabulary, syntax, genre, method of narration, judgment of what is real and what is fantasy; everything, in short, that goes by the name Revolution of the Word. This revolution had begun earlier on the Continent, but now all forces joined and came to a climax and a self-consciousness. What is its meaning as a creative response to introjected norms?

The syntax and style of speech convey character, the so-called system of defenses and projections. Consider, as an analogy, the Rorschach test. In this test of "personality-type," the most important indices are not the content of what is seen in the blots, but the form of perception, e.g., whether color is seen or overlooked or there is shock at seeing color; whether color is seen free or in delineated areas; whether large details, small details, the whole are seen, and in what order; whether what is seen is on the periphery, in the center, down the middle line, always on the surface or sometimes in depth; whether the white spaces are seen as well as the inked ones; whether movement is projected, and so forth. It is these formal differences that project the type of feeling, the "personality." And so in literature. It is the formal actions, the structure, texture, diction, syntax, mood and tense, trope and image, concreteness and abstraction, directness and periphrasis, and so forth, that deeply communicate the character. To experiment with these things is the same as saying, "Not only do I disagree with you, but I am trying to make myself a different kind of person from what you made me, or what you are." Considered genetically, it is a going back to the time one first learned to speak and be a "person" at all. At the same time there is still the attempt to communicate by using the accepted machinery of communication, orthography, books, publication, as if to say, "Won't you become a different person? Try to understand me if I speak this new way."

Just as the previous naturalism was a kind of recovery of the traumatic scene, the Revolution of the Word was what later came to be called "character analysis." The parallel nonartistic movement of the time was medical psychoanalysis and progressive education, attempts to heal not institutions but personality disorders. And the secondary politics of the advance-guard tended to be the "permanent revolution," the expression of a worsening crisis in a period of expansion.

The insulted audience ridiculed the artists and charged them with bad faith and willful incomprehensibility. This meant that the audience felt that it was being not so much hostilely assaulted as disregarded. And this was indeed a correct feeling, for the artists were not regarding the audience as "persons"; it was the personality they shared with the audience that they were trying to disgorge. Alternately, the audience called the artists irresponsible children and felt that they themselves were bewildered children, and this was indeed the ambiguous nature of the case, for both were experimenting in learning to speak.

Unlike the grimness of naturalism, the Revolution of the Word was playful, euphoric, libidinous, dreamy, barbaric, exotic. To attack the institutions and ideology as the naturalists did, was to be infected with the guilt and punishment of instinct that had first resulted in the introjections. But to "pierce the character-armor" as did the Revolution of the Word, was to release pent-up drives. In principle such release is accompanied by intense anxiety. Nevertheless, as long as the period was economically booming and politically hopeful, it was possible to achieve wide toleration of the anxiety, especially by regarding the innovations as sophisticated (extremely "grown-up") and superficial (not "meant"). However it was, just as the standard literature of the 'twenties and 'thirties accepted the earlier advance-guard subject matter, so the 'forties consolidated much of the Revolution of the Word, especially in poetry, and the 'fifties have played with it still more freely, using it as a lingua franca for dissidents.

4. SOCIAL SOLIDARITY AND "IRRESPONSIBILITY"

With the Depression and the looming of another war after all, the buoyancy vanished and the general anxiety became intolerable. In such circumstances, surface defenses are tightened and no inward adventure is possible. At once the advance-guard seemed to vanish from the scene. In the opinion of most critics twenty years later, it vanished for good and my history has no further relevance. But I shall show how in this continually deepening anxiety there has always been an advance-guard reaction, begun in the 'thirties and running afoul, and now—at the end of the 'fifties and into the 'sixties—beginning to affirm itself strongly, though not yet hitting on the right course. (If indeed the advance-guard had vanished in the 'thirties, we should have to reconcile ourselves to having no genuine literature at all—as seems to have been almost the case for two decades!—for it is impossible to *accept* the norms of anxiety, a clinging to security, and still create something.) But let us proceed step by step.

In the 'thirties, the Revolution of the Word began to be called "irresponsible"; and its obscurity, which had previously been shared in as entertaining and challenging, was rebuffed as Ivory Tower and of no consequence. To the artist this meant that now indeed he had no social role and he could call himself "alienated" or estranged, with what profound effect we must soon discuss. There was, however, an immediate reaction in the tightened circumstances of the anxious surface.

This was the literary manner of so-called "Socialist Realism"; for the most part it was merely reactive and without creative meaning, but if we carefully anatomize it, we can see that it contained something new. (1) The socialist-realists fully accepted the early-century program of reform, and with a deadly monotony reiterated the naturalistic subject matter. (2) They couched it in a banal dramatic manner, full of standard evaluation, that made the old-fashioned message quite reactionary in effect (as Trotsky, for instance, was quick to point out). (3) With this, however, there was a new sentiment: the solidarity of the artist and audience; that art is a solidary action; the artist is not physically or culturally isolated from the audience, though he may purposely attack it. This sentiment, which still has vitality, went back to such different advance-guard roots as Dada, the theater of participation, and the Bauhaus. But (4) instead of finding a creative expression of solidarity, the sentiment at once degenerated into opportunistic propagandizing of party formulas, first of the minority then of the majority.

The valuable new sentiment of solidarity—which we expect to appear in a crisis of fear, and which did appear—was debauched by the miserable pretense of the art, which renounced the artistic responsibility of inventing something new. It was a pretense, for whereas the naturalists had suffered an illusion, that their society, which they accepted at face value, could be reformed, these artists did not inwardly believe it at all. And outwardly, as it turned out, they eventually migrated to Hollywood or advertising or government service, there to endure ulcers, Stalinism, sinusitis, and such other complaints as come from aggressing against oneself and laying the blame elsewhere. The charge of "irresponsibility" was a projection; it was they who were irresponsible to their own creative selves. And finally, when the Second World War broke out, it was the official spokesmen who used the word "irresponsible" and took up the call for social solidarity.

Let us review the situation as it passed into the 'forties and toward our present day. On the one hand the norms that a young person perforce introjected were now extraordinarily senseless and unnatural—a routine technology geared to war, a muffled and guilty science, a standard of living measured by commodities, a commercial art, a moral "freedom" without personal contact: it is not necessary to go over this familiar ground. Then we should have expected the activity of artists of the late 'forties and the 'fifties to have been more than ever advance-guard. But the general anxiety and their own anxiety were such that there could be no audience recognition of any product of inward daring, if anyone could dare to produce it. (I think some of us continued.) What an artist would say spontaneously would now seem hopelessly irrelevant, likely even to himself, and he would have no means to communicate it, nor perhaps even incentive. This was a clinch. The tendency of some artists would therefore be to fall silent, to accept their estrangement—and this seems to have been the case. (Instead of writers, we got the epidemic "revivals" of Melville, Henry James, F. Scott Fitzgerald, etc., even Nathanael West. This is too pathetic to dwell on.)

But of course the silence—the "silence, cunning, and exile"—is a physiological impossibility. Creative vitality simply expresses itself. The advance-guard action, then, took the form of concern neither with the subject matter nor the method, but with the use, and attitude, of being an artist at all. In the language of the accompanying philosophy, this was the "existential" problem for the artist: not what to think nor what kind of person to be, but how to persist at all, being an artist. (As usual, the advance-guard problem has slightly anticipated the current general problem: how to persist, being alive.) The literary revival—in America it was a discovery—of Kierkegaard made sense, for the age was again very like the Congress of Vienna.

The problem we faced—how to be an artist at all— was different from that blithely tackled by Dada in the early 'twenties, for at that time, in buoyant circumstances, it was possible to decide that art was pointless and to take revenge with irksome acts of anti-art; but in straitened circumstances one cannot allow himself such luxuries.

5. AFTERMATH OF WORLD WAR II

One would not call the aftermath of World War II buoyant and confident of progress. Probably one should not even call it an age of anxiety, as Auden did. Rather, from the clinical point of view, we have seen the phenomena of shell shock, a clinging to adjustment and security of whatever quality, and a com plete inability to bear anxiety of any kind, to avoid panic and collapse. For instance, in 1948 I lectured on Kafka to a college audience composed of ex-soldiers. This audience unanimously insisted, with frantic emphasis, that Kafka was a freak whose psychotic vision had no relevance to anything in "real life." Where there was such insecurity as this, as not to allow even the possibility that all might not be well, we could expect little creativity of any kind.

Correspondingly, for at least a decade after the war, the literary atmosphere for the reception of any deep-springing art, advance-guard or otherwise, was miserable. Certainly the literary magazines were never so poor in forty years in this country. In the interest of a secure academism, including an academism of the 'twenties, they printed nothing that could arrest attention (although some things that were fine and solid). Perhaps no new things were submitted. At least the impression was created among young persons, who get incentive from such periodicals, that nothing astonishing was being done and nothing could be done. One felt, indeed, that this was the intention of the editors.

It is the thesis of this essay that advance-guard is only one species of art and is, in principle, not the best art. Yet it comes to be the case that where the literary climate is unfavorable to the destructive élan of advance-guard, there is little genuine creation of any kind. The best period is one in which every new work destroys the convention of its predecessors, yet, advancing to just the next step—the result of an achieved habit and assimilated tradition—it carries its audience along. The possible, and usual, period is one in which the integrated artist employs productively the destructive work of an immediately previous advance-guard—and this is common within an artist's own career, his own youth being his advance-guard. But where the advance-guard dies, the language dies.

6. NEW DIRECTIONS APPARENT AROUND 1950

Now consider, as we have been doing, the introjection of the norm of shell shock, equivalent to clinging to security. Genetically this takes us very far back, to the infantile fright of total abandonment. The average person feels it as a lack of concern and a passionless going about one's business. (Hannah Arendt has well described this indifference and excessive busyness in the spectacularly guilty and shell-shocked Germans post Hitler; but the ill has been much more universal than she seems to be aware of.) A self-aware person feels the introjected shell shock as his estrangement. The advance-guard artist, however, unwilling to accept this introject as his own, revives from the fright of total abandonment, begins to wail and reach out—to the audience, for a new possibility. He becomes first a cry baby, then an unwanted lover. That is, to persist at all, being an artist, the advance-guard artist tries to create a new relation of artist and audience. The art of the artist is to invent ways needfully to throw himself on the mercy of the audience. By this aggression he saves the audience from its numb shock. To explore this, let me describe three advance-guard tendencies apparent around 1950, and that still are working themselves out. Let me call them the direction of Genet, of Cocteau, and of a writer who proceeds from a remark of Goethe.

(1) Conscious of estrangement, serious standard writers, in their self-portraits and choice of protagonists, have more and more been describing marginal personalities—criminals, perverts, drunkards, underground people—or persons in extreme situations that make them "existent" rather than universal. Their artist no longer considers himself an accuser or advocate, an explorer or a radical, but as one beyond justification, as if to say, "Your judgment is indifferent to me." In plot, the melodrama of the sensational popular writer

is now the sober content of the standard writer. The meaning of it is, clearly, the assertion of the repressed vitality in despite of the lifeless or shell-shocked norms, but it accepts the normal judgment and fails to create a new valuation. This is, of course, to give up the possibility of humane synthesis altogether. Therefore, one kind of possible advance-guard action would be to assert the marginal as the central and to prove its justification, thereby demolishing the norm.

This is what Genet has tried. In a famous speech on delinquency, he explains himself succinctly. He says that as a man he has little sense of moral values, they do not concern him. His only contact with life is the act of writing. But when he comes to write about the law-abiding or the esteemed, his pen stands still, his images do not soar, the rhythm limps. As soon as he takes up his criminal types, however, he has plenty to say, his style warms up. Therefore he must, he does, present the criminals in a more heroic light; and therefore he has come to understand that they are the superior people. Genet uses the action of art, that is, his existential role, to find vital norms, necessarily offensive and alone, for him, justifying. (Naturally, they are the norms of his own inner problem, which seems to be a conflict between accepted castration and flaming exhibition. It is interesting to contrast this with the almost similar conflict of our Hemingway, accepted castration and stoical endurance, which has made him the classical writer for the serious young men of the Organized system.)

Genet pursues his prophetic role with a careful calculation of his audience. E.g., in *Les Pompes Funèbres* the chief person is at once introduced as honorably glorying in a masochistic idolatry for a Nazi soldier occupying Paris, with whom he happily performs what the audience will consider the ugliest possible sexual act. Yet Genet manages to keep confronting the reader with such fullness of affection and of desire to be accepted—and profound thought and remarkable language—that finally the normal valuation is indeed swept away, and there is confusion, grief, and contact.

As the shock of the infantile fright of total abandonment relaxes, the first creative act is to wail, "Help! I am abandoned." This puts it up to the listener. What the method says is this, "I have proved we are *both* lost; therefore, instead of your clinging to a false adjustment, let us cling together." The audience must respond to it by trying to annihilate the outcry, as if it had not been heard, or to prevent others from hearing it. The snub that the audience administers is not, then, one of outrage but of embarrassment before a poor relation, as in the joke where the millionaire tells his butler, "This beggar is breaking my heart, throw him out!"

(2) To an academic critic, the later plays and films of Jean Cocteau seem to bear out the rule mentioned above, that an artist's early work is the advance-guard that is consolidated in his later, standard work. The only problem would be how from such a likely sowing comes such poor fruit. But Cocteau himself has explained his intentions otherwise, and has given his theory of the right direction for advance-guard. We must attend to it, for during this century he has been the advance-guard's chief philosopher.

It is inadmissible, he says in *Foyer des Artistes*, for the poet to allow his audience to be lost to commercial entertainers. The heat of the audience is necessary for the persistence of the artist. Now, what attracts the audience is, in principle, corn, vulgar sentiment. Therefore the artist must at present, with all the honor and truth of genuine art, convey this corn, and so Cocteau has chosen to do. That is, what seems to be curiously stupid standard work is really a daring advance-guard effort to answer the crucial question of how to unmake alienation.

Nevertheless, the works are stupid. "Precisely," the creator might say; "they were not made for you." Perhaps the problem is too hard and the poet is suffering an illusion and undergoing a kind of (profitable) martyrdom. The corn in these works of Cocteau is still alien to himself, he cannot energize it with feeling. To put it bluntly, it is not yet low enough to be quite uncorrupted. (Let me say that in the film *Orphée* Cocteau fortunately gave up the noble program for which he was unprepared, and again made something fine. Plastically and poetically, *Orphée* is by no means equal to *Le Sang d'un Poète* of which it is the sequel, but the grim honor with which it treats its subject—what it means to be the youth-thieving poet now "stinking with money and success"—makes a very poignant work.)

Anyone who chooses this direction, of seducing the audience, must without talking down find a level of subject matter so elementary that he and the audience really share it in common, meaning by it the same thing. There must be such common subject matter, for all of us walk on the ground, breathe, and so forth, and these things are common and not subject to the corruption of self-alienation. Somewhere between this level and the level of shell shock and commercialized sentiment, there must be a border line of subject matter felt by the artist and not quite devitalized in the audience. It is here that the advance-guard must operate. (Is this the intention of the *Nouvelle Vague?*)

As the shock of total abandonment relaxes, the infant reaches out with coaxing and flattery, or with teasing and being nasty, saying, "How can I please you? How can I annoy you?" Trying still to please at too adult a level, Cocteau merely flatters the normal audience without offense. The sanction of the audience against him is to make him a commercial success and appoint him to the French Academy. The advance-guard artist must invent something more direct and childish that will win a smile or a slap of which all are at once ashamed.

(3) But finally, the essential aim of our advance-guard must be the physical re-establishment of community. This is to solve the crisis of alienation in the simple way. If the persons are estranged from one another, from themselves, and from their artist, he takes the initiative precisely by putting his arms around them and drawing them together. In literary terms this means: to write for them about them personally, and so break the roles and format they are huddled in. It makes no difference what the genre is, whether praise or satire or description, or whether the style is subtle or obscure, for anyone will pay concentrated attention to a work in which he in his own name is a character. Yet such personal writing can occur only in a small community of acquaintances, where everybody knows everybody and understands what is at stake; in our estranged society it is just this intimate community that is lacking. Of course it is lacking! Then give up the ambitious notion of public artist. The advance-guard action is to create such community, starting where one happens to be. The community comes to exist by having its culture; the artist makes this culture.

We know that for various moral and political reasons such movements toward community have occurred widely, sporadically, since the war. But no such community can flourish on moral, economic, or political grounds alone, for—whatever its personal satisfactions— its humane integration cannot compete with the great society, however empty it is. As a friend to all such places, I would urge them to attach to themselves their artists and give them free rein, even at the risk of the *disruptive* influence of these artists.

As soon as the intimate community does exist—whether geographically or not is not essential—and the artist writes for it about it, the advance-guard at once becomes a genre of the highest integrated art, namely Occasional poetry, the poetry celebrating weddings, commencements, and local heroes. "Occasional poetry," said Goethe, "is the highest kind"—for it gives real and detailed subject matter, it is closest in effect on the audience, and it poses the enormous problem of being plausible to the actuality and yet creatively imagining something unlooked-for.

An aim, one might almost say the chief aim, of art is to heighten the everyday, to bathe the world in such a light of imagination and criticism that the persons who are living in it without meaning or feeling find that it is meaningful and feelingful to live.

Obviously, if the artist, responsible to his art, commits himself to his bold insight and genuine feeling, and brings it home inevitably to the audience by writing man to man *ad hominem*, the Occasional poetry that he creates is not likely to flatter or comfort. Rather it will always have the following ambiguous effect: on the one hand it is clearly an act of love, embarrassing in its directness, for to give one's creative attention to anyone is a gesture of love; on the other hand, given the estrangement of the aliens from one another, it will always seem, and be, an act of hostility, an invasion of privacy, a forcing of unwanted attention. To the extent, then, that this advance-guard does not succeed in welding a community secure enough to bear criticism and anxiety—and how can a single-handed poet accomplish much?—the sanction against it is absolute and terrible: exclusion from the circle of frightened acquaintances.

7. THE NATURE, ADVANTAGES, AND DISADVANTAGES
   OF ADVANCE-GUARD

Let me now review the course of this argument as a whole. We started by distinguishing advance-guard as a species of genuine art with a social-psychological differentia: that an important part of the advance-guard artist's problem is the destruction of introjected social norms. This explains the peculiar offense of advance-guard to the audience. Tracing the history of the introjected norms and the advance-guard response, we singled out three phases: the phase of the rejection of institutions by naturalistic revelation and hostile withdrawal of feeling; the phase of the rejection of normal personality by experiments on the language (character analysis), arousing anxiety; and the phase of the rejection of self-alienated adjustment by direct contact with the audience, rousing the embarrassments of offered but unwanted love.

We are now in a position to restate more fundamentally the difference between integrated art and advance-guard. What, psychologically, is the meaning of an art that has a sociological differentia in its definition?

We must say, with Otto Rank, that the action of art asserts immortality against the loss, waste, and death in oneself and the world; and the artist appoints himself to the re-creation—who else will do it? Now the advance-guard artist is essentially concerned with the immortal perfection of the particular society of which he is a member, whereas the more integrated artist, taking his environment for granted, is concerned with the universal human condition as embodied in his own problem.

Here too the usual opinion is just the contrary of the truth. The advance-guard artist is considered as going his own irresponsible way, heedless of his audience, and dwelling in an ivory tower. But the truth is that his relation to his audience is his essential plastic medium—so that he is often careless with the material medium; he is excessively socially responsible. On the other hand, the usual sentiment is accurate, for standard art the audience can take or leave, but advance-guard is irritating and obstrusive and cannot be disregarded; it is a loving and hostile aggression on the audience.

In the little history we have sketched, we have seemed to come full circle: in the beginning it was the naturalistic artist who withdrew, in the end it is the shell-shocked audience that withdraws. But throughout there is the attractive and repulsive tampering of the artist and audience with one another. In order to reconstitute a better society within himself, the artist destroys the existing society. This is naturally resisted. Yet people, too, are dissatisfied with their state and want to get on, and they are fascinated by any new direction.

What are the peculiar advantages and disadvantages of advance-guard? We have pointed out that an advance-guard artist must divert energy to an internal problem that is not constructively his own, but only destructively; this hinders an ease of flow and symmetry of form. (In the best cases the parts of an inner conflict are fused and transformed in the coming solution; in advance-guard there are some elements that are merely to be attacked and destroyed.) On the other hand, there is no doubt that his concern for the destruction and reconstruction of society as a part of his art draws on powerful energies of its own, unavailable to standard artists: both the memory of a very early time of satisfactory interpersonal peace—an "age of gold"—and the present-day revolutionary ferment. It is impossible for any artist to ignore the problem of social renovation. In the best, expansive period, all the agents of society are engaged in the renovation, and the artist need not particularly concern himself with it, it "takes care of itself"; that is, he need not inquire where he is man, where artist, where citizen. In other ages, the advance-guard artist "wastes himself" on the social problem—it is his vocation, for it exists within him; but the standard artist ignores it at the price of losing the glancing brilliance of actual relevance (I do not mean the slick shine of commerical relevance), and he may soon become merely academic.

From the point of view of society, again, it is certainly no advantage to be manipulated "for its own good" by artists, and it is even worse when the aim is to make society into a work of art. Yet there is, in life, an important factor that can be called "the art of life"—concern and distress for the style we live—and in a disintegrated culture like our own, very few are busy with it, and among these is the advance-guard artist. And from the point of view of the artist, again, in a shell-shocked society like ours there is a general estrangement, and the artist is estranged, in the sense especially that he feels helplessly without status. But being more conscious of his estrangement, he is really less estranged than the others, and he is used to inventing means of communication, patterns, irritants, bridges; this is his forte.

An artist feeds on fame. It is only this, to quote Rank again, that alleviates his "guilt of creation" by gaining him accomplices. Here the advance-guard artist is in an ironical situation. More than others, he needs accomplices, not only *post factum*, but as collaborators *in delictu*, in constructing the social art-object in a rebellious atmosphere. Yet his hardly veiled hostility and embarrassing love diminish his chance of personal fame and drive off his collaborators. On the other hand, he is less lonely. He more easily identifies himself, with pain, with the whole social framework; and with hope, with its future in young persons.

In America, as we proceed further into the 'sixties, there seems to be plenty of advance-guard writing again; just as for the previous twenty years there seemed to be none. But these judgments of audiences and critics are pretty illusory: they depend on the degree of the audience's own anxiety. When anxiety is very strong, oblivion is a characteristic sanction of the outraged audience; the advance-guard offense is present, felt, and "annihilated," excluded from the possibility of being real. The artists go underground, and when they reappear they bring with them the underground.

Good interim writing—1954

As we read through anthologies like *The Partisan Reader*, New Directions' *Spearhead*, or the English *The Golden Horizon*, it is gratifying and reassuring to find a large number of perfectly durable pieces of fiction written by my generation. Pieces that have "anthology" written all over them, for they are standard and without serious flaw, and they will be, or already are, at home in collections from all times and places. Of course every one of these works is different, for they are genuine and sound out the individual voices of their authors. If they were not genuine they would not be durable. Yet I think we can by now show a class resemblance in many of the best of them that is distinct from any other literature and makes them stand for a generation as its style. Without mentioning individual pieces, let me explore an important property of that common style.

There is achieved a classical objectivity by maintaining a relativity of points of view, instead of, as in previous classical writing, embodying the cultural norm. (We have no such norm; we have a society of subcultures.) In this style there is always the sense of the possibility of telling what is being told from a number of different scientific, philosophic, or esthetic points of view. The event is explicable sociologically *and* psychologically *and* mythically *and* as an existential crisis of the author *and* it is a phenomenon for naturalistic description *and* an occasion for the nuances of sentiment *and* a plotted drama, etc. These points of view are not felt as clashing, nor as if one were more true than the others; rather, all are equally true and, by composing them, the artist conveys what is. Of course, all are not equally explored by every author; the varying weights of handling give the texture of various pieces.

Now, a first effect of such equi-valence of perspectives is that in the composition of the whole each patch, so to speak, is given purely, with its own color, rhythm, and proper articulation. Sections are often sharply and strongly contrasted. A description, say, of what is on the table will be given as a picture or a reasoned catalogue or an ecological detail, not, or not merely, to set the stage, to create an atmosphere, to indicate social class, or to incorporate symbols. A socio-psychological interpretation will be expert and even professional, but it does not reveal any ultimate secret— there *is* no ultimate secret; nor does it necessarily stir to action or give the sense of scientific analysis or case history. Where there is action, the plotting is good, but it does not carry everything away in its climactic surge nor ever come to a great surprise; it too is a colored line in the composition. Indeed, the analogy I keep thinking of is that these stories are like the classical paintings of the past fifty years, where the colors, without admixture of black or white, are laid on in plain sizable patches; the shadows are also pure colors; there is no chiaroscuro; there is an avoidance of illusory depth; and the composition is lovely.

When such parts compose in good pieces, the effect is clear and animated but not dynamic. I do not mean that the stories are static, but rather factually quiet, as if to say, "There it is." The whole is on the surface, for the perspectives are obvious and even explicit, but the effect is not superficial, for the parts have solidity and value. The tone is not warm or climactic, but it is not cold or pointless, rather dry and bright. The reader is not carried away, yet when he is finished, he does not ask, "So what?" Rather he says, "Well! So that's it."

What is this style accomplishing, for every successful style functions as a workable way of making experience hang together? Let us contrast it with various achievements of the previous two or three generations. Our style does not allow for character study and the full-blown drama of passion, for it neutralizes identification. It does not evoke a mood and objectify an inner world, for it is not understated or allusive, it tells everything; its "subjectivity" is frankly objectively auto-biographical. Yet it has neither thesis nor theme, for its thoughts and depictions are limited in their place and application; they are true and worth while, but they do not add up to a case, nor is anything on trial. The authors can be neither foolish nor misty nor profound. It is a style weak in sentiment, for it is neither personal nor antiromantically impersonal; rather it gives the personal and impersonal equal valence side by side. It is useless for the pitiless unmasking of naturalism, with the consequent revulsion and indignation, for it refuses to stick to one color and to the lack of evaluation that is a hostile evaluation; it does not disown the subject matter by keeping it "out there."

So much negatively; and we seem to have exhausted most of what serious readers want from stories. But they can't get what they want. Then, positively what do we have? We have an acceptance of any and all factors and the making of a pattern. Now, making of the pattern *proves* that a pattern can be made. But this is an enormously worth-while contemporary achievement! It proves that art still works. For we are notoriously in an age when all assumptions have been undermined, all standards have been demolished, no one is adequate to the fund of knowledge, we cannot cope with the liberation of repressions, ethics (and/or social science) have not kept pace with the advances in technology. I do not doubt for a moment that all of this is so. Nevertheless, these disarmingly unpretentious but tough-textured art-works show that, as ever, an honest exercise of the senses, the feelings, the wits, and the spirit can make a livable experience. This is not the grandest thing in the world, but it *is* something to go on.

It is interesting to see how this style obviates once-formidable problems of content. For instance, frankness; it is impossible in this style to be pornographic, the surface is too astringent. Where everything is told adequately and that's that, nothing is tendentious. The ugly, again, becomes an interesting shape with a certain weight and certain textural relations. One would say of some of these stories as of certain pictures, "Really very good, but I shouldn't like to live with it on the wall." But most astonishing is the vanishing of almost any trace of irony. By making every perspective actual, what starts out as high sophistication ends up as a refreshing naïveness. The fact that the author is contemptuous or is suffering is part of what he composes, it is not the drive of his composition that emerges with the ending. And, as in a psychoanalytic interview, a nightmare is simply another objective datum. But if, by rare chance, the author has hit on a subject matter in which every point of view yields something beautiful, gentle, promissory, or assuaging, then the effect of this flat and ingenuous mode of composition is paradisal, and readers laugh and weep.

I like this style. It has being and unity and is, in so far, good. It is our duty to learn it and study its successful pieces, for they are ours. Its best writers, like good authors of all times, have learning, observation, sensibility, intelligence, and stubborn individuality and integrity. Yet there is something I do not like. The authors are knowledgeable, but the works do not have enough tendency to explode and shatter the veil of the surface, revealing something that nobody knows. The authors of my generation are withholding their strength, they lack daring and absolute aspiration. There is no hint of experimentation in these pieces; rather there is the knowing use of the techniques, attitudes, and subject matters that our predecessors won for us. This is all very well for a brief interim, but I think that the interim has lasted too long.

Underground writing, 1960

The history of literature is the adding on of new themes and scenes, along with new techniques, styles, and author attitudes. Nevertheless, a special problem is raised by our present tendency to write up, as if in one feverish co-operative effort, everything that is underground and hitherto unmentioned. We apparently want to break down in principle any barrier between underworld and public world, and between what is kept silent and what is literature. Why do we publicize the underworld, why don't we let it remain under?

As with every other spontaneous act in our unsatisfactory era, this effort commences either as a reaction of despair or as a generous gesture of reform; but with astonishing rapidity it is corrupted to the style and effect of the global Thing it means to attack. Because the writers are themselves inwardly betrayed, their frankness rapidly becomes lewd and their impulse to direct action often turns into punk fascism.

To get our bearings, let us recall that in other times the underworld was kept under not necessarily because it was base or shameful. For instance, the ancient

Mysteries seem to have been the important community religion of the Greek folk, far more than was the vastly written-up cult of Olympus. Yet they were by no means for publication, so we have few texts from which to learn much about them. From antiquity through the Middle Ages, even in so verbal a subject as philosophy, the highest tradition of certain sects was passed on secretly from the master only to the disciple who had the right character. And of course in less verbal disciplines, apprentices did not learn from books, and there were no books. Socrates and Plato were dubious about writing things down, and in the Chinese tradition, Lao-tse and Confucius, disagreeing on everything else, agreed on this: "We do not speak about the divine."

In most societies there has been silence or reticence also about much of the middle part of life. Concerning Periclean Athens, for example, I should dearly love to have some direct vital statistics, e.g., what were the free and slave populations? At what age (barring plague) did men die? People simply took such affairs for granted and did not write them up. And of course throughout history nothing is said about happy sex or happy married life, although romantic love, sexual failure, and marital failure have been literary topics par excellence. This reticence does not necessarily mean that sex was considered private or that the societies were antisexual. No such conceptions exist in antiquity, not to speak of many more primitive societies. But what is there to write? It is the kind of thing that you *do*. Romantic sexuality is written up precisely because it touches on what you can't do; it is a kind of completing of unfinished situations. (In so far as sex is an art, however, there is a place for speech and writing and even for how-to-do-it manuals; we have some charming ancient ones. But unfortunately, just where instinct is most distorted, there is the strongest drive for "proving" and impersonal technique rather than for culture and art, and I suppose that our own manuals, at least, often cater to this drive.)

At the bottom of the ladder, finally, throughout most of history, illegal low life has, prudently, not courted publicity. It would have been considered a point not of prestige, as with us, but of simple idiocy, for the secrets of a thieves' or addicts' gang to be exposed and written up. One did not blab. The exceptions are remarkable and force us to speculate. There is evidence that Villon wrote his jargon poems for the *coquillards*, the gang, themselves, as if they were a proper community; yet the poems are published and courtly in form, and they merge harmoniously with his lamentations of low life in proper French and with his standard poems about the general human condition. In his own life, we know, he bestrode the two worlds; the fact that he also did so in writing makes us think of the breakdown of medieval culture, the upsurge of the vernaculars, the disasters of the Hundred Years' War. Villon is an interesting contrast to our Genet, an artist of equivalent stature. Villon surveys the scene of his low life from the point of view of universal humanity; Genet finds animation only in his low life and struggles to find in it some universal humanity. Another obvious example is Defoe, in the seamy age of Walpole. Here we seem to get something more like "modern" reporting.

So we return to our own disposition to write up the unutterable, the unmentionable, and the underworld. I want to explore three different general motives for this, so I won't mention any names, since every writer should be treated fairly as an individual.

2

First, of course, this underground reporting is simply part of our wretched universal reporting and spectatoritis. On the one hand, it is technological. "Objective" reporting of "scientific" data makes no distinction in what it surveys, any more than a camera shies away. In the past history of literature and painting, a new scene, like a new technique, was painfully won to meet a new expressive need; but mechanical reporting eats up every scene omnivorously, and the great presses print off anything that has the format of objective reporting and might sell. The same occurs with the "scientific method" of so-called sociology; any kind of problem "area" is given the works, and the result has no relevance to solving the problem.

Also, we verbalize a lot in this way because active life does not come off for us. It is an easy way of being on the scene without being involved—just as the sociologists can sharpen their tools and work the area without doing any agriculture. In this respect, *Contact* or *Kulchur* or *Big Table*, with their criminal, underground, or Beat issues, are no better than *Life* or *Look*. We substitute journalism for philosophy, poetry, and politics. We regard our existence as though it were already history or nothing better than fiction; and since the essence of existence, its presentness and challenge, is omitted, we get inaccurate history and weak fiction. Thus, far too much gets written, and yet the proper function of letters is neglected or swamped. As part of the popular culture, the scenes of the underworld are like the rest of the chewing gum.

3

A second motive for the publication of the underworld is more promising, but disappointing in the performance. It is that, since the legitimate world has become lifeless and contemptible, we explore in the illegitimate for vitality. We seem to propose, by affirmation and publication, to make *this* the public world or at least an acceptable part of the public world. The need is pathetic, but beggars aren't choosers. It is no news that, just to live on to tomorrow, many of us have to be illegal. (For instance, I have experienced in a lawyer's office that very few of my friends could appear in court as character witnesses. Though they are fine folk, they could not survive a superficial cross-examination. Certainly I could not.) Thus it is probably a wise course to counterattack ideologically and creatively and get everybody used to the dirty words and the illegal scenes. This is a customary job of advance-guard writing.

We must distinguish two contrasting aspects of our illegitimacy. Given our moronic system of morals and property, it is impossible to live without sinning and trespassing; and in the tight organization of modern society, any spontaneous gesture is a threatening nonconformity. Then to be illegitimate may be simply the continuing defiant affirmation of free love, anarchism, progressive education, and productive work like arts and crafts, that belonged to the bucolic age of Greenwich Village. Our difference is that we have come a further step from bohemianism in honest poverty. It is harder to be decently poor; urbanism and technology are still further out of human scale; civil liberties are harder to defend. The result is that, especially among the unseasoned, a larger number resign from the fight altogether.

But also, given the inhuman pressures and temptations of commercialism, regimentation, and community fragmentation, inevitably there are criminality, flight to the margin, and personality disturbances that are not properly efforts for natural satisfaction in difficult circumstances, but are hostile reaction-formations. Such are the spite, conceit, fantasies of power, and the throwing of tantrums that are the usual tone of hipster letters. The kind of reactive vitality that used to characterize delinquent hoodlums now spreads to middle-class, middle-aged gentlemen who can write books; and naturally it rings bells on Madison Avenue, where there is the same resentment of earnest effort.

Rebellious humanism and reactive hipsterism are by nature incompatible. The positive satisfaction of life; or life striving for satisfaction, being frustrated, and becoming angry—these pay off in a real world of real contacts. There is no need to win "proving" victories, to be one-up in every encounter. Conceit becomes boring and violent methods are rarely constructive. Nevertheless, as the case is *socially*, these two aspects of illegitimacy, humanist and hipster, are lumped together and damned together, and often have to live together. It becomes necessary for a writer to vindicate them together. We who simply want community, productive culture, justice, and pleasure understand that, as Kropotkin said, "So long as one person is in prison, I am not free." Besides, some of us suffer, perhaps neurotically, from a thankless compassion that supports the conceited, wasteful, and violent because they are like sick children.

Unhappily, in the peculiar market of publication, bad writing drives out good. Rebel humanism has an unpopular style; it seems never to pose the "problems" that everybody is talking about—how could it, since the problems are falsely posed? Even muckraking, a proper function of humane letters, e.g., disclosure of police brutality, has a miserable way of becoming sado-masochistic, just as "pacifist" films, on the whole, exacerbate violence. But most fatally, serious humanistic writing really *is* old-fashioned and out of touch. Consider, simply, that a man who for years has accurately understood the worth of Hollywood, the networks, and their related world—which soon includes the whole apparent world—and who has treated them appropriately, that is, with contempt and neglect, such a man will finally have little to say to an audience for whom, perforce, those things have been the *only* world, even though known to be a phony world. One cannot understand, for instance, why Nathanael West is admired, for oneself signed off from California with Aldous Huxley. But the young people must regard that world as important, since it is the only one they have experienced, and it seems that West teaches them a possible attitude to survive by.

The mass public, of course, takes to its heart just that aspect of the illegitimate which is reactive to its own official ideology and mores and which, inevitably, shares the same psychology of power, sensation, and success. The seamy scene of hip literature is an attractive forepleasure, and the acting out of every office clerk's conceit and castration complex provides a relevant thrill. This reportage serves the same function for the philosophy of the mass audience as the bathos of Tennessee Williams does for its sexuality. The poet caters to the tender pornographic side, combining lust with punishment; and the hipster prose writer caters to the conceited power side, combining know-how with putting down. This is utterly boring.

In my opinion, there is something dishonorable and exploiting, queasy-making, about hipster writing—and, similarly, much of the school of Sartre. Life strategies that are brutal necessities for folk who are in clear and present danger, and that precisely would not be written up, are toyed with by intellectuals who evoke fantasy dangers so that they can thrill to extreme situations; and indeed thereby they create unnecessary real dangers, as if life weren't hard enough. It sounds as though they were calling up the underground for spite, as a psychological reaction to blocked creativity—not otherwise than the resentful Stalinists of the 'thirties. The rhythm becomes jabbing and the tone shrill; the fantasy is for the cool to seize power, even via Jack Kennedy. But our real need is otherwise. The case is that our society is in a chronic low-grade emergency. To alleviate this, so that outgoing life can revive, requires patience, fortitude, and music; curtly rejecting anything phony, but having faith in abiding goods and powers. Instead, these writers, lacking the stamina of natural strength, cop out and plunge into the pointless brawl.

4

Let me suggest another motive for writing up the underworld that I think is more reasonable. By making all scenes equal, by writing one's situation as it is, whatever it is, writers might hope to get rid of "standards" altogether and perhaps of "writing" altogether. (Unfortunately, the writers who seem to have this motive, e.g., some of the Beats, are both so ignorant and so hopped up, that they don't know what they're after and sell themselves short.)

This is to revive old-fashioned nihilism, to clear the decks. In the nineteenth century, in a scarcity economy, the nihilism was more politically revolutionary and religiously Christian; in the "affluent society" it consists of quitting and being religiously Taoist and pacifist. The aim is certainly not to substitute the underground as a new power, but to form a new community from scratch. I have shown elsewhere that this is a happy direction for an advance-guard.

A nihilist program is a beautifully democratic approach to literature. It seems designed for the millions of the inarticulate who say, "If I could only write, I have a story to tell!" All of the faithful are encouraged to be creative, a very different thing from making whole art-works, the products of a complicated culture. One is permitted to be fragmentary; by learning the trick of spontaneous association, one can achieve exciting poetic moments; by employing the primitive rhetorical devices of repetition, incantation, and crescendo, it is possible to read a scattered page aloud as if one had made a whole poem; and of course by writing "wd" and "cd" and using the slash mark on the typewriter, one is in the swim. Music (bongo) and painting are also Everyman's.

A critic cannot help being bemused, for indeed this Beat art is a remarkable historical product. Consider how the most exquisite efforts of modern art to break free of convention and get back to the elements of expression—one could mention Mallarmé's symbolism, Rimbaud's visions, Pound's and Eliot's fragmentation and pastiche, Apollinaire's and Cummings' ideograms and typography, W. C. Williams' neo-Wordsworthianism, Viennese atonality, Webern's pointillism, Stravinski's and Varèse's percussion, Bártok's rhythm, polyrhythms from Bali and New Orleans, Picasso's abstraction and collage, Matisse's fauvism, Kandinsky's nonobjectivism, Mondrian's and Albers' elementarism, Pollock's action and Kline's gesture—how all of these intensely cultivated sources have met up with the deliberately programmatic realism of Sherwood Anderson, Joyce, Lawrence, Céline, and others, to give a lingua franca to amateur boys. They have a means of esthetically expressing how they are. None of their art is inventive, little of it is any good, yet there is in it a valuable contribution, its very communitarianism, and supported by the sense of a community—the very opposite of the dueling of the hipsters—literature is cultivated as an action on the audience, to increase the community. When they have read their poems at one another, they can barge in for bed and board like Samoans.

Culturally they, and we, are not up to this nihilism. Those who abdicate from the economy and university of the big society become a sect rather than a universal solvent. The "scene" soon becomes a stereotyped subject matter, with monotonous repetition of jejune experiences and standard props, rather than a modest account of just where one happens to be thrown, with its materiality and wonder. Public readings become boringly drunken rituals. And to one's astonishment, the creative community spits with envy at proper writers. The situation is bitterly ironical: on the one hand, we who are cultivated artists and realize how little that's worth (though let me speak no ill of the Creator Spirit) would gladly see our culture relapse into the human community; yet every youth feels thwarted by his writer's block and spiteful because he doesn't know anything.

To sum up: the resigned beatnik publicizes his scene as the only world; the impotent hipster calls up the underworld to put down everybody else; and the technological popular culture makes an amalgam of underworld and public world that is as nourishing as chewing gum. Yet I don't think it is at present possible to return to a classical silence. Our literary task must be to get rid of distinctions altogether and recognize only the human beings as existing.

5

What are the "human beings"? When there are dominant groups and minorities, legal and underworld groups, the minorities and the underworld are necessar-

ily "in the right," for they exist as a repressed poten-
tiality within the dominating majority, and there is
nothing to do with such a repression but undo it. If
they did not symbolize something within the preponderant group, there would be no "Negroes," "homo-
sexuals," or "Jews," but only varieties of people; and
the underworld would be either citizens or frank out-
laws at war with us. Once they emerge into notice as
"problems," the minorities and the underworld are a
lively revolutionary force.

It is an inner boundary that creates dominant groups
and minorities, and the success of a revolution is to
eradicate the boundary, to liquidate the problems. It is
not to give equal justice to different classes—though
justice is always indispensable; it is surely not to transform the downs into ups, which would be simply a
compulsive acting-out of the repressed resentment and
rebellion. To give an actual social example: for the
whites the "Negro problem" is their own psychological
problem, to be psychiatrically treated. (For the Negroes, of course, it is also a problem of personal dignity
and social justice, to be solved by resisting and fighting.) Now the bother with much underground writing
at present is that it is a fetishism of the underground—
it does not eradicate the boundary. Base or noble
properties are assigned to addicts and addiction, or to
breathless violence, or to queer society. This is no different from socialist realism or the religion of Catholic
writers. But no behavior or ideology is in fact such a
big deal; for only the human beings exist. The literary
problem is not to present the scene but to show the
man destroyed, fulfilled, or chastened in the scene.
Also, unless this is done, we do not even get the
scene but only its props, for there is no exploration of
causes and ideals. Some writers, sensing this superficial-
ity, treat the scene as symbolic of "real life"; but this

gambit is bound to be boring, for it requires extraordinary spirituality to write allegory, and the "real life" of these authors is very thin gruel.

To one with any memory or history, it is evident that the need for prejudice, for inner boundaries, goes deeper than the particular content people are prejudiced against at any time. Right-thinking people were just as upset by tobacco as they are now by marijuana. Reading in popular novels of 1880, one eerily senses the same dismay about marriage across class lines that is now felt about marriage across color lines; and, especially among Jews, marriage across religious lines used to be mourned like death. It is as if people cannot feel they exist except by affirming, with a shudder, that they are different from something that they are against.

But to be rid of it, we must *indeed* do without the boundaries. This might mean, for instance, taking it for granted that a chap (like young Freud), busy with God's work and touchingly in love with a well-bred girl, is also sending himself on cocaine, and that's just how it is; or to give a common example, that a splendid teacher is naturally queer for his students. As might be expected, it is just this matter-of-fact attitude that is shocking to the audience and unacceptable to the publishers, whereas any kind of "underground" writing has become perfectly acceptable. The problem for modern writing is not treating some "underground" property, but simply coping with the facts of life with reason, compassion, learning, and imagination.

This brings me, finally, to the dilemma that, in my opinion, is the most serious that faces an earnest writer at present. This is the fact, which I mentioned above, that especially for younger readers the dominant scene in our society—of role-playing, front personalities, and phony achievement—is the only culture and manners that they think they have experienced, it is the "real world," even though they dissent from it. This simulacrum of life is not worth criticizing in detail, and since literature is the criticism of life, there is no function for literature. With regard to this dominant scene, the only possible literary tone is the apocalyptic one, which of course some writers have hit on.

But the case is not so desperate, for the dominant scene only seems to occupy the world. This phony world stays in existence precisely by the tension of an inner boundary: people conform against their better impulse because they are afraid to be different and excluded; and they compel others to the same behavior in order to protect the image they have invested their lives in. It is a structure of conceit made by the polarity of proving and success versus failure and shame; and its characteristic feelings, if they can be called so, are face-saving and embarrassment. In *Growing Up Absurd* I pictured this world as a Closed Room with a Rat Race as the center of fascination, powerfully energized by the fear of being outcaste. If this is so, the underground writing we have been getting is only one more expression of the same world. But contrariwise, if, as I urge, our writers refuse to take seriously the boundaries, the distinctions between respectable and outcaste, and begin to consider only the human beings as real, then even the younger readers must recognize that they too have had a different experience than they thought.

This idea gives a curious literature—I myself essayed it in *The Empire City*—about a kind of real persons living in an illusory system, with such comic and dreadful adventures as then befall them. They are sane; their behavior seems crazy, but it is society that is crazy; but they bitterly suffer, for one lives in the only society that there is. Or imagine this theme in a more elementary work, say, a film about children: we would show nothing but shots of children, laughing children, jumping children, children bawling beat by mamas in the park, children playing ball, children whose hands are slapped because they touch their genitals, children crying themselves to sleep, children in disgrace because they have pissed in their pants in school, children twisting the arms of other children.

Some problems of interpretation: silence, and speech as action

In interpreting a text, Professor Kristeller has recently warned us, we must not read between the lines, or we must do so very grudgingly. (Especially when, as with the pre-Socratics, there is only one line to read between.) What a man meant is what he said. As a student of literature, and even more as a poet, my bias is certainly the same. I have found that by scrupulously saving the minute details of a great text, I have learned new things, my preconceptions have been changed, I have been moved in ways that I had not expected. And as a poet, I have often been impatient when a critic has used my little hard-won book to write a lazy book of his own, without bothering to understand me at all. I sometimes wonder why a critic thinks I bother to write, if my meaning is only the commonplace banality that he reads onto my page— especially when I have explicitly pointed out that it is what I do *not* mean!

Nevertheless, the professor's wise maxim cannot stand as a general rule of interpretation, for it misunderstands the nature of language. In all critical and historical studies there is a kind of regulative principle, namely, that those people made sense understandable to us, they share our common humanity. And it must have been with them, as it is with us, that very often the meaning of a man and his situation is not expressed in speech and even less so in writing. Sometimes it is irrelevant to speak, sometimes one cannot or dare not speak. Sometimes the mere act of speaking is a lie. Sometimes speech is a systematic avoidance of meaning, and sometimes one must speak indirectly. Sometimes speech is the beginning of conveying meaning, but the essential meaning occurs in some other action than speech. All these are commonplaces of ordinary experience, and a critic, coming afterward and looking for the historical philosophical, or poetic essence of a situation, must bear them in mind as likely possibilities. Scholars tend to suffer from a fetishism of texts. To them it is the most obvious thing in the world that the truth and reality of men are conveyed in books. But if we go back to the origins of our Western academy in the Pythagoreans or Socrates, we seem to be told that this is neither possible nor desirable. In the tradition of Lao-tse even vocal speech is suspect.

Speech is not merely a communication of ideas and descriptions from one head to another. Perhaps it is essentially so in the reports of natural philosophy and in accurate journalism; but much more primarily, and for the most part, speech is an action, a peculiar action in a series of other actions, to be explained by all the causes relevant to sequences of human actions. I think we have here one important reason for the immense complexity and the inevitable vagueness and speculativeness of humanistic and literary studies. Not only must they start with the formidable apparatus of philology, logic, and poetics, in order to *have* a text, but then they must go on to rhetoric, history, psychology, and anthropology in order to see how the "literal meaning" *is* the meaning. Scholars may not like the imprecise, but, as Aristotle says, it is the sign of an ignorant man to be more precise than the subject warrants. In our own classical times, let us remember, all such studies were considered as Rhetoric, that is, as occupying a middle position between linguistic and practical analyses.

With this much introduction, I want in this essay to point to three or four contexts in which, bearing in mind the nature of speech, it is necessary, in order to interpret a text, to go beyond the text.

2

Often speech is an irrelevant or inappropriate action. Then, if there is a speech or text to be interpreted, this is in itself problematical. If my friend says, "Please pass the salt," I pass the salt, saying nothing. I might pedantically say, "Here is the salt"; but if I say anything more, I have missed his meaning. This is simple, but consider an only slightly more complicated situation where the misunderstanding of the essential irrelevance of speech is momentous; in my experience, it is one of the hardest neurotic symptoms to liquidate in psychotherapy. Suppose we have the two premises: "I want so-and-so" and "So-and-so is there and nothing hinders." The conclusion of this syllogism is an action, to go and take it; it is not a verbal proposition like "I could take it," "I ought to take it," "May I take it?" or anything of that sort. *Any* verbal statement in such a case is a sign of obsessional doubt, disowning responsibility, or some other neurotic maneuver. (One is reminded of the academic book reviews that exclaim, "What can Professor B. mean when he says, etc.?"— when indeed the professor sits in the office across the hall from the reviewer who could knock on his door and ask him. To be sure, such an action would bring down a vast edifice of protocol in a cloud of plaster. And of course many battles of book reviews have no relation to inquiry, being written for ceremonial reasons or for spite.)

In general, many events will not normally be spoken about and a fortiori not be recorded, simply because a quite different action is relevant. This has no relation to their importance. As I have pointed out elsewhere, there is an almost total absence of plays and poems about happy marriage, for there is nothing to write. Conversely, the vast plethora of romantic literature has been correctly interpreted, as by De Rougemont, to indicate a nonacceptance of the sexual. Let me give a beautiful example of delicate understanding in this line by Johann Sebastian Bach, a powerful interpreter of texts. In his cantata setting of Nicolai's *Wachet Auf,* in the part where the Bridegroom is searching and the Bride is waiting, the duet is in serious opera style. When they find each other, the style is operetta, almost like Sir Arthur Sullivan. But when they *are* together, Bach simply repeats the chorale, and Nicolai's words are, metaphorically, about the Pearly Gates:

> *Kein Aug hat je gespürt*
> *kein Ohr hat je gehört*
> *solche Freude, des sind wir froh*
> *io, io!*
> *ewig in dulci Jubilo.*

The reticence refers, of course, to the ineffability of mystical experience, but it means also that in the connubial metaphor there is nothing more to say. So Bach adds nothing. Here we have a typically Christian text; but along the same line, may I suggest that, with all due respect for the keen scent of the author of *Mimesis,* his comparison of the Christian and Greek texts with respect to the pregnancy of their meaning might fail to take into account that the Greeks were in many ways psychologically and socially healthier than we. They write with a sharp foreground against an empty background because this is un-neurotic perception; a good Gestalt has an empty background undisturbed by repression. The Greeks did not need to fix in literature certain dualistic difficulties which they could still cope with in the travails of the flesh and in the secret mysteries of the community. It does not occur to Auerbach that the Christian *saying* might be problematical. But as Kafka pointed out, "*Man kann nicht Erlösung schreiben, nur leben.*"

To generalize still further, we are faced with the dilemma of the *argumentum e silentio*. The absence of a text might mean that there was no such event. But in some cases it surely means that the event was too frequent, too practical, and too important to get recorded in mere texts. Recall the maxim, "A happy people has no history." This does not mean there is monotony, but that prudent and natural activity is not a matter for records. Consider, for example, how the ceremonial art-works of some of the Polynesians are burned on the day after the festival. And let me again cite a giant of humanistic interpretation, Shakespeare. At the beginning of his Histories he shows us old John of Gaunt as the wise statesman who rebukes Richard II for his bad management, but who is by no means willing to interrupt the legitimate succession to the throne. Then John dies and we are at once plunged into seven plays of bloody civil war. If prudence had prevailed, the poet is saying, there would be no Histories.

As another example of a pregnant *argumentum e silentio*, let me offer a speculation in American history. During the first thirty years of the Republic only 5 to 10 per cent were enfranchised and as few as 2 per cent bothered to vote. But the conclusion to be drawn from this is not necessarily that the society was undemocratic.

On the contrary, apart from the big merchants, planters, clerics, and lawyers, people were likely quite content, freed from the British, to carry on their social affairs in a quasi-anarchy, with unofficial, decentralized, and improvised political forms. It was in this atmosphere that important elements of our American character were developed.

3

But there is a valid and exactly contrary use of the *argumentum e silentio*. There may be no text not because speech was irrelevant compared with some other action, but because speech itself was in the situation so powerful an action that it was forbidden or later excised. This is the case with official censorship. The libelous, whether true or not, is censored because it is an act; the pornographic is censored because it leads to likely acts; the blasphemous because it breaks a taboo in the utterance; political opinion when there is incitement to riot; *lèse majesté* is censored because certain thoughts must not exist—e.g., the deposition scene has dropped out of *Richard II* in the first two quartos. In such cases the interpreter will take the known absence of a text or the evident deletion of certain passages as very significant. But we know from overwhelming common experience that the implicit censorship of social condemnation leads to important reticence or various dodges, like esoteric writing, which then must be read as esoteric. An amusing example is the delicious periphrastic style of Thorstein Veblen which, it has been held, he concocted in order that his students might not have any simple radical proposition of the professor to report home to papa! But the case is more disastrous when, because of absolute social taboo, we are left in the dark on vital information. To mention a case of great importance to a psychologist of art: What sexual outlet, if any, did Beethoven have? Did he at least masturbate? How did he masturbate? Any one who would say that these are irrelevant questions doesn't know what he's talking about. A scholar *must* speculate about them; and yet he knows that, given the kind of texts possibly available from that period, he cannot possibly get textual evidence. Yet he cannot modestly say, "We don't know," because there is only one Beethoven, and we must explain him one way or other. So the scholar has to resort to far-fetched psychoanalytical guesses between the lines, and face the scorn of his critics.

Habent sua fata libelli, books have their destinies. Since, as Kierkegaard urged, a book is the act of a man in a concrete situation, it is often essential to study the public fate of a book in order to understand the weight and bearing of its literal meaning. By and large, where censorship of certain ideas is strong, the ideas are taken seriously. E.g., in Czarist Russia nearly every important political and moral writer was at times in jail or exile. Even if their books appear to be abstractly theoretical, they are implicitly heavy with concrete reference; and the interpreter must explicate this, for it is the meaning that the ideas had in fact for both author and public. On the other hand, the kind of total freedom that we have for such writings may be evidence that reasoned ideas don't much influence our institutions. Indeed, the fact seems to be with us that such ideas can first become effective when they enter the mass media, and it is at this point that they are strictly regulated in style and content. With us it could almost be said that *format* is the chief meaning to interpret. To break the format is the censorable act.

In historical studies the problems of the absence of texts have risen globally as our focus of interest has shifted away from kings, war, and intellectuals to social conditions and everyday morals. Texts are scarce because sometimes such important pervasive matters did not have to be noticed in writing, and sometimes, according to the ideology of the scribes, they were not worthy of being noticed in writing. Historians have then delved manfully for every kind of unlikely laundry list and other relic, and by reasoning, often between the lines, they have made them speak.

4

Next, there are those cases where a text cannot be taken literally because it is deceptive. Most simply: the text is willfully deceitful, slanted, or unfairly selective, as in outright forgeries, propaganda, or histories that are really campaign documents. From the Renaissance on, the exposure or reasonable domestication of such texts, by internal and external evidence, has been the spectacular work of interpretation, naturally sometimes overreaching itself in debunking or in the beginnings of "higher criticism," genre of Reimarus. At its best, however, this cutting of a text down to true size is a typical act of the Enlightenment. It is not reading between the lines but reading with skepticism and sophistication.

But the problem is very different when it is felt that the text is deceitful and the speaker could not help deceiving. He was self-deceiving, or betrayed by prejudice, cultural, or class bias. Or perhaps, to go to the extreme, the whole logic of his thinking and even his perception was such that he *could not* tell the truth or even make sense according to our notions. From the beginning of the nineteenth century there has been an increasing emphasis on this kind of interpretation; consider the spectrum from D. F. Strauss and Marx to Lévy-Bruhl and Freud. The texts are shown to mythologize or ideologize or rationalize, or they are prelogical altogether, really dreams. Then what else is there to do but read between the lines? In the appropriate situations, there is nothing else; but I do not think it is enough understood that this kind of interpretation is *argumentum ad hominem*; it says, "We cannot make sense of the text as it stands, either literally or by internal and external correction; but if we transform the speaker and put him in *our* realm of discourse, then we can see what he really means to say." To make a fair analogy, the interpreter treats the text as if it were psychotic.

Suppose a psychotic holds an idea that is imbedded in his system, and we try to reach him, either to understand what he really means or to tell him what we mean, perhaps to dissuade him from jumping out the window. Ordinary dialogue is fruitless. His logic may be impeccable, or his dreamy logic may seem consistent to himself. More important, there may be no sharing of perceptual evidence; he may blot out what we point to or, more likely, its *weight as evidence* may to him be entirely different. Kinds of facts that are basic and irrefutable in our experience, prove little to him; whereas some chance circumstance is to him vastly significant. When such a man is a patient, the usual recourse in institutions is to physico-chemical or, better, physiological and nonverbal interpersonal efforts to alter the man and so alter the speech. But similar problems arise outside of institutions. A child in a tantrum, a youth in love is unreachable. Whole populations suffer from endemic prejudices or emotional epidemics. In a culture a superstition may have an overwhelming social consensus and so predetermine all thought and literature, like religion in ages of faith or the present-day belief in the omnicapability of Scientific Method to deliver truth or happiness. In such cases one soon despairs of mutual understanding unless there is a change on one or both sides as to what is accepted as reality.

In my opinion, there is great humanistic power in the argument *ad hominem* if it is a two-way affair, if *both* sides risk their unexpressed presuppositions, in a dialogue not of speeches but of men speaking. Some of our best modern criticism has had just this character. As a corrective to the previous attitude that important speech and text had to be reduced to our kind of experience, there was bound to be the response that perhaps our kind of experience is inadequate. To correct Lévy-Bruhl's excessive devaluation of the logic of primitive man, Franz Boas modestly urged that primitive man's syntax and arithmetic are as reasonable as anybody's, if we take them relative to his needs, technology, and institutions. This is plain sense; but at once there follows from it, in Boas's school, that every society, including our own, must be taken as a functioning whole and interpreted in its own terms. The resulting cultural relativism has had, I think, a salutary pedagogic effect for ourselves, leading to a radical unsettling of our own presuppositions. (Of course, such a theory springs from an already unsettled culture.)

Let me give a different kind of example. Albert Schweitzer's interpretations of the New Testament depend on the thesis that those people thought they had a real experience of a new heavens and earth, making them believe things senseless to us. But perhaps they did have the experience; then it is we who are thrown off balance. A variant is the method Buber sometimes uses in *Moses:* the people experienced something so extraordinary that they were threatened with losing their wits; and the texts we have are rationalizing reaction-formations, in order to grip again to our common world. This is like Bergson's ingenious theory that the apparent species are not the forms of life but are the negative impressions of the *élan vital* in inert matter. Using a different metaphor, Karl Barth says that the Bible consists of burnt-out volcanoes from which we may guess the fire that was there—the theory of his *Dogmatics* is that the fire recurs when the preacher ascends the pulpit. Barth explicitly speaks of criticism as a two-way affair: we question the Bible and the Bible questions us.

This is a new kind of theological reading. People started by reading the Bible literally in faith. When it was intolerable to plain sense or rational philosophy, they began to allegorize it. They then subjected it altogether to a rational philosophical reading, "like any other book," as Spinoza said. And now they have come out on the other side of the philosophical reading with a new kind of theological reading. To return to our analogy with the psychotic: the assumption now is that our sane criticism is not humanly sufficient; perhaps the psychotic fantasies of the sacred texts make more sense for our existence after all; they even might be "literally" true if, by grace, one could share their "wholly other" experience. We see again the power of the formula *credo quia absurdum,* and if so, the necessity and plausibility of the formula *credo ut intelligam.*

But more generally, quite apart from theology, it seems to me that the man-to-man encounter, going through the text and beyond the texts, and risking one's own logic in the interpretation, is indispensable for humanism. Especially when texts are weird, repugnant, or foolish, we must maintain the common sensibility of mankind. Experience teaches us that it is very unlikely that the other knew the truth, and it is quite certain that we don't.

5

Most of the readings that we have just been discussing seem to commit the "genetic fallacy." They make the truth or falsity of the texts depend on their origins and backgrounds, whether the text is interpreted as an ideology, a rationalization, a function of its culture, or a reaction to a divine seizure. But I think the situation can be described more accurately as follows: These critics are talking directly not about the truth of the proposition at all, but about the existence of the speech as an act—how and why did it come to be? Compared with this, the truth, in many cases, might not be very important. The test whether or not the truth is important is this: if the origin is exposed or the background is altered, is or is not the proposition dropped? Does it continue to be affirmed or cease to be affirmed? Let me say that to anyone who has practiced psychology and has seen many a stubbornly held true rationalization of vital importance to a patient, as he thinks, simply vanish under analysis because it has become boring and of no practical use to him when he has learned its source, the logic condemning the genetic fallacy is rather trivial in moral and psychological matters. It is a fetishism of propositions. I do not mean that moral propositions are not importantly true or false, but that the importance of their truth or falsity cannot be dissociated from *how* they are held by the man: on what grounds? from what background? were they imposed on him, or self-imposed, or has he really grown into them? The very same sentence that is a platitude when said by any man is importantly true when said by Goethe.

6

Speech is a man's act, it expresses a truth, and it is a real thing in itself. The relations of these are problematic, often ambiguous. Any interpretation makes an assumption about the metaphysical status of its text, whether it is a man speaking, a proposition, or a kind of thing. For instance, when texts are authorities, a characteristic behavior of interpreters is to *save the texts,* as if they were themselves independent things. We know how this often leads to pious fictions of allegorical interpretation, not unlike legal fictions; but indeed the authoritative text *is* a pillar of the immutable social reality, like other laws. But consider how in some of the Zen anecdotes they seem to make exactly the opposite assumption and flout and deride the sacred Buddhist texts; I take it that this is part of the Taoist tradition in Zen, that speech cannot tell the way, for "the Way that can be told of is not an unvarying Way—it was from the Nameless that heaven and earth sprang." Since in this philosophy we want to get rid of ideas, the more authoritative the speech, the more it must be put down. Also, in the main line of Western poetics, from Aristotle down, texts are taken to be things; poems are "like animals whose end is in themselves." To be sure they are also "imitations" and have some relation of truth to a model. The entire history of Western literary criticism is taken up with this ambiguity.

Speech is sometimes interpreted primarily as an action. Let me give a beautiful illustration. When Milton in *Tetrachordon* has to choose between the two possible readings of Malachi ii, 16—"Let him who hateth put away, saith the Lord" or "The Lord saith . . . that he hateth putting away"—his decision is that God, speaking through his prophet, cannot speak of Himself indirectly in the third person, but always speaks full-faced in the posture of command. Milton's method here is identical with Buber's in *I and Thou.* We have seen that in legal interpretations of texts, it is primarily the act and effect of speech, rather than its truth, that has the most weight. But also in the analysis of modern poetry, the poem is regarded first as an act or gesture, or as an act with its effect, and much less importantly as either a self-contained "animal" or as a communication of a model truth.

7

Let me offer an interpretation of my own to show the importance of assuming the right metaphysical status of the text. In the Book of Job the obvious crux, which various commentators wrestle with variously, is that the argument seems to have no logical validity. The poems of the end, Warhorse, Behemoth, and Leviathan, do not refute the hero's reasoned dissatisfaction with the consolations and criticisms of his three cronies. I think, however, that a more careful consideration of a few sentences in the first two chapters will show that any possible "logical" answer would be precisely irrelevant, whereas the movement from reasoning to presentation and action-speech is exquisitely relevant to the problem as posed. (Assuming that the prologue is a later level of the text, I take it to be an ancient, and correct, interpretation of the meaning of the text.)

What do we know about Job? He is a man prosperous and righteous. But his righteousness is peculiar; it is portrayed for us in one detail, i, 4-5: that when his sons have feasted, he cleans up after them and offers purifying prayers, because "It *may be* that my sons have sinned and cursed God in their hearts. *Thus did Job continually.*" We are told no more, but it is enough, for this kind of doubt, projection, and perseveration are unmistakably revealing. This is an obsessional character, as we would say, one who wards off, by repeated rituals that prove his own purity, a sin that he readily projects upon others. By this means he constructs himself an invulnerable righteousness, forgetting that he is a creature in the world. Satan accurately describes him by saying, "Hast not thou made a hedge about him?"—so long as he is prosperous, he will never be touched by life. Further, the peculiar detail of the boils is typical for obsessional cleanliness. Finally, the only other thing that we know about him is his wife's

remark: "Dost thou still retain thine integrity?" (ii, 9).
I take it that this is the angry sarcasm of a bereaved
and despairing woman who has lived long with a self-
righteous, invulnerable, and abnormally unfeelingful
man. We do not read, for instance, that Job weeps at
the death of his sons; he merely performs the ritual
acts. Contrast, e.g., 2 Samuel, xviii, 33, David "went
up to the chamber over the gate, and wept."

The middle of the story follows inevitably. Job's tone
is alternately complaining, resentful, self-cursing, resigned. At no point does he lose control of himself or
the situation, in either bawling or hot anger. His anger
is irritation, the counterattack against the consolers
and critics who attack his invulnerable position. In
principle, rational argument cannot reach him, for in
principle he has constructed himself perfectly in the
right. It is summarized by saying, xxxii, 1, "he was
righteous in his own eyes." Therefore the feeling of all
the characters, and of the readers, becomes impatience.
The three cease to reply to him.

It is this ceasing from the obsessional duel in which
he has trapped them that allows some primary feeling
to occur. It appears in the wrath and enthusiasm of
Elihu, who is defined emphatically as a *young* man
and who says, "Behold, my belly is as wine which
hath no vent; it is ready to burst like new bottles."
(xxxii, 19.) Elihu's tone makes possible the denoue-
ment. He is angry but he does not reprove Job, which
would only throw him back on his defenses. Rather
he invites him forth with his warm enthusiasm, and he
offers him the bait of a mighty identification.

"There are questions," said Franz Kafka, "which we
could never get over if we were not delivered from
them by the operation of nature." Just such a question
is what to do with the stubborn obsessional character
of a Job. It can be touched only by an action. And so
the story climaxes. God confronts him "out of the

whirlwind." (William Smith, giving the Biblical uses of this term, says, "They convey the notion of a wind that sweeps away every object it encounters, and the objects so swept away are tossed and agitated.") God does nothing but present Himself, and He has no argument but the encounter itself: "Here am I, and who are you?" It is therefore at this juncture that the text, preluded by the livelier tone of Elihu, changes in metaphysical character and becomes the spine-tingling poem. The poem is both a vivid *thing* and an action on the reader. To my sensibility, the power of the poem makes credible the incident of the Whirlwind. In the story, in turn, Job is not persuaded by a reason but moved by a fact, and so repents.

The one point I would here make is that the powerful poetry of the climax of Job is conclusive just because it is poetry, a kind of presentation and action; whereas, given the character of Job, any continuation of argument in a lower-pitched language would come to no conclusion. Job is changed because he is moved. As it is set up, he is done poetic justice by having a great fact to identify with; in comparison with which, his own stubborn self-righteousness, heroic though it was, was a small thing. Therefore the work has a happy ending.

Interpretation of this text, then, must also flexibly change in its assumption of the nature of the speech. The interpretation of the argument must test the logic of the argument; interpretation of the poem must prove the excellence of the poem; and the interpretation of the whole must be a kind of philosophy of language that can unify both reasoning and feeling, truth and act.

We are here touching on one of the most puzzling, never finally resoluble, problems of the human condition, the relation of knowledge and ethics. There is no doubt that the thinking of prophets, scientists, and artists has been powerfully normative for behavior. Nevertheless it is a fair challenge to ask how any proposition about reality can possibly be normative; how can we get from "is" to "ought"? Modern logicians tend to deny the possibility and to hold that ethical sentences are, ultimately, not propositions but commands or expressions of feeling. There is a pathos in this positivism, for these philosophers are dedicated to natural science, yet their logic makes it unthinkable to develop a naturalistic ethics. Then the search for truth and the searchers for truth are at the moral mercy of any kind of venality, fanaticism, bullying, or caprice.

But the case is less desperate if, as we have been urging, there is always a complex relationship between act and truth, between speaker and speech. Logical validity depends on what we take sentences to be, how much is to be included in the meaning of the sentence. For instance, the statements of scientists are behaviors of a character of men, and that character has very often been, we know historically, normative in the most crucial matters, hostile to superstition, humble and loving toward nature, and frank to publish for the consensus of all observers. Whether or not we can logically ground ethical sentences depends on how complexly and humanly we take our primitive propositions, how much of the speaker and his behavior we want to include in their meaning. Further, it is certainly false that feelings and emotions have no cognitive value; they are structures of the relation of organism and environment, and they give *motivating information* (how else would an animal survive?). And even more, by the working up of feelings and emotions into articulate literary speech—which is a storehouse of perceptions and memories, nicely discriminating and structured from beginning to end, and, not least, embodying the social wisdom of the vernacular—we are given ethical premises grounded in the nature of things. Indeed, if we consider the human sciences, we may say that the concrete "complex words" of stories, plays, and eloquence are more adequate observations and hypotheses of reality than any formulae and samplings of psychologists and sociologists; but besides, they are exemplary and moving. In brief, students of poetry, history, philosophy, and natural philosophy, do not *in fact* find the gap so unbridgeable between "what is the case?" and "what ought we to do?"

Vocational guidance

In vocational guidance there is a necessary conflict between economists and educators. The economist studies how the economic and technological machine is running and will be running for the next ten years, and he advises how much labor and what kinds of skills will be in demand. He tests for aptitudes to man this machine better. He does not omit the factor of individual satisfaction, since it is evident that workmen are more efficient when the work suits them, just as it is now understood that enterprises are more efficient when working conditions are better, when there are better interpersonal relations and more security. (Relations would be still better if the workmen identified with the enterprise as their "own," but persistent efforts of social engineers to create such a feeling have not been very successful, being too much at variance with the facts of present-day management.) In general, the aim of economists is fairly high use of the productive capital, fairly full employment, and a good rate of expansion.

An educator, on the other hand, attends to the

young persons who are to man that machine, and so he has a different aim. He is interested not merely in a boy or girl's finding a job, making a living, and adjusting to society's needs, but also in each individual's actualizing his powers and growing up into a worthwhile person. He deals in longer-range considerations than the economist. He takes into account family and cultural background, and he forecasts the forty or fifty years of working life. He is likely to deal in vague heuristic concepts like "nature" and "alienation from nature," to indicate whether or not a job is a good one for a young person. If there is a good "flowing" relation between a person's nature, background, education, and work, the work will be done with force, grace, intelligence, spontaneity, and inventiveness; it will be a major factor in happiness. But alien work is betrayed by behavior symptomatic of not belonging or pressured conformity, of lack of interest, of merely playing a role or having a job. The ideal is for a youth to find a vocation, a kind of work in the community that is his identity and provides a structure for his life, a use of his powers, a sense of being justified. When the educator tests for skills, therefore, his purpose is to find a job in the economic and technical machine that will be an opportunity for growth. He may urge a youth to try his hand at various likely jobs until he hits on the one that brings out his excellence. And if, as happens, there is no right job in all the *Occupational Handbook*, this is not taken as a failure of the youth, although he is economically a dead loss. The educator—now perhaps called a psychologist—simply redoubles his efforts to bring him out with productive noneconomic activities—now called occupational therapy. In the long run, the aim of the educator is to produce not merely full employment in an expanding economy, but also a productive and inventive society of workers with a noble standard of life.

Such an educator cannot be easily impressed into the service of Society; he must be in conflict. He has a twofold task: to protect the developing human powers that are abused by many of our ways of working, and therefore to try radically to alter much of our economy and society in order to build an educative society. This seems to be very impractical, but is it? Fundamentally, our chief resources are our human resources. If we waste them by having people work at a tiny fraction of their capacities, it is a poor bargain to gain an efficient, even automatic machine—not to mention the morbidly destructive social effects of alienated labor, anomie, delinquency, the sensationally useless American standard of living, and so forth. I do not at all mean that a highly scientific industrial technology is necessarily inhuman and produces anomie; on the contrary, I am persuaded that a scientific, technical way of life can be powerfully cultural and part of a noble humanism. It can be rich with meaning for all its workmen, rather than empty of meaning except for a few top managers, planners, and technicians. This was the ideal of Proudhon, Prince Kropotkin, Karl Marx, Thorstein Veblen, John Dewey. How to implement the ideal in each era of technology must be studied. It is not machines that hurt us but how we use them, our technical and social arrangements, and our low standards for the jobs themselves. By and large, nobody is at fault for our present plight; we have not yet learned how. Modern conditions are too new. But we are at fault if we continue to avoid the problem as a crucial one. Therefore there *ought to be* a conflict between the educators and the engineers, because this will lead to experimentation and finding solutions hitherto unthought of.

Let me mention an example of disagreement within pedagogy itself. Confronted with the emergencies of the Cold War and the need to expand the economy, Dr. James Conant surveyed the junior high schools and the high schools. On the basis of tests and grades, he decided that only 15 per cent of the youth were academically talented enough to study sciences and mathematics. He felt that most should have a realistic vocational training aimed at the actual industries and other jobs in their communities. Characteristically, he was much concerned about centralizing and enlarging the schools in order to have better equipment and more uniform standards. In all of this, Dr. Conant was acting the part of a social engineer.

Remarkably different was the attitude of the conference of distinguished scientists and teachers of science that met at Woods Hole in 1959 to decide on methods and curriculum for teaching science in these same primary and secondary schools. (The conference has been reported in Jerome Bruner's *The Process of Education*.) Since these men were interested in producing scientists and not test passers or technical assistants, they concluded that the methods must be classical progressive-educational methods, unblocking intuition, giving the youth confidence in himself, learning by doing, working with the life interests of each age group. The curriculum, they said, must comprise big structural ideas of the field, not the accumulation of the latest facts and theories. They want to produce men with the habit of science, as Aristotle would have called it, who see the structure *in* their present world, who do not merely know all *about* it. These scientists and educators do not seem to be much concerned about equipment or standard performance—indeed, they encourage guessing—but they insist that the primary textbooks and demonstrations must be prepared by the giants of science, since only such men can convey the simple underlying structures. And with regard to the aptitude of the kids, they insist that almost any child at any age can grasp the most advanced conception. "When I teach well," says one, "I find that seventy-five per cent of the students are above the median!"

Now we cannot call these Woods Hole people "impractical"—they know what they are after, and how hard it is to get. What I would suggest is that, in the broader field of all jobs and vocations, and not merely the scientific, we might well imitate their thinking.

2

I can propose three or four "impractical" notions that would facilitate the flowing relation of nature, culture, and work, so that our machine can be manned by grown-up men and women rather than by cases of arrested development and resignation, or thwarted and resentful potentialities.

One thing that is overlooked by placement engineers is the meaningfulness of the job as such: is it *worth* doing, is the product good for anything? They are so concerned about the economics of the system that they forget that objective utility must be the chief structure and chief motivation for work. When even simple utility is absent, naturally everything degenerates to status seeking and emphasis on methods rather than goals. Young people are quite simple-minded about this. We see that in emergencies, almost everybody comes across with remarkable spirit. But it is impossible to tell oneself, "During the forty years of my working life, I shall spend six to eight hours a day doing what is no good," without profound resignation and alienation. Consider as an ideal case the work camps for youth, whether the Civilian Conservation Corps, or the camps sponsored by Senator Humphrey, or Quaker Youth for Service, or even camps for delinquents: in all these, it is felt that the work must be unmistakably socially useful, whether conservation or urban renewal or painting a poor widow's kitchen. It is only such work that makes a youth feel that he is indispensable and becoming a man. Yet in our present nicely expanding economy, many a job cannot meet this standard.

Another sad fact is that, in many jobs as we do them at present, a person is too small a cog in the machine; he does not know enough what he's doing. Psychologically, for creative experience it is not necessary to know the whole—that might even be a hindrance to growth —but one must know a large mind-sized chunk. Yet our present minute subdivision of labor is not inevitable; indeed, in very many cases it is demonstrably inefficiently centralized, for instance. We must figure out other technical arrangements, more opportunity for the individual to work on, and train for, larger wholes. And he must have more opportunity to criticize and make inventions. Let us keep in mind the wisdom of the Woods Hole scientists, that it is the big structural ideas that are absorbing, motivating, confidence breeding, and stirring to initiative.

This brings me, alas, to an idea that is even more impractical. What is wrong with our society is, in the end, not the kinds of jobs it offers, for nearly all of them are potentially worth while and useful. It is how people work on their jobs. They are not *allowed* to make them useful. It is no secret that initiative is discouraged and common sense often outraged. The use of a man's full energies and capacities is severely frowned on, and plain honesty will sometimes get him fired. Let's face it, the educator who believes in productive life as a great means and goal of human growth will find himself inculcating in the young attitudes of sincerity, understanding, and initiative that will sometimes get them fired. It happens that I am often called to talk to the students of architecture and community planning at various schools. We, and the members of the faculty, agree that it is invaluable training for a young architect to learn to criticize the program for a project rather than merely to carry it out; for the program is often misconceived, based on ignorant assumptions, and it sometimes needlessly prevents a handsome and workable solution. "But what," I ask, "when you are in a big office and the building you have to work on has a bad plan, or the City Planning Commission has hired you for some Urban Renewal that is socially disastrous—ah, then what?" Our present tendency to centralize and departmentalize is unusual in its effect of excluding, muffling, or baffling original, gifted, and outspoken men.

Finally, I want to make an obvious, but neglected, psychological comment about "getting a job" altogether, especially as it applies to a poor youth in our society. For school drop-outs, unemployment is regarded as predelinquent. The youth who "gets a job," however, is considered to be on the right track and making a normal adjustment. Certainly he is not then a social nuisance, and he does gain some independence from his family. Nevertheless, if the job is not worth while or suited to the young man, and therefore is not educative and does not provide him a new structure of values, "getting a job" tends to be merely a response to the internalized superego demand, "Go out and support yourself," and this is an important factor that keeps him psychologically adolescent. The job may soon rouse a resentment that is often lasting and channeled against later married responsibilities. (I think this situation is often a contributory cause of alcoholism, which spites the demand.) On the job, the youth, unprotected even by a union, acts out a relation with the boss that is little different from his childish relation to his father. He is tied to the job, just as he was to his home. Conversely, he rebels against the job out of resentment. Either way, he has no freedom to make rational choices. So the chance of growth through real work and of finding identity in vocation is muddied up by irrelevant emotions, rather than fired by relevant emotions. Nor does it help if the youth enviously sees his more fortunate peers continuing in school and going on to better jobs. Surely we ought to keep all this in mind and manage better.

These are radical ideas. The criterion of socially useful work attacks our profit system. The criterion of a job that exercises capacities and offers a field for real training and subsequent initiative is pretty close to Syndicalism, it threatens management. The need for sincere criticism and energetic performance undermines the conformity of our bureaucratic corporate system and the feather-bedding of labor unions. To support our poor youth requires a better community than we have. Naturally, then, an educator to whom these are basic considerations is in conflict.

It is a troubling situation. For a youth to grow, there must be a fairly stable environment; one cannot change too much too fast. There must be a going concern for him to take his place in. Yet at present that going concern is simply not good enough.

Youth work camps

The idea of work camps for unemployed teen-agers has always been attractive, it has somehow seemed "right." So it recurs whenever, as now, the competitive labor market begins to fail these youth. The camps are first set up as a facility for delinquent youth—the first such camps in California antedated by a few years the Civilian Conservation Corps of the Depression, and now in New York we have set up delinquent camps. Then they are proposed for "predelinquent" youth; and then for all who are not easily employed though otherwise unproblematic. Various reasons are given. The camp situation is therapeutic for the emotionally disturbed; it gets them out of their (and our) environment. Work is therapeutic. Youth are taught work habits and even particular skills that serve them on their "return to the community." And public projects like conservation are carried through. (Indeed, the actual productive work done proves—surprisingly, as in the case of the CCC—immensely valuable; it was an economic use of human resources otherwise wasted.)

These arguments are sound, but I do not think they

hit the essential "rightness" of the idea of work camps, which is simply: that *there is an intrinsic relationship among middle adolescence, living in camps, and the need for work and a certain kind of work.* Camps and the right work are not, for that age, a device for an emergency but are a natural institution of society. One does not "return" from them to the community, they are part of the community, akin to the Youth House of primitive cultures. Under certain conditions, parts of the complex are informally provided in the active community itself, for instance, when the city itself has real vocations and there is a general institution of apprenticeships. But at present it is worth while to explore this philosophical idea of the youth work camp, because it is a standard to judge what is wrong with our own community and its work.

To begin with, a residential camp is a subcommunity away from the parental home. In America we are so committed to the psychological value, if not sanctity, of the family that we have insensibly slipped, in modern urban and technological conditions, into the error of a later and later "maturity." The mayoral prescription to curb youth by stricter home supervision is not only unrealistic but disastrously unhealthy. Consider the trap that American youth is maneuvered into: they are put off to a later and later sexual maturity and independence, and forced into an earlier and earlier career choice. There is no period for adolescence.

The community of youth must exist in a certain sociological isolation from the massive adult world, it must have its own rules. In principle this does not require the country or forest setting that is the usual image, though that has obvious attractions; a street gang isolates itself very well. We shall see that many youth-valuable and socially-valuable work projects require being in or near town, and therefore every effort should be made to devise an urban residential camp.

A difficulty is the wildness and in-groupness intrinsic in any transitional stage. Hell-raising and the need for space are good things, but how to institutionalize them? (In Scheme I of *Communitas* my brother and I therefore locate all the high schools and junior colleges in the forest belt.)

A second interesting property is the mean size of the camps. One is struck by the unanimity of the writers. "A delinquent camp," says the latest manual (George Weber), "should be limited to a maximum of 60 boys, and fewer are desirable." By law, California delinquent camps "must not exceed 100 in population, including staff." (Lee Cary.) The two delinquent camps in New York number 50 and 60. The CCC nondelinquent camps averaged 110, but the discipline was admittedly too military. Senator Humphrey's proposed camps will therefore average 40 to 50. One is reminded of the kind of figure mentioned for a residential progressive school, 50 to 100. Clearly in this median figure, not too few and not too many, there is implied a face-to-face community where everybody knows everybody; and yet there is a complexity of social relations beyond cliques or even gangs, so that a youth must learn to take himself also as a public person. Living together in such a community provides a continuum between intimate acquaintance and the public self, the citizen. In modern mass-society, this is the school of democracy, and possibly there is no other school.

It is relevant to leave home during *middle* adolescence. The youth is now past the anxieties of the onset of adolescence (age 11-14), which might still require, as our Mayor says, "the love and warmth of family affection." Now there is sexual and self-affirmation, and therefore fights at home. Contrast this period with the much earlier "separation from mother" (age 6). That was part of finding oneself in friends like oneself, ultimately in one's gang and uniform. But the break during 14 to 18 consists in finding oneself in the public real world.

The crucial question is this: *What can give structure to this new identity, to replace the parental identity?* And the answer I want to suggest is: *Objective productive work, leading to the discovery of unique vocation and career.* On such a view, a man's work and kind of work are as important to him as in Luther's religious view that "a man is justified by his calling." Yet our society does not think about it!

2

Go back a moment to comparison with the primitive Youth House. This is a community of peers, but there is no need to provide for it an objective work, for *all* the work in such a community is cultural and useful and performed co-operatively or with a simply understood division of labor. From early childhood the youth has already been involved in it, trying out various skills.

Our nearest equivalent to such normal growing-up is, perhaps, middle-class youth going off to schools and colleges, continuing the academic work they have done since childhood and learning the verbal and symbolic skills of a bookish and technological adult world. They do not have a very communal Youth House in their schools; and their careers, and academic preparation, do not, for the most part, have much flesh and blood. Yet they are our model for the unproblematic in the "automated society."

For noncollege youth, however, merely "getting a job" is *not* unproblematic, it does not provide objective productive work. As I have pointed out above, it does not provide a normal next adjustment. For the wrong job, just to get a job, *prevents* growth. The job gives economic independence, but the employer turns into a substitute father, and the youth (and man) repeats the pattern of resentful dependency. Further, the job market being what it is, the job rarely has any relation to aptitude. If there is "guidance," it is of the sort that tests him to see where he can be useful in the economic machine, chopping off an ear or finger if necessary. No effort is made to find the job that will be useful for him, and there is no chance of trying out useful possibilities. (Why, at least, is the underprivileged or the nonbookish boy not given vocational scholarships, for exploration and training, if the college boy is given aid?) Finally, the job is not presented to the youth as a worth-while occupation with useful products to be proud of; often in our society the enterprise is not worth while, and the products are useless.

It is remarkable how both informed opinion and popular sentiment have insisted that the camp work have exactly contrary characteristics. The product must be publicly useful, manly, and admirable; conservation, planting trees, stocking ponds, etc., have this popular image. To say it wryly, the CCC jobs, like the WPA, were not allowed to compete with private "enterprise"; that is, the boys could not work for profits and be useless, but had to fall back on the worth of the products. One hears touching tales of the CCC boy returning twenty-five years later with his own son to point with pride to the park pavilion he helped build. And indeed, in some cases, like the Red Rocks amphitheater in the Denver Rockies, he might well be proud, for it is a lovely thing.

Further, the notion that work is an "experience" and that skills should be tried out as part of education, is considered an advantage. Variety of work, such as domestic work and field work, is considered an advantage. The work is done co-operatively or in a division of labor arranged by the community; this helps make it one's own work. The youth is paid—typically, the army minimum for enlisted men—only so that he can have spending money; his support is his by right as a member of the community. How strange it is that the excellent things that the public insists on for work camps seem to be irrelevant to the ordinary jobs in society!

In all these ways, we can speak of productive work as providing an objective structure to replace the family authority. There is the background of a community of peers, but the work is something more than the interpersonal relations of the camp. It is a real project to grow on, to *project* on, in the real world, to find one's identity and hopefully one's vocation.

(We can see here the structural defect in the street gang. Being cut off from the adult real world, where the future values are, its enterprises are marginal and it has to make a structure of its own interpersonal relations: pecking order, enforced loyalty, and finally gang fighting with its similars.)

3

There is a sharp distinction between the meaning of work in the delinquent and the nondelinquent camp. In the delinquent camp, work is a therapeutic discipline, precisely to impose an authority and "reality principle" where just these are lacking, perhaps in the so-called psychopathic personality. Such work must also be useful, not made, work, in order to build self-respect, for the youth says, "I have done that, therefore I am." Naturally I am speaking of good camps, not reformatories, where the work is likely to be either punishment or slave labor. In a nondelinquent camp, however, the work is an end in itself, as process and product. The youth does not strengthen his ego against the discipline of work, but "loses himself" and grows into the work, to find himself new and larger on the other side. This entails, of course, programming great jobs of work.

So far the programmers have not been very inventive; they are bureaucrats and haven't called on inventive people to help them. Even conservation, which is always first-rate, has usually not been made cultural and meaningful enough by scientific explanation and experiment led by the neighboring university.

Youth needs counseling and guidance, and here again we can distinguish between delinquent and nondelinquent guidance in terms of the meaning of the work. The disturbed delinquent—let me hasten to say that many committed "delinquents" are by no means disturbed but have gotten into trouble by influence of environment or even simply bcause society has foolish rules—the problem of a disturbed delinquent is likely to be inability to work at all, for he resists the objective demands of any job. He feels inferior and absents himself. A counselor will not then try to get him to work, but will use the lapse to explore his personality. Obviously in a good delinquent camp, the productive work cannot be the goal, for, temporarily, *not* to do the work may be in the boy's interest. In a work-centered camp, however, counseling is the same as good work-supervision: it springs from the product and the process and aims at discovering further vocation. A young worker may lack interest in the product as worth while, and the therapy for this is cultural: giving information, showing meaning and importance. Or a boy may work badly; e.g., a boy who inhibits his aggression and has tight shoulders may not know how to drive a nail with confidence and beauty. The best therapist in such a case may be a master craftsman, who loves the making, the style. He will not need to explore problems of personality, for they project and heal themselves in the art and craft. After a while, more formal vocational guidance may be added, informing the youth what jobs are available for him in the future, how to get them, where to get further training. Perhaps he will want to return to school, for which he has now discovered his own use.

I have thus in an abstract way brought together the problems of a stage of adolescence with the need for residential camps with a program of real work. Leaving his family and choosing a community of his peers, a youth finds a structure to replace his parents in objectively valuable work, till he finds identity and vocation. So the youth camp is, in type, an institution of normal society.

4

Paradoxically, the success of a great program of work camps designed for the advantage of youth depends on the worthwhileness of the work projects for the community at large, since only the community can give objective cultural norms. In principle, the invention of a master program of projects is prior to the location and staffing of camps, and provides their context.

How topsy-turvy our thinking is! When we benevolently worry what to do with the millions of dropouts (35 per cent of the high school population), we start with this "problematic youth" and try to find employment useful for them and useful for society; and perhaps we hit on the idea of forest work camps, postponing for a year the question what they will do when they "return to the community." Surely the normal procedure would be the reverse, to think what we need for a better quality of life and to rejoice that we have these new human resources to help meet the need.

There used to be an organization called the National Child Labor Committee, to protect youth from being exploited by parents and profiteers of industry. This organization has now changed its name to the National

Committee on Employment of Youth, to protect youth from wasting away unemployed. We are in a unique dilemma. Given our "surplus productivity," we might do well to aim at a large *planned* paid unemployment, as Galbraith has suggested. No politician would dare this proposal, yet to judge from the lax boondoggling and expense-account "production," it seems to be the undercurrent of public thinking. And there is a general acceptance of the desirability, or at least inevitability, of automation involving unemployment grossly underpaid (by social insurance and dole). Yet it is also felt that especially for youth and the aged, who are the least employable, unproductive life is a moral and psychological disaster!

Consider our dilemma as a problem of administration and finance. Like any communities, the Work Camps are multipurposive. Their advantages are ecological, educational, moral, economic, judicial. Therefore it should be easy to get funds for them from several groups. But of course the opposite is the case: since many will be benefited, nobody is competent to administer or responsible to finance. This difficulty of coping with any multipurpose enterprise, any community, is a fair index of the state of our society. In a great city there is a plethora of community problems— housing, delinquency, traffic, schooling, unemployment, etc., etc. These are dealt with by a bewildering maze of departments, but there is no community plan— even though the problems *cannot* be solved in isolation, for the isolated "solution" of one problem (housing) in fact aggravates the other problems (traffic, delinquency). The normal approach, "This is irrefutably a fine thing, so let's get together and do it"—this is precisely infinitely difficult for us. And when by exception a great multipurpose enterprise like the TVA *is* implemented, with whatever crippling safeguards, it is a wonder of the age.

5

We do not invent great programs, because not enough *mind* is put to the task. It is not to be expected that the departments of Labor and the Interior, or even a county administrator of Correction, will dream up remarkable work projects. A fine architect might, and might even do it gratis as a patriotic action, but we do not much rely on such men and such motives. Students of architecture at the university might think up something for youth to build; out of fifty of their inventions, one might be both remarkable and feasible. But the university is not on speaking terms with the government. Or in another genre, a social case worker might have a most vivid sense of some alteration or installation that would make all the difference to a harried family, and that youth could do. (This is the line of Carl May's Youth for Service; e.g., "The boys built a retaining wall at a neighborhood center. They scrubbed the kitchen and painted the bedroom and bath at the home of two elderly sisters.")

Camps have usually been located in a country or forest setting, for conservation, park maintenance, the construction of recreational facilities. But urban conservation and urban renewal are equally important. And most important, to my mind, is that fifty thousand small towns in America are ugly, shapeless, and neglected—nowhere to belong to, nothing to be proud of. These will not in fact be improved by private promoters whose notion of a community center is not a green but a supermarket. Maybe some of them can be improved by artists and youth.

There is another valuable kind of work, the living theater, where youth can work as builders, stagehands, and actors. To offset the standardized mass communications, we need hundreds of Little Theaters throughout the country. These would not ordinarily be thought of as work-camp projects, but why not?

I am suggesting a very broad spectrum of projects; and this is why. We are at a crisis in America, when we must either improve the quality of our life or begin to give up. The idea of work camps as an adventure for all youth, as a normal institution of society, is itself a new quality of life. In such a ferment, of real community, real work, and real goods, bubbling up in every likely and unlikely place, we could tolerate the system we have. I am not sure that the youth "returning to the community" would tolerate it, having known better. But increasingly they do not tolerate it anyway.

Crisis and new spirit

A recent sampling of the students of a high school in the East found that "25 per cent of the freshmen, 30 per cent of the sophomores, 62 per cent of the juniors, and 70 per cent of the seniors, admitted cheating on tests." (The poll was honorably published in the school paper.) It would seem that the school itself teaches the boys and girls to cheat. But now let me explain that this school is not a blackboard jungle, but comprises the highest academic talent in a populous region, selected by examination. The cheating is not to pass rather than fail, but to get 97 rather than 94. The reporter of the poll says laconically, "As college pressure mounts, so does the crime rate." And let me quote another score: "69 per cent have already decided on a career—among the seniors 79 per cent. Forty-six per cent have chosen science." This is at fourteen to sixteen years of age!

To these children, it is clear by these melancholy figures, American society is already a tightly organized system. One must get good grades now; the rewards at the further end will be, for many of the 46 per cent, good jobs in Westinghouse, Bell, one of the drug companies, or the Pentagon. The school issues frequent administrative bulletins warning against black marks on "Your Permanent Record" that will jeopardize Careers. We can imagine how the kids tremble when they cheat.

Addressing the students, I proposed that the grading was a bad idea; but many of them defended it, asking, "How else can we get into the prestige colleges?" It did not occur to them that anything in the system could be changed. I became indignant; didn't they want to become *scientists?* and I told them the conclusions of the Woods Hole conference on the teaching of science, that learning to be a creative thinker is a kind of experience that cannot be graded on IBM machines or taught by teaching machines. It involves an adventurous and progressive-educational approach to nature, whereas grading is simply an in-built teaching machine for answers, reinforcing the conditioning by fear. Yet I felt guilty about disturbing the boys and girls, for they were trapped. A few weeks later I had the opportunity to address the parents and give them a piece of my mind. It is their pressure and their way of life that entrap the children; let *them* change things.

When Dr. James Conant proposes that in the interest of a "new national concern," less attention should be centered on the "individuality of each child," and that the fraction of bright children must be induced to take sciences—has he thought it through to anything like the situation I have been describing?

2

I have chosen this account of a high school to start a discussion of present-day morale in the colleges, in order to get a broader context, of the kids in the parents' world before college. It is the same world in which, after college, they will meet the criminality of the General Electric and Westinghouse executives, the outrageous pricing by the drug companies, the hoaxes on TV, and so forth. Business peculation, like cheating on examinations, did not begin yesterday. But it used to be a neurotic aberration or an act of ruthless ambition. Now it is felt to be intrinsic in the grading and career system itself. Let me quote college students on this. When the executives of the electric companies were jailed, the student paper of the Harvard Business School said editorially that these men were "placed by society and the pressure of capitalist conformity in a position where they can succeed only by violating the laws."

Consider what this means. There is a system of corporations and public relations which pre-empts all opportunities; apart from it there are no careers. Therefore it exerts an irresistible pressure to succeed according to its mode of grading, no matter how.

In this context we can quickly dismiss with deserved contempt a criticism of the colleges that we have been hearing from the so-called "neo-conservatives" and the Luce publications. The colleges, they claim, undermine morality by teaching that there are no fixed and universal values. In courses in anthropology they teach that ethics are relative to patterns of culture. Existentialism is atheistic, it denies man's essential nature. Logical positivism reduces knowledge to empirical probabilities and asserts that ethics consists of emotive commands. (In the 'thirties, historical materialism was the culprit. When I was a boy, it was Darwin and Nietzsche.) In the words of Vivian Grant, who was a gifted young disciple of Ayn Rand, "What the content of today's education has accomplished is to destroy the student's confidence in his own mind. Today's 'intellectuals' are persuading the student that thought is futile." My favorite among such sentences, however, is the pronouncement in *Time:* "The ultimate cause of anxiety in the United States may be pragmatism. . . . It leads to the notion that philosophy, the search for truth beyond mere language or mathematical symbols, is impossible. Few things could produce more anxiety in people who either believe in, or want to believe in, a moral order." This is really vulgar. Later in this discussion I shall try to show that a couple of these wicked philosophies are probably the only possible moral regimen for the youth of today; but *Time* is interested in debater's points and not social facts.

Really, it is not necessary to look in philosophy for the causes of futility. It is demonstrably the present dominant system of society (including the Luce publications) that leads young people to feel that thought is futile, since change is impossible and it is dangerous to be oneself. But to be sure, the colleges do abet the evil. It is because they do not stand out *against* that system of society, but adopt its style and, alas, cooperate with its aims. The University is the bearer of our ancient culture, of pure science, of the universal community of mankind; of the disputation of the Middle Ages, the scholarship of the Renaissance, and the critical spirit of the Enlightenment. It is this University that, almost entirely in many cases and somewhat in all cases, allows itself to become a mere granter of degrees and union cards, the step on the ladder after high school and before junior executive or well-paid technician. Many of its courses teach nothing but skills for the smooth functioning of a foolish economy and a monstrous war machine. It serves as an employment agency for firms that buy up brains. It accepts grants that dictate the course of research. In the interest of getting endowments and aggrandizing its plant, it sacrifices free criticism to public relations. It hires "safe" men. It interferes in the private life of both faculty and students. It exacts loyalty oaths, though in principle the University must be universal. It is run by Trustees and Regents instead of by the community of the Faculty. In all these ways the University is little different from any other organ of a venal, publicity-hungry, and excessively role-playing society. It is my experience that the majority of professors and instructors, though they are not soaring geniuses, are earnest, hard-working, and dedicated to learning; but it is very difficult in the present circumstances for them to act as responsible men and women.

What then happens with the students who, at this intensely formative period of their lives, are not in touch with responsible adults?

3

Let me quote again from the high school poll I started with: "The most read magazine was *Life*. A close second was *Mad*." That is, the picture magazine that publishes the slick ads, and the cartoon magazine that scoffs at them. In the past year I have visited twenty colleges, and I have been dismayed to see just this differentiation, between *Life* and *Mad*, deepening into polar groups of students, hostile to one another, the conformist and the totally disgusted. (Here again, instead of changing them, college life has simply reinforced the morals they came with.) The conformists are willing, eager, or at least able, to regard the college as part of the system. They go for grades, some of them no doubt cheating. They keep their records clean, avoiding any but prestigious political action, and in very many cases, getting their sexual satisfaction on the sly in a cynical and dirty way. (I am speaking of the young men; the young women have to suffer this behavior.) And even before they are asked, as W. H. Whyte has pointed out, they seek out the corporation talent scouts. Some of them are already subsidized, much as athletes are. E.g., during her work period at Bard, my daughter was an office girl at one of the oil companies, and it offered to pay her tuition through college if she would contract to return after graduation. She is bright, but she had shown no particular talent in carrying the mail from the eleventh to the fourteenth floor; but perhaps that year they needed to pad the expense account.

At the other pole, those totally disgusted with the system include the college as part of the system. They burk their studies, failing to realize that the University also means Newton and Darwin, Sophocles and Kant, and that they are losing their chance of a profound and well-rounded training. But they take their extra-curricular activities seriously, engaging in antisegregation sit-ins, protesting against the civil defense, and even sitting on submarines. Abashed, they insist on the right to unashamed sexual experiment. Off campus they listen to good music and read books too hard for them that they ought to be studying in class. Finally some of them quit school or flunk out, and perhaps have a spell as proper Beats with beards and tiny pads. A chief use of Black Mountain College was that it could successfully cope with these flunked-out dissenters from the Ivy League, in an atmosphere of creative arts and affectionate community. Another such school that has sprung up, Emerson at Pacific Grove, is significantly weaker in curriculum.

What a deep pathos there is in this polarizing. The conformists appreciate and learn to use the great resources available to modern man, but their goals are humanly pretty worthless. The dissenters, who are sensitive, ingenuous, and idealistic, withdraw and become incompetent and socially worthless. Meantime, poorly represented are the old spirited groups of the center: the young idealists, the "tough-minded" young radicals, the literary clubs of geniuses confident of their unique talents, the inspired scholars who badger the professors for more work, the ambitious who are going to make a billion dollars, even the snobbish patricians who maintain college "standards."

4

Nevertheless! although the above description is my experience, I also experience a new spirit altogether. There is an even startling appearance of students who suddenly take themselves seriously as a community and have a formidable program. They want the rights of youth. Being in school, they want to learn something real. They want more contact with the teachers. They want the faculty to lead them. They want the University to stand for something in the world. To my surprise, it is upon these kids that the social criticism by Riesman, Mills, Whyte, myself, and others, has been having an effect. (God bless them! they take our books at face value, just as some of us meant them.)

At student meetings, whether sponsored by the Columbia *Spectator* in New York, or by the Christian Union at the University of Vermont well sprinkled with farm boys and girls, the students ask one fundamental question: "What is there for us to *do?* Do you have any suggestions for action?" This is accompanied by frustrated irritation because their previous efforts, this year, to press live issues—either a change in the dormitory rules or Fair Play to Cuba—have been met with indifferent disdain by most of their fellow students. Let me report a remark of the chaplain at the University of Vermont: "You young people are new at making an effort. You expect to get something on a silver platter. The problem is not that you're met with disdain, but that you take it so hard, as if you weren't sure of yourselves."

They are not sure. Yet they do communicate with

one another in a real way that is different from the empty one-upping of the conformist generation or the communal soliloquy of the Beat generation. Perhaps this mode of communication is the thing most worth noticing. They argue rudely *ad hominem*, making personal remarks, yet matter-of-factly, with surprisingly little malice. It is just bad manners. Where does this style come from? My guess is that their one-upping was first sharpened to the hipster manner of combative direct confrontation, leading to intensely self-conscious dueling; but then this destructive dueling was suddenly transformed and humanized by the filtering down to them of modern interpersonal psychotherapy, which confronts *without* the need to put down or save face. In my opinion, it is upon this generation that all the professional and amateur psychoanalysis of the past decades has had an effect. The young chaplain's remark was itself typically psychotherapeutic. Such communication forges a bond.

The essence of the new spirit in the colleges is simple. It is awaking from the mesmerized conviction that nothing can be done because the organized system is overwhelming, and suddenly finding themselves in a manageable community of their own where something can be done. To a superficial observer, it seems that they are just bent on making trouble and that any issue will do, large or small. But that is not the tone of it. What they are doing is testing a daring hypothesis: "Social action on our terms is not impossible." (In this context, the nonviolent action against segregation in the South is proving to be immensely important.) Naturally, such an hypothesis is self-confirming, since the concerted action produces solidarity and self-confidence, and therefore *creates* a new social situation in which they must be reckoned with.

Another fundamental issue is voiced as a complaint: "The teachers don't commit themselves. We ask for

guidance because we don't know anything. They are
not forbidding, but they won't lead. Also, they are too
distant." The tone of this is not disrespectful, but disappointed. But the students are not resigned. Let me
present a contrast. The remarkable special issue of *i.e.:
The Cambridge Review* devoted to Harvard 1956, had
the following brief chapter on Professors: "The average undergraduate has no contact with them, and realizes that is the way things should be, when he does
talk to them. There are rare exceptions—about two or
three—who happen to be men too—as a hobby, you
might say." (This is put deliciously.) The contrast is
that in 1961 a certain number of students seem to
have conceived a quixotic program, probably unique
in academic annals: "How to force our teachers to be
men."

From the students' point of view, the logic of this
strange idea is impeccable. The University is their
community. The teachers are the natural leaders. The
University should stand for something in society, provide criticism, intellectual guidance. Therefore the
teachers have to lead. These students are not interested
in having professors impose society's views on students;
they want them to make articulate and wise the wishes
of students in society! Obviously such students do not
sympathize with the problems of dealing with Trustees,
Regents, Legislatures, and Donors. In a curious way
they are dreaming up, in the heart of the vast machine
of the American institution of learning, the old idea
of the medieval and Latin college run by the community
of faculty and students. What they fail almost completely to understand, however, is the disinterested
dedication to academic learning. One has the impression that in the past thirty years—perhaps since the
Depression, pell-mell after the First World War—
young people have lost touch with the *relevance* of the

intellectual tradition and must recapture it in their own way.

Let me give an example of a significant "success" of the New Spirit—in these matters it is hard to know what is success and what is failure. At a very great Eastern school, some professors happened to make a tape for the school radio criticizing some building plans. Public Relations banned the tape, since it hurt the "image" of the institution and might jeopardize endowments. Getting wind of it, the student newspaper splashed it in headlines as a scandal. The student director of the radio station went directly to the top of the school and insisted on buying the tape from the administration for broadcast, since he would not have any censorship imputed against "his" station. The president of the university agreed to the sale. (As of this writing, however, he has not produced the goods, despite the loud squawk of the student paper.)

Another example, of an interesting "failure." At a large Catholic college in the Middle West, the editors of the literary magazine—an instructor and a senior—wanted to use a story of a well-known writer. It contained a single forbidden word and the author good-naturedly advised them to alter it or abbreviate it. But the editors insisted that just that word was esthetically right in its place, and any subterfuge would be shameful. The Fathers promptly confiscated the issue on grounds of "disciplinary consistency," since there was a strict rule against writing dirty words on the toilet walls! Now the instructor-editor has decided to quit the school. The senior, in turn, was destined for expulsion; but because of the rallying of his fellows to his aid, the administration allowed him to graduate. Obviously we are not proceeding according to the rules of the Organized society.

5

Student apathy of the past twenty years was importantly due to the Communist betrayal of youth-politics in the 'thirties, when the students were "had," used for tactical purposes by the Kremlin. Spirited students at present seem to want nothing to do with ideologies or "big" politics altogether. Their social action starts close to home, in problems directly relevant to themselves as youth and collegians. For instance, when they fight segregation, the motive is simple brotherhood, with astonishingly little mention of abstract concepts of Justice or Christianity. They oppose nuclear war and boycott "civil defense" because that is everybody's concrete problem. They do not have enough general politics to oppose the draft. Student sentiment for Castro, I am convinced, has been not political, but springs from their notion of him as a young leader of a student band that rebelled against aged tyrants; and conversely, few students, except for the Negroes, are interested in the war in the Congo. They want the Peace Corps as exciting and worth-while work, but not if it is part of the Cold War and not if there is FBI clearance. One group wants the Peace Corps under the United Nations, to avoid monkey business. The missionary and service aspects do not cause much stir.

But this very close-to-home practicality can, of course, lead to far-reaching principles. I am impressed by the insistence on plain speech, without diplomacy. A good example is a current controversy on dormitory rules at Columbia. As is inevitable in a huge school in New York City, the administration keeps pretty shy of sexual matters; there have been almost no "incidents" and no punishments. Then why fuss about rules? But students attack this expediency as hypocritical, saying that it confirms the guiltiness that has caused all their adolescent misery. Here the principle is (psychologi-

cally) important, and they quote Wilhelm Reich.
They seem to want the University to *declare* for the
sexual revolution.

On this logic, as soon as they think of it, the students
of physics will want a public declaration against scientific secrecy; the students of law will want a University stand on civil rights; the students of medicine
will want a stand on the American Medical Association,
and so forth. This is what they call "making the studies
real" and "forcing the teachers to commit themselves."
As I have said, it is hard for them to see that a
scholarly nonattachment, remaining above the battle,
is not necessarily being afraid. Yet to my mind, as a
teacher, this mood of theirs opens a remarkable opportunity for great teaching. If we handle it right,
professors can make these students see that it is also the
University of Newton and Darwin, Sophocles and
Kant, and perhaps that there is even something to be
said for Justice and Ethics with capital letters.

Another kind of case occurred at Sarah Lawrence
this spring. The girls made a fuss because a fine
teacher was dropped without a reason given. They felt
that they had a right to be informed and not be
"treated like children." In fact the reason was a clash
of personalities in the faculty so that, to keep the
peace, somebody had to go. When this embarrassing
"secret" was allowed to be circulated, the girls accepted the facts of grown-up life.

There is a need for simple personal communication.
Certainly teachers must protect themselves from the
cannibalism of the young that would eat their hearts
out; but caution can go so far that academic life becomes frigid. For instance, recently at Hamilton there
was a hassle between administration and faculty, and
many students were indignant because they thought
good teachers were treated shabbily. Learning about it
from the students, I brought it up with some of the

teachers. They were astounded that the students knew; they were deeply touched that they cared. "If I had known that was how they felt," said one teacher wistfully, "I should have made a different decision and fought it out."

6

How widespread is the new spirit? How strong and viable is it? There is no telling. But it *is* a direct response to a universal crisis, and there are more and more cases of its operation; so it might be a powerful and even explosive force. But it is a phenomenon in schools; the students have economic security and live in a community. Can such a spirit persist after Commencement Day?

It is a profoundly moral spirit. If somehow the colleges are teaching this, they are teaching the most important lesson needed in America, and one that can be learned, apparently, only by the young: that human action is possible, it is possible to change our aims and procedures; that community is possible, we need not be fragmented individuals in a system out of human scale. In these respects, the dominant system of society is cynically, timidly, or hopelessly immoral. In detail, the morals of the students displease their parents; they displease the neo-conservatives who say there are no "values"; and they displease the radicals who regard them as unpolitical. I agree that young people today are weak in lofty universal ideals; but it is more important, I think, that they stop role-playing and one-upping, conforming and seeking status, or rebelling out of resentment. There is a certain amount of experimental "making trouble," but it *is* a testing, an experiment; it is not rioting and panty raids.

This brings me back to the subject I started earlier, the actual relevance of the modern philosophies that are academically taught and that have been criticized as undermining morality and producing anxiety. To assess them, we must be quite clear about the ideas that *in fact* possess these young people and determine their style of thinking. Here is a thumbnail sketch:

I have mentioned the flood of books of social criticism. But of course the youth have been more strongly influenced by their "own" writers, by the Beats and by college magazines, like *Big Table, i.e., The Black Mountain Review.* Positively, these have taught honest speech, confronting *ad hominem* without pulling rank, and a kind of community of youth even at the price of being outcaste. Behind such writing, of course, have been Henry Miller, Genet, and so forth, who have taught acceptance of one's experience as it is, whatever it is, without regard for official values or conventional norms. Besides, the young people have read dismayed accounts of the "American" scene and self-dismay at sharing in it, e.g., in Salinger and Nathanael West. And they avidly read the magazines that are cynical about this "American" scene but exploit it, like *Esquire* and *Playboy*. We thus have a spirited literature for the polarizing mentioned above: those who disgustedly withdraw from the unchangeable society, and those who cynically conform to it.

But further, in the past couple of years, superseding the Beats, there has spread a Hipster literature. This also accepts the scene as unchangeable, but tries to avoid the polarizing choice by asserting: "Cultivate your own experience at the expense of the only society there is. Be cool. Play roles." This stance is the same as that taken by Thrasymachus in the beginning of the *Republic* and seems to be highly immoral. But, in fact, hipsterism—like Mailer, its chief philosopher—is a desperate complex of moral indignation, pretty acute self-awareness, painful moral confusion, and tantrums and violence. It is the ideology of an underprivileged group struggling for fulfillment. *In an important sense, youth is always such an underprivileged group*, and must take to such ideas.

This, I submit, is the actuality of the intellectual climate of the students who now come to the study of academic ethics. The classical, Biblical, chivalric, and humanistic ideals that used to nourish us well are not in fact comprehensible to these young. Modern history has been too catastrophic. Our society is at present too base. We must not hope to inculcate complete and universal principles of action; these arouse only suspicion. Also, let us be frank, most teachers do not know them with enough confidence, do not *live* them with enough confidence, to be able to prove them.

In this context, among the academic philosophies, it is European and Oriental existentialism and American pragmatism that, in my opinion, prove to be relevant and are actually influential. And this is a good thing. The students grasp them because they are believable to them; and the lesson they teach is that in the absurd situation of a dehumanized society, it is possible to act and cope. This is what Camus was saying. That is, far from being demoralizing, causing anxiety and making life problematic, these philosophies, especially in combination, begin to recover morality for those who *are* anxious and baffled. By their existentialism they learn words to affirm themselves as and where they are, to be authentic and not have to play roles or satisfy standards that are empty to them, and to dissipate corporate "images" and political ideologies. In the version of Martin Buber, existentialism gives them a firm relation to their fellows in a face-to-face community. And in the existentialist aspects of Zen and Tao, which are the aspects that influence them, they learn to notice the possibilities in the present moment, so they no longer feel trapped.

From the pragmatism of James and Dewey they learn that any concrete problem of their own can initiate a useful process. They need not feel frustrated by cut-and-dried career goals, national goals, and moral goals that do not in fact animate them, but that make them lose confidence in themselves because they are ignorant and unskilled. Their youthful age is as real as any, and its natural motives are the best possible if they keep growing. They learn to respect experiment, instead of being afraid to perform awkwardly because they will be disdained. They learn that ideas must be tested by present action; but that, also, faith finds means. They learn that no society is unchangeable and unamenable to practical intellect.

PAUL GOODMAN, a native New Yorker, was born in 1911. After graduating from City College in New York, he received his Ph.D. in humanities from the University of Chicago. Mr. Goodman has taught at the University of Chicago, New York University, Black Mountain College, Sarah Lawrence, and has lectured widely at various universities throughout the country. He is associated with the New York and Cleveland institutes for Gestalt Therapy and the University Seminar on Problems of Interpretation at Columbia. Mr. Goodman has written for *Commentary, Politics, Kenyon Review, Resistance, Liberation, Partisan Review,* etc. His fiction includes *The Facts of Life, The Break-Up of Our Camp, Parents' Day,* and *The Empire City,* and he has also published a volume of verse, *The Lordly Hudson. Kafka's Prayer* and *The Structure of Literature* are books of criticism. In the area of social studies, in addition to being the co-author of *Communitas* and *Gestalt Therapy,* he has written *Art and Social Nature, Growing up Absurd, Drawing the Line* (a pamphlet), and *Community of Scholars.* Mr. Goodman is married and has three children.

THIS BOOK *was set on the Linotype in* ELECTRA, *designed by* W. A. Dwiggins. *The Electra face is a simple and readable type suitable for printing books by present-day processes. It is not based on any historical model, and hence does not echo any particular time or fashion. It is without eccentricities to catch the eye and interfere with reading—in general, its aim is to perform the function of a good book printing-type: to be read, and not seen. The book was printed and bound by* H. WOLFF, BOOK MANUFACTURING CO.

VINTAGE POLITICAL SCIENCE
AND SOCIAL CRITICISM

V-428   ABDEL-MALEK, ANOUAR   *Egypt: Military Society*
V-365   ALPEROVITZ, GAR   *Atomic Diplomacy*
V-286   ARIES, PHILIPPE   *Centuries of Childhood*
V-334   BALTZELL, E. DIGBY   *The Protestant Establishment*
V-335   BANFIELD & WILSON   *City Politics*
V-198   BARDOLPH, RICHARD   *The Negro Vanguard*
V-185   BARNETT, A. DOAK   *Communist China and Asia*
V-87   BARZUN, JACQUES   *God's Country and Mine*
V-705   BAUER, INKELES, AND KLUCKHOHN   *How the Soviet System Works*
V-270   BAZELON, DAVID   *The Paper Economy*
V-42   BEARD, CHARLES A.   *The Economic Basis of Politics* and Related Writings
V-59   BEAUFRE, GEN. ANDRÉ   *NATO and Europe*
V-60   BECKER, CARL L.   *Declaration of Independence*
V-17   BECKER, CARL L.   *Freedom and Responsibility in the American Way of Life*
V-228   BELOFF, MAX   *The United States and the Unity of Europe*
V-199   BERMAN, H. J. (ed.)   *Talks on American Law*
V-352   BERNSTEIN, PETER L.   *The Price of Prosperity*, Revised Edition
V-211   BINKLEY, WILFRED E.   *President and Congress*
V-81   BLAUSTEIN & WOOCK (eds.)   *Man Against Poverty: World War III—Articles and Documents on the Conflict between the Rich and the Poor*
V-513   BOORSTIN, DANIEL J.   *The Americans: The Colonial Experience*
V-358   BOORSTIN, DANIEL J.   *The Americans: The National Experience*
V-414   BOTTOMORE, T. B.   *Classes in Modern Society*
V-44   BRINTON, CRANE   *The Anatomy of Revolution*
V-37   BROGAN, D. W.   *The American Character*
V-234   BRUNER, JEROME   *The Process of Education*
V-196   BRYSON, L., et al.   *Social Change in Latin America Today*
V-30   CAMUS, ALBERT   *The Rebel*
V-33   CARMICHAEL AND HAMILTON   *Black Power: The Politics of Liberation in America*
V-98   CASH, W. J.   *The Mind of the South*
V-429   DE CASTRO, GERASSI, & HOROWITZ (eds.)   *Latin American Radicalism: A Documentary Report on Left and Nationalist Movements*
V-272   CATER, DOUGLASS   *The Fourth Branch of Government*
V-290   CATER, DOUGLASS   *Power in Washington*
V-420   CORNUELLE, RICHARD C.   *Reclaiming the American Dream*
V-311   CREMIN, LAWRENCE A.   *The Genius of American Education*
V-67   CURTIUS, ERNEST R.   *The Civilization of France*
V-234   DANIELS, R. V.   *A Documentary History of Communism*
V-235   (Two volumes)
V-237   DANIELS, ROBERT V.   *The Nature of Communism*
V-252   DAVID, et al.   *The Politics of National Party Conventions*
V-746   DEUTSCHER, ISAAC   *The Prophet Armed*

V-747   DEUTSCHER, ISAAC   *The Prophet Unarmed*

V-748   DEUTSCHER, ISAAC   *The Prophet Outcast*

V-333   ELLIS, CLYDE T.   *A Giant Step*

V-390   ELLUL, JACQUES   *Technological Society*

V-379   EMERSON, T. I.   *Toward A General Theory of the First Amendment*

V-47   EPSTEIN & FORSTER   *The Radical Right: Report on the John Birch Society and Its Allies*

V-353   EPSTEIN & FORSTER   *Report on the John Birch Society 1966*

V-422   FALL, BERNARD B.   *Hell in a Very Small Place: The Siege of Dien Bien Phu*

V-423   FINN, JAMES   *Protest: Pacifism and Politics*

V-225   FISCHER, LOUIS (ed.)   *The Essential Gandhi*

V-707   FISCHER, LOUIS   *Soviets in World Affairs*

V-424   FOREIGN POLICY ASSOCIATION, EDITORS OF   *A Cartoon History of United States Foreign Policy—Since World War I*

V-413   FRANK, JEROME D.   *Sanity and Survival: Psychological Aspects of War and Peace*

V-382   FRANKLIN & STARR (eds.)   *The Negro in 20th Century America*

V-224   FREYRE, GILBERTO   *New World in the Tropics*

V-368   FRIEDENBERG, EDGAR Z.   *Coming of Age in America*

V-416   FRIENDLY AND GOLDFARB   *Crime and Publicity*

V-378   FULBRIGHT, J. WILLIAM   *The Arrogance of Power*

V-264   FULBRIGHT, J. WILLIAM   *Old Myths and New Realities* and Other Commentaries

V-354   FULBRIGHT, J. WILLIAM (intro.)   *The Vietnam Hearings*

V-328   GALENSON, WALTER   *A Primer on Employment & Wages*

V-461   GARAUDY, ROGER   *From Anathema to Dialogue: A Marxist Challenge to the Christian Churches*

V-434   GAVIN, JAMES M.   *Crisis Now*

V-475   GAY, PETER   *The Enlightenment: The Rise of Modern Paganism*

V-277   GAY, PETER   *Voltaire's Politics*

V-406   GETTLEMAN & MERMELSTEIN   *The Great Society Reader: The Failure of American Liberalism*

V-174   GOODMAN, P. & P.   *Communitas*

V-325   GOODMAN, PAUL   *Compulsory Mis-education* and *The Community of Scholars*

V-32   GOODMAN, PAUL   *Growing Up Absurd*

V-417   GOODMAN, PAUL   *People or Personnel and Like a Conquered Province*

V-247   GOODMAN, PAUL   *Utopian Essays and Practical Proposals*

V-357   GOODWIN, RICHARD N.   *Triumph or Tragedy: Reflections on Vietnam*

V-248   GRUNEBAUM, G. E., VON   *Modern Islam: The Search for Cultural Identity*

V-430   GUEVARA, CHE   *Guerrilla Warfare*

V-389   HAMILTON, WALTON   *The Politics of Industry*

V-69   HAND, LEARNED   *The Spirit of Liberty*

V-319   HART, H. L. A.   *Law, Liberty and Morality*

V-427   HAYDEN, TOM   *Rebellion in Newark: Official Violence and Ghetto Response*

V-404   HELLER, WALTER (ed.)   *Perspectives on Economic Growth*

V-283   HENRY, JULES   *Culture Against Man*

V-465 HINTON, WILLIAM *Fanshen: A Documentary of Revolution in a Chinese Village*

V-95 HOFSTADTER, RICHARD *The Age of Reform*

V-9 HOFSTADTER, RICHARD *The American Political Tradition*

V-317 HOFSTADTER, RICHARD *Anti-Intellectualism in American Life*

V-385 HOFSTADTER, RICHARD *Paranoid Style in American Politics*

V-749 HOWE, IRVING (ed.) *Basic Writings of Trotsky*

V-201 HUGHES, H. STUART *Consciousness and Society*

V-241 JACOBS, JANE *Death & Life of Great American Cities*

V-433 JACOBS, PAUL *Prelude to Riot: A View of Urban America from the Bottom*

V-332 JACOBS & LANDAU (eds.) *The New Radicals*

V-369 KAUFMANN, WALTER (ed.) *The Birth of Tragedy and The Case of Wagner*

V-401 KAUFMANN, WALTER (ed.) *On the Genealogy of Morals and Ecce Homo*

V-337 KAUFMANN, WALTER (tr.) *Beyond Good and Evil*

V-470 KEY, V. O., JR. *The Responsible Electorate: Rationality in Presidential Voting 1936–1960*

V-361 KOMAROVSKY, MIRRA *Blue-Collar Marriage*

V-152 KRASLOW AND LOORY *The Secret Search for Peace in Vietnam*

V-341 KIMBALL & McCLELLAN *Education and the New America*

V-215 LACOUTURE, JEAN *Ho Chi Minh*

V-327 LACOUTURE, JEAN *Vietnam: Between Two Truces*

V-367 LASCH, CHRISTOPHER *The New Radicalism in America*

V-399 LASKI, HAROLD J. (ed.) *Harold J. Laski on The Communist Manifesto*

V-287 LA SOUCHÈRE, ÉLÉNA DE *An Explanation of Spain*

V-426 LEKACHMAN, ROBERT *The Age of Keynes*

V-280 LEWIS, OSCAR *The Children of Sánchez*

V-421 LEWIS, OSCAR *La Vida: A Puerto Rican Family in the Culture of Poverty—San Juan and New York*

V-370 LEWIS, OSCAR *Pedro Martínez*

V-284 LEWIS, OSCAR *Village Life in Northern India*

V-392 LICHTHEIM, GEORGE *The Concept of Ideology and Other Essays*

V-474 LIFTON, ROBERT JAY *Revolutionary Immortality: Mao Tse-Tung and the Chinese Cultural Revolution*

V-384 LINDESMITH, ALFRED *The Addict and The Law*

V-267 LIPPMANN, WALTER *The Essential Lippmann*

V-204 LOMAX, LOUIS *Thailand: The War that Is, The War that Will Be*

V-469 LOWE, JEANNE R. *Cities in a Race with Time: Progress and Poverty in America's Renewing Cities*

V-407 MACK, RAYMOND *Our Children's Burden: Studies of Desegregation in Ten American Communities*

V-193 MALRAUX, ANDRÉ *Temptation of the West*

V-324 MARITAIN, JACQUES *Existence and the Existent*

V-386 McPHERSON, JAMES *The Negro's Civil War*

V-102 MEYERS, MARVIN *The Jacksonian Persuasion*

V-273 MICHAEL, DONALD N. *The Next Generation*

V-19 MILOSZ, CZESLAW *The Captive Mind*

V-411 MINOGUE, KENNETH R. *The Liberal Mind*

V-316 MOORE, WILBERT E. *The Conduct of the Corporation*

V-251 MORGENTHAU, HANS J. *Purpose of American Politics*
V-703 MOSELY, PHILIP E. *The Kremlin and World Politics:* Studies in Soviet Policy and Action (Vintage Original)
V-57 MURCHLAND, BERNARD (ed.) *The Meaning of the Death of God*
V-274 MYRDAL, GUNNAR *Challenge to Affluence*
V-337 NIETZSCHE, FRIEDRICH *Beyond Good and Evil*
V-369 NIETZSCHE, FRIEDRICH *The Birth of Tragedy and The Case of Wagner*
V-401 NIETZSCHE, FRIEDRICH *On the Genealogy of Morals and Ecce Homo*
V-285 PARKES, HENRY B. *Gods and Men*
V-72 PEN, JAN *Primer on International Trade*
V-46 PHILIPSON, M. (ed.) *Automation:* Implications for the Future (Vintage Original)
V-258 PIEL, GERARD *Science in the Cause of Man*
V-128 PLATO *The Republic*
V-309 RASKIN & FALL (eds.) *The Viet-Nam Reader*
V-719 REED, JOHN *Ten Days That Shook the World*
V-192 REISCHAUER, EDWIN O. *Beyond Vietnam: The United States and Asia*
V-212 ROSSITER, CLINTON *Conservatism in America*
V-267 ROSSITER & LARE (eds.) *The Essential Lippmann*
V-472 ROSZAK, THEODORE (ed.) *The Dissenting Academy*
V-288 RUDOLPH, FREDERICK *The American College and University*
V-408 SAMPSON, RONALD V. *The Psychology of Power*
V-435 SCHELL, JONATHAN *The Military Half*
V-431 SCHELL, JONATHAN *The Village of Ben Suc*
V-403 SCHRIEBER, DANIEL *Profile of a School Dropout*
V-375 SCHURMANN AND SCHELL (eds.) *The China Reader: Imperial China,* I
V-376 SCHURMANN & SCHELL (eds.) *The China Reader: Republican China,* II
V-377 SCHURMANN & SCHELL (eds.) *The China Reader: Communist China,* III
V-394 SEABURY, PAUL *Power, Freedom and Diplomacy*
V-220 SHONFIELD, ANDREW *Attack on World Poverty*
V-359 SILVERT, et al. *Expectant Peoples*
V-432 SPARROW, JOHN *After the Assassination: A Positive Appraisal of the Warren Report*
V-388 STAMPP, KENNETH *The Era of Reconstruction 1865-1877*
V-253 STAMPP, KENNETH *The Peculiar Institution*
V-244 STEBBINS, RICHARD P. *U. S. in World Affairs, 1962*
V-374 STILLMAN & PFAFF *Power and Impotence*
V-439 STONE, I. F. *In a Time of Torment*
V-53 SYNGE, J. M. *The Aran Islands* and Other Writings
V-231 TANNENBAUM, FRANK *Slave & Citizen:* The Negro in the Americas
V-312 TANNENBAUM, FRANK *Ten Keys to Latin America*
V-322 THOMPSON, E. P. *The Making of the English Working Class*
V-749 TROTSKY, LEON *Basic Writings of Trotsky*
V-206 WALLERSTEIN, IMMANUEL *Africa:* The Politics of Independence (Vintage Original)
V-405 WASSERMAN & SWITZER *The Vintage Guide to Graduate Study*

V-298 WATTS, ALAN W. *The Way of Zen*
V-145 WARREN, ROBERT PENN *Segregation*
V-323 WARREN, ROBERT PENN *Who Speaks for the Negro?*
V-729 WEIDLE, W. *Russia:* Absent & Present
V-249 WIEDNER, DONALD L. *A History of Africa:* South of the Sahara
V-313 WILSON, EDMUND *Apologies to the Iroquois*
V-208 WOODWARD, C. VANN *Burden of Southern History*

VINTAGE HISTORY AND CRITICISM OF
LITERATURE, MUSIC, AND ART

V-418 AUDEN, W. H. *The Dyer's Hand*
V-398 AUDEN, W. H. *The Enchafèd Flood*
V-22 BARZUN, JACQUES *The Energies of Art*
V-93 BENNETT, JOAN *Four Metaphysical Poets*
V-269 BLOTNER & GWYNN (eds.) *Faulkner at the University*
V-259 BUCKLEY, JEROME H. *The Victorian Temper*
V-51 BURKE, KENNETH *The Philosophy of Literary Form*
V-75 CAMUS, ALBERT *The Myth of Sisyphus*
V-171 CRUTTWELL, PATRICK *The Shakespearean Moment*
V-471 DUVEAU, GEORGES *1848: The Making of a Revolution*
V-4 EINSTEIN, ALFRED *A Short History of Music*
V-261 ELLIS-FERMOR, UNA *Jacobean Drama:* An Interpretation
V-177 FULLER, EDMUND *Man in Modern Fiction*
V-13 GILBERT, STUART *James Joyce's Ulysses*
V-363 GOLDWATER, ROBERT *Primitivism in Modern Art*, Revised Edition
V-114 HAUSER, ARNOLD *Social History of Art*, v. I
V-115 HAUSER, ARNOLD *Social History of Art*, v. II
V-116 HAUSER, ARNOLD *Social History of Art*, v. III
V-117 HAUSER, ARNOLD *Social History of Art*, v. IV
V-438 HELLER, ERICH *The Artist's Journey into the Interior and Other Essays*
V-20 HYMAN, S. E. *The Armed Vision*
V-38 HYMAN, S. E. (ed.) *The Critical Performance*
V-41 JAMES, HENRY *The Future of the Novel*
V-12 JARRELL, RANDALL *Poetry and the Age*
V-88 KERMAN, JOSEPH *Opera as Drama*
V-260 KERMODE, FRANK *The Romantic Image*
V-83 KRONENBERGER, LOUIS *Kings and Desperate Men*
V-167 LA ROCHEFOUCAULD *Maxims*
V-90 LEVIN, HARRY *The Power of Blackness*
V-296 MACDONALD, DWIGHT *Against the American Grain*
V-55 MANN, THOMAS *Essays*
V-720 MIRSKY, D. S. *A History of Russian Literature*
V-344 MUCHNIC, HELEN *From Gorky to Pasternak*
V-118 NEWMAN, ERNEST *Great Operas*, Volume I
V-119 NEWMAN, ERNEST *Great Operas*, Volume II
V-107 NEWMAN, ERNEST *Wagner as Man and Artist*
V-383 O'BRIEN, CONOR CRUISE *Writers and Politics*
V-161 PICASSO, PABLO *Picasso & the Human Comedy*
V-372 PRITCHETT, V. S. *The Living Novel and Later Appreciations*
V-24 RANSOM, JOHN CROWE *Poems and Essays*
V-412 SAARINEN, ALINE B. *The Proud Possessors*
V-89 SCHORER, MARK *William Blake*
V-108 SHAHN, BEN *The Shape of Content*
V-275 SHAPIRO, KARL *In Defense of Ignorance*
V-415 SHATTUCK, ROGER *The Banquet Years*, Revised
V-366 SHATTUCK, ROGER *Proust's Binoculars*
V-186 STEINER, GEORGE *Tolstoy or Dostoevsky*
V-278 STEVENS, WALLACE *The Necessary Angel*
V-39 STRAVINSKY, IGOR *The Poetics of Music*

V-100	SULLIVAN, J. W. N. *Beethoven:* His Spiritual Development
V-243	SYPHER, WYLIE (ed.) *Art History:* An Anthology of Modern Criticism
V-266	SYPHER, WYLIE *Loss of the Self*
V-229	SYPHER, WYLIE *Rococo to Cubism*
V-166	SZE, MAI-MAI *The Way of Chinese Painting*
V-179	THOMSON, VIRGIL *Music Reviewed 1940-1954* (Vintage Original)
V-214	THOMSON, VIRGIL *The State of Music*
V-162	TILLYARD, E. M. W. *Elizabethan World Picture*
V-35	TINDALL, WILLIAM YORK *Forces in Modern British Literature*
V-82	TOYE, FRANCIS *Verdi:* His Life and Works
V-62	TURNELL, MARTIN *The Novel in France*
V-194	VALÉRY, PAUL *The Art of Poetry*
V-347	WARREN, ROBERT PENN *Selected Essays*
V-122	WILENSKI, R. H. *Modern French Painters*, Volume I (1863-1903)
V-123	WILENSKI, R. H. *Modern French Painters*, Volume II (1904-1938)
V-218	WILSON, EDMUND *Classics & Commercials*
V-181	WILSON, EDMUND *The Shores of Light*
V-360	WIMSATT & BROOKS *Literary Criticism*

V-365	ALPEROVITZ, GAR *Atomic Diplomacy*
V-334	BALTZELL, E. DIGBY *The Protestant Establishment*
V-198	BARDOLPH, RICHARD *The Negro Vanguard*
V-42	BEARD, CHARLES A. *The Economic Basis of Politics* and Related Writings
V-60	BECKER, CARL L. *Declaration of Independence*
V-17	BECKER, CARL L. *Freedom and Responsibility in the American Way of Life*
V-191	BEER, THOMAS *The Mauve Decade:* American Life at the End of the 19th Century
V-199	BERMAN, H. J. (ed.) *Talks on American Law*
V-211	BINKLEY, WILFRED E. *President and Congress*
V-513	BOORSTIN, DANIEL J. *The Americans: The Colonial Experience*
V-358	BOORSTIN, DANIEL J. *The Americans: The National Experience*
V-44	BRINTON, CRANE *The Anatomy of Revolution*
V-37	BROGAN, D. W. *The American Character*
V-72	BUCK, PAUL H. *The Road to Reunion, 1865-1900*
V-98	CASH, W. J. *The Mind of the South*
V-311	CREMIN, LAWRENCE A. *The Genius of American Education*
V-190	DONALD, DAVID *Lincoln Reconsidered*
V-379	EMERSON, THOMAS I. *Toward A General Theory of the First Amendment*
V-424	FOREIGN POLICY ASSOCIATION, EDITORS OF *A Cartoon History of United States Foreign Policy—Since World War I*
V-368	FRIEDENBERG, EDGAR Z. *Coming of Age in America*
V-264	FULBRIGHT, J. WILLIAM *Old Myths and New Realities* and Other Commentaries
V-463	GAY, PETER *A Loss of Mastery: Puritan Historians in Colonial America*
V-31	GOLDMAN, ERIC F. *Rendezvous with Destiny*
V-183	GOLDMAN, ERIC F. *The Crucial Decade—and After:* America, 1945-1960
V-95	HOFSTADTER, RICHARD *The Age of Reform*
V-9	HOFSTADTER, RICHARD *American Political Tradition*
V-317	HOFSTADTER, RICHARD *Anti-Intellectualism in American Life*
V-120	HOFSTADTER, RICHARD *Great Issues in American History,* Volume I (1765-1865)
V-121	HOFSTADTER, RICHARD *Great Issues in American History,* Volume II (1864-1957)
V-385	HOFSTADTER, RICHARD *The Paranoid Style in American Politics and Other Essays*
V-242	JAMES, C. L. R. *The Black Jacobins*
V-367	LASCH, CHRISTOPHER *The New Radicalism in America*
V-386	MCPHERSON, JAMES *The Negro's Civil War*
V-318	MERK, FREDERICK *Manifest Destiny in American History*
V-84	PARKES, HENRY B. *The American Experience*
V-371	ROSE, WILLIE LEE *Rehearsal for Reconstruction*
V-212	ROSSITER, CLINTON *Conservatism in America*
V-285	RUDOLPH, FREDERICK *The American College and University:* A History
V-394	SEABURY, PAUL *Power, Freedom and Diplomacy*

V-530	SCHLESINGER, ARTHUR M.	*Prelude to Independence*
V-52	SMITH, HENRY NASH	*Virgin Land*
V-345	SMITH, PAGE	*The Historian and History*
V-432	SPARROW, JOHN	*After the Assassination: A Positive Appraisal of the Warren Report*
V-388	STAMPP, KENNETH	*The Era of Reconstruction 1865-1877*
V-253	STAMPP, KENNETH	*The Peculiar Institution*
V-244	STEBBINS, RICHARD P.	*U. S. in World Affairs, 1962*
V-110	TOCQUEVILLE, ALEXIS DE	*Democracy in America, Vol. I*
V-111	TOCQUEVILLE, ALEXIS DE	*Democracy in America, Vol. II*
V-103	TROLLOPE, MRS. FRANCES	*Domestic Manners of the Americans*
V-265	WARREN, ROBERT PENN	*Legacy of the Civil War*
V-368	WILLIAMS, T. HARRY	*Lincoln and His Generals*
V-208	WOODWARD, C. VANN	*Burden of Southern History*

A free catalogue of VINTAGE BOOKS *will be sent at your request. Write to* Vintage Books, 457 Madison Avenue, New York, New York 10022.